The Legends of Oldham Athletic

The Legends of Oldham Athletic

by Garth Dykes

breedon books
PUBLISHING

Dedication

For my A Team
ANN, ANGELA and ALISON
With love

First published in Great Britain in 2006 by

The Breedon Books Publishing Company Limited

Breedon House, 3 The Parker Centre,

Derby, DE21 4SZ.

ISBN 1 85983 531 7

Printed and bound by BIDDLES LTD,

King's Lynn, Norfolk.

Contents

OLDHAM EVENING
Chronicle

Acknowledgements

This book is the product of many years' work on the general history of my favourite football team and owes a great debt of gratitude to many willing friends and helpers – football people all. My dear partner Ann is not a football person, but her love and support, not to mention encouragement and understanding, makes all things possible. Thank you Annie.

I am, as ever, particularly grateful to Jim Creasy; not only for his continuing help in the matter of players' births and deaths, but for his invaluable input in all aspects of inter-war and other periods of football history. Jim has enriched the works of numerous other writers, in addition to my own.

A special thank you also to my friends and fellow football researchers Michael Braham, Mike Davage, Barry J. Hugman and Mike Jackman for their considerable help. Although sadly no longer with us, I feel compelled to acknowledge the great help I received during the lifetime of two particular friends: Peter Windle (1951–2002), to whose memory my earlier title *Latics Lads* was dedicated, and Douglas Lamming (1914–2005), a widely admired and respected author, whose giant footsteps I have attempted to follow.

My dear sister, Hilary, would not thank me for describing her as a football historian, but as a historian's helpmate she has done a first-class job in supplying vital details from the archives of the Oldham Libraries Department.

Finally, my thanks to Steve Caron and Susan Last of Breedon Books Publishing for the opportunity to select and describe 100 Latics' players for inclusion in this volume. As might be expected, football humour being what it is, comments questioning the existence – past or present – of 100 Oldham Athletic 'Legends' have been rife. However, with a pallet of around 1,000 players to choose from, I feel I know better. I cannot, however, expect everyone to agree with my selection, but I hope that readers will enjoy *Legends of Oldham Athletic*.

Garth Dykes
Leicester
June 2006

Photographs

Are courtesy of the *Oldham Evening Chronicle*.

Additional photographs are from the author's own collection in addition to those kindly loaned by Steve Hobin and Gordon Lawton.

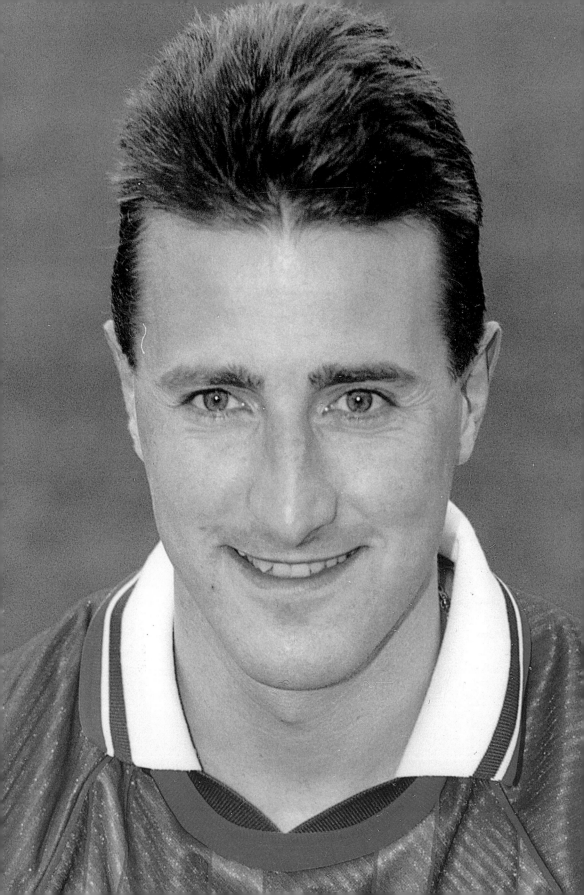

Neil Adams

Date of birth: 23 November 1965, Stoke-on-Trent

Oldham Athletic record:
Appearances: League 149(36), FA Cup 12(1), League Cup 17(2)
Goals: League 27, FA Cup 3, League Cup 1
Debut: Manchester City (h) 14 January 1989, lost 0–1

Also played for: Stoke City, Everton, Norwich City

Neil Adams joined Stoke City from local junior football in July 1985 and after just 12 months at the Victoria Ground earned an upward move to Everton. He made his League debut for the Potters at Charlton Athletic on 21 September 1985 and netted his first League goal in a 2–1 win at Sheffield United on 14 December. He had played in 31(1) Division Two matches and scored four goals when Everton paid £150,000 for his signature, and he made his debut in a 1–1 draw at Coventry City on 30 August 1986, Everton's goal being scored by Ian Marshall, another player with subsequent Latics connections.

Everton won the Football League Championship in Adams's first season at Goodison, and he was capped by England at Under-21 level against Sweden. Playing against Athletic in the fourth round of the Littlewoods Cup in November 1987, he scored Everton's winner – four minutes from time – in the 2–1 victory.

In the following season, manager Joe Royle returned to his old club to secure Adams's services, initially on a one-month loan. He played his first game on the right side of midfield as cover for club skipper John Kelly, who was serving a period of suspension. His loan was later extended, and with his Everton contract expiring in the summer a £100,000 fee was negotiated for his permanent transfer.

Adams enjoyed five excellent seasons as a most valued member of the senior squad. As a wide player the service to his strikers was always of the highest quality, while in roles as diverse as central-midfield and wing-back his energetic style and ability to make a telling pass served the team well during momentous times at Boundary Park.

During his first spell, Athletic won the Championship of the Second Division and made Wembley appearances in the Littlewoods Cup Final against Nottingham Forest and the FA Cup semi-final against Manchester United.

In the season dubbed 'The great escape', Athletic preserved their Premier League status by a whisker in the month of May 1993. Successive victories against Aston Villa (a) 1–0, Liverpool (h) 3–2 and Southampton (h) 4–3 – the latter achieved despite a Matt Le Tissier hat-trick – rounded off a season of high drama. Goal difference settled the final relegation place, which was occupied by Crystal Palace, who accompanied Middlesbrough and Nottingham Forest in their descent to Division One. Adams scored nine goals during the season, a vital contribution, bettered only by Ian Olney, who scored 12. His total included a personal highlight when he scored twice against his old club Everton at Goodison Park in a 2–2 draw on 27 February. One week later he scored the priceless only goal of the game against Manchester United at Boundary Park.

Later in the following season, Adams was transferred to Norwich City for a fee of £225,000. In five years with the Canaries he appeared in 164(18) League matches and scored 25 goals. He returned to Athletic on a free transfer in July 1999. He joined a struggling Division Two side – the season opening with five straight League defeats. Neil scored two League goals and one in the FA Cup in a disappointing season that ended for him in February, with a foot injury that required surgery.

Adams scored Athletic's first goal of the new season, 2000–01, in a 4–1 home victory against Port Vale. He was also on the mark one week later at Walsall. Sadly, however, he suffered a cruciate knee-ligament injury at Stoke City in October and was released when his contract expired in the summer. At 35 years of age, he decided to retire and was quickly offered a coaching position with Norwich City.

Leslie Adlam

Date of birth: 24 June 1897, Guildford
Died: October 1968, Guildford

Oldham Athletic record:
Appearances: League 279, FA Cup 11
Goals: League 9, FA Cup 1
Debut: Newcastle United (h) 30 March 1923, drawn 0–0

Also played for: Farnham Breweries, Guildford United, Queen's Park Rangers, Cardiff City

Leslie Adlam made a late start in professional football after serving as a Company Quartermaster Sergeant in the Royal Engineers in Greece and Salonica during World War One. He was demobilised in February 1920 and resumed his previous employment as a railway clerk. Returning to local soccer, in 1921–22 he helped Farnham Breweries to win the Championship of the Surrey Senior League without losing a match. His major contribution was an astonishing 87 goals, more than half of his team's total of 154. An upward move to Guildford United followed in August 1922, and he had scored 27 goals in 19 outings for the Surrey club when he was recommended to the Latics by their former full-back Jimmy Hodson, Guildford United's manager at that time.

Adlam cost Athletic £300, and he came north as a centre-forward. In the month of his signing he made his debut in the Central League and scored twice against Preston North End Reserves and once against Manchester United Reserves. In the same month he was given his debut in Division One. A weakness in the forward line had been obvious from very early in the season and despite being a young player of some promise, he lacked experience and his introduction failed to solve the problem. Athletic were relegated from the top flight, having failed to score in 23 League games, more than half the total played. As the local correspondent, who was under orders to write an article retrospective of the team's fortunes (or, in this case, lack of them!) during the season, ruefully admitted 'I am placed in somewhat of a dilemma, as no one cares for the task of rubbing it in!'

Adlam featured little in Division Two in 1923–24, with three new forward recruits in Howson (Bradford City), Longmuir (Blackburn Rovers) and Alex Campbell (Swansea Town) stepping up the competition. During the course of the season, Leslie's role was switched from forward to half-back in the Central League team.

Although the Latics flirted with relegation during 1924–25, it was the term that saw Adlam installed at right half-back. He quickly adapted himself to the new position. At 5ft 10in and 12st 10lb he was nicely built for the job, but his chief asset was his unusual energy. Wherever the ball, you would expect to see him. He seemed to be in constant action throughout every match, never flagging in his efforts to keep his forwards well supplied with the ball.

From the mid-1920s onwards, Athletic were well served at half-back, with Adlam and Jimmy Naylor virtual ever presents. He recorded his 200th senior appearance in November 1929 and was awarded a benefit match later in the same season. An attendance of 12,481 witnessed the 2–2 draw against Bristol City at Boundary Park. Two days later Blackpool were the visitors, and they won 2–1, a result that virtually ended Athletic's hopes of promotion from Division Two.

Adlam missed just one match during 1930–31 and scored four League goals, but in November of the following season he was transferred, along with Ted Goodier, to Queen's Park Rangers for a combined fee of £1,500. The pair certainly improved their new team's results, as nine straight victories resulted from their first seven League and two FA Cup appearances.

A final move in League circles to Cardiff City was followed by a coaching appointment in France. Two years later, Adlam was traced in familiar territory when he appeared as a reinstated amateur for Guildford Post Office in his 38th year.

David Ashworth

Date of birth: c.1868, Waterfoot in the Rossendale Valley
Died: 23 March 1947, Blackpool

Oldham Athletic record:
Manager: April 1906–April 1914 and January 1923–July 1924

Also managed: Newchurch Rovers, Stockport County, Liverpool, Manchester City, Walsall, Caernarfon, Llanelli

Affectionately known as 'Little Dave' and said to stand no more than 5ft tall, David Ashworth first played for Newchurch Rovers and, despite his lack of inches, was once described as 'a fearsome full-back'. He then became club secretary-manager before moving on to refereeing, later graduating to the Football League list. His appointment as Athletic's manager virtually coincided with the club's return to Boundary Park from Hudson Fold in May 1906. Having sampled every aspect of the game, his experience was put to good use. A veritable hound for sniffing out young players, he was considered the ideal man to lead the club out of the Lancashire Combination and into the Football League.

Usually seen wearing a bowler hat and sporting a waxed moustache, Ashworth's somewhat stern appearance disguised a keen sense of humour. Legend has it that he was said to wear his moustache with both ends turned upward after a win, both downwards after a defeat, and with one end up and one down after a draw!

Both ends of his whiskers must have spent the majority of his first season in an elevated position, as the team set a blistering pace from the outset. A very short 'retained list' from the previous season – when the side finished 13th in the A Division of the Lancashire Combination – left plenty of room for new signings. Among the best of the new recruits were Harry Hancock from Blackpool, who scored 29 goals during the season; Matt Brunton from Accrington Stanley, who played in every match in 1906–07 and scored 33 goals; David Walders, along with brother Jack, who joined from Burnley; David Wilson and goalkeeper Edwin Daw, both recruited from Bradford City.

In the 38-match League tournament the side began with six straight victories. They scored 105 goals, conceding only 33, and were very worthy champions. In the FA Cup competition five qualifying rounds were successfully negotiated, and in the second round proper a plum draw brought Liverpool to Boundary Park. A record crowd of 21,538 squeezed into Boundary Park where the magnificent run ended, with Liverpool winning 1–0.

Athletic were just one of six non-League clubs who applied for election to the Football League in May 1907. Their initial application was unsuccessful, but in the following month Burslem Port Vale resigned and Athletic were elected to Division Two in their place.

Far from overawed in loftier company, the Latics' first four seasons in the League brought only five home defeats, and in 1909–10 a late surge of 14 wins in 16 matches earned promotion to Division One on goal average. The years leading up to World War One were glorious ones, six men winning caps as Athletic players – Hugh Moffatt and George Woodger played for England, David Wilson and Joe Donnachie for Scotland and Wales selected David Davies and Evan Jones.

'Little Dave' rather surprisingly moved on to Stockport County in April 1914, leaving his successor, Herbert Bamlett, the nucleus of a side good enough to finish as runners-up in Division One in 1914–15.

Taking over as Liverpool's manager in December 1919, Ashworth guided them to the First Division Championship in season 1921–22. In January 1923 Athletic's directors induced him to return, but he arrived too late to save the side from their first ever relegation. After one season in Division Two, when Athletic finished in seventh place, he departed to Manchester City in July 1924. He managed Walsall from February 1926 and later scouted for Blackpool. He died at the Victoria Hospital in Blackpool in 1947, at the age of 79.

Andy Barlow

Date of birth: 24 November 1965, Oldham

Oldham Athletic record:
Appearances: League 245(16), FA Cup 19, League Cup 22
Goals: League 5
Debut: Birmingham City (h) 25 August 1984, lost 0–1

Also played for: Bradford City on loan, Blackpool, Rochdale

Andy Barlow played Rugby League football at school and represented Oldham Under-11s in a curtain-raiser to the 1977 Rugby League Challenge Cup Final, Leeds v Widnes, at Wembley in May 1977. However, soccer eventually claimed him, and some 13 years later he was at Wembley again with the Latics in the Littlewoods Cup Final against Nottingham Forest.

Very briefly on schoolboy forms with Forest as a 16-year-old, the popular, locally–born defender spent 11 seasons of first-team football with his home-town club, making his League debut at Boundary Park on 25 August 1984 against Birmingham City in Division Two. An unfortunate own-goal by Kenny Clements gave the relegated Blues a winning start to their season. He played in 31(2) League matches in his first season, which concluded in great style. A Mike Quinn hat-trick and two from Roger Palmer accounted for Carlisle United, the 5–2 result being the best away victory of the season. The match also featured a brilliant penalty save by Andy Goram, his sixth spot-kick save of the campaign.

Barlow waited three years before scoring a League goal and promptly celebrated by scoring two in the same match on 14 February 1987, ensuring that promotion rivals Ipswich Town were beaten 2–1, thanks to his match-winning double. In a season when Athletic gambled by splashing out £180,000 on Kevin Moore and Tommy Wright, they were never out of the top three all season, but in a dramatic last week they lost in the Play-off semi-finals to Leeds United.

The following season could be neatly divided into two halves; relegation candidates to mid-December, promotion candidates thereafter. Following a 2–2 draw with Bournemouth at Dean Court in early December, only four out of the following 25 matches were lost. It was a season of change and injury problems; highlights included 20 goals each for Andy Ritchie and Roger Palmer – Palmer netting three hat-tricks and his 100th League goal.

Barlow was married in the summer of 1989 and went on to enjoy a wonderful season. His combination on the left flank with Rick Holden launched numerous adventurous forays in a season when Athletic totalled 110 goals in their 65 matches. He appeared in all but two of the games, including the Wembley Littlewoods Cup Final against Nottingham Forest, in which he was the only home-town player in the Latics team. Despite the heartbreak of a 1–0 defeat in the searing Wembley heat, he had plenty to celebrate in a season that earned him a new four-year contract.

Barlow was one of just three players who made maximum appearances in the 1990–91 Second Division Championship side, who turned the near-misses of 1989–90 into glorious triumphs. In another season of high scoring, 93 goals were registered, Ian Marshall topping the list with 18. For those supporters who attended the season's dramatic final match against Sheffield Wednesday, they are unlikely to forget that it was Barlow who earned the 92nd-minute penalty, successfully converted by Neil Redfearn, that sealed the 3–2 win and the Division Two Championship trophy with it.

On the eve of Athletic's return to the top flight, Barlow suffered knee-ligament damage in an accidental collision with Ian Thompstone in training. Without experienced cover for the left full-back position, manager Joe Royle acted immediately to bring in Glynn Snodin from Leeds United on loan. He was sidelined until early October but recovered to make 28 League appearances. In the following season, Neil Pointon took over the left full-back role, and Barlow suffered a further serious knee injury in the second match of season 1994–95 at Port Vale, bringing his Athletic career to a premature end. He subsequently gave excellent service to both Blackpool (80 League matches) and Rochdale (67 League matches). As a regional coach for the PFA, he has remained involved in the game following his retirement as a player.

Earl Barrett

Date of birth: 28 April 1967, Rochdale

Oldham Athletic record:
Appearances: League 181(2), FA Cup 14, League Cup 20
Goals: League 7, FA Cup 1, League Cup 1
Debut: Plymouth Argyle (h) 28 November 1987, lost 0–1

Also played for: Manchester City, Chester City (on loan), Aston Villa, Everton, Sheffield United (on loan), Sheffield Wednesday, England (3 caps)

Versatile defender Earl Barrett began on YTS Forms with Manchester City, becoming a professional at the age of 18. He was loaned to Chester City in February 1986 in order to gain first-team experience, and in 12 appearances he assisted the Sealand Road club to win promotion from Division Four. Returning to Maine Road, he was given his Manchester City debut in the final fixture of the season against Luton Town. After failing to win a first-team place as City dropped out of Division One, his three-and-a-half year stay ended when he joined the Latics in November 1987 for a bargain fee of £35,000.

Despite a first season when he was troubled by injuries, the lightning-quick defender was a key figure in the Latics' most memorable season, which sadly ended without any tangible reward. Appearances in the 1989–90 Littlewoods Cup Final and the FA Cup semi-final both ended in disappointment, as did the brave bid for a promotion Play-off place. The mental and physical strain of the 65-match senior programme proved just too much, but it was greatly to Barrett's credit that he was the only player to appear in every match of the season. He additionally scored his first goals in senior football, chipping in with four in the impressive overall total of 110 for the season.

In a season when manager Joe Royle collected three Barclays monthly awards, Barrett's consolation prize was his selection as an over-age player in the England Under-21 squad for the European tournament in Toulon, France, in May 1990.

A storming start to season 1990–91 showed that the players had put behind them the disappointment of not achieving promotion. Despite injury problems during the campaign, Barrett again made maximum appearances, as did Andy Barlow and Jon Hallworth. Promotion was clinched when Athletic beat Ipswich Town at Portman Road at the end of April. Three thousand Latics fans made the long journey to East Anglia to witness a piece of history, the 2–1 victory which put their club back in the First Division for the first time in 68 years.

Further drama followed as the Second Division Championship race went right to the last day of the season. Already promoted Sheffield Wednesday were the visitors for the final match, witnessed by 18,809 spectators. After 30 minutes the Latics lost Gunnar Halle through injury and were a goal behind after just 90 seconds. With 50 minutes on the clock they trailed 2–0 to a slick Wednesday side, who could have been even further ahead had they taken full advantage of their superiority. Even the most optimistic fan feared the worst, but a most unlikely victory was snatched, against all the odds. Goals by Ian Marshall, Paul Bernard, and a heart-stopping injury-time winner – scored from the penalty spot by Neil Redfearn – saw the Latics safely home, and Earl Barrett was the proud recipient of the title trophy. In the close season he made his full England debut in Auckland. A major upset seemed likely when Athletic's newly-capped defender gave his side the lead, with an eighth-minute headed goal in their first Division One match against Liverpool at Anfield. Taking the game to their aristocratic rivals, the Latics were well worth their interval lead. Second-half goals from Ray Houghton and John Barnes, however, denied the Latics an opening-day victory.

In February of the same season, Barrett moved to Aston Villa in a £1.7 million transfer and assisted them to finish as runners-up in the Premier League in his first season. He also collected a League Cup-winners' medal with Villa in 1994. An identical fee reunited him with his old manager, Joe Royle, at Everton in January 1995. His first appearance for Everton was a stormy affair, Barrett being one of two Everton players to be sent off by referee David Elleray. Following a brief loan spell with Sheffield United in January 1998, he joined Wednesday on a free transfer. He retired just prior to Christmas 1999 having failed to make a complete recovery from a serious knee injury sustained in October 1998.

Keith Bebbington

Date of birth: 4 August 1943, Cuddington, near Nantwich

Oldham Athletic record:
Appearances: League 237, FA Cup 10, League Cup 8
Goals: League 39, FA Cup 6, League Cup 1
Debut: Leyton Orient (h) 20 August 1966, won 3–1

Also played for: Northwich Victoria, Stoke City, Rochdale, Winsford United

Raven-haired and handsome, Keith Bebbington joined the Latics in August 1966. Manager Jimmy McIlroy, himself a former teammate at Stoke City, made a double swoop on his old club when he signed him and George Kinnell for a combined fee of £25,000. While George Kinnell was sold for a quick profit – £20,000 to Sunderland – after only two months, Bebbington remained a fixture at Boundary Park for six years, replicating his period of professional service with Stoke City.

Bebbington first joined the Potters on amateur forms as a 15-year-old, and, despite a trial period with Northwich Victoria in between, he was signed as a professional in August 1960 and made his first-team debut two years later.

Stoke City fielded a front line with four internationals in the early 60s – Stanley Matthews, Dennis Violet, Jackie Mudie and Jimmy McIlroy – so there was no shortage of stiff competition. Bebbington totalled 123(1) League and Cup appearances that included appearances in the 1964 Football League Cup Final – a two-leg affair in those days – against Leicester City. Keith scored in the first leg at Stoke, which ended 1–1, but Leicester City won 3–2 at Filbert Street to win the Cup 4–3 on aggregate.

Bebbington served under three different managers in six years at Boundary Park – Jimmy McIlroy, Jack Rowley and Jimmy Frizzell – and he found favour with them all, averaging nearly 40 matches per season throughout his stay. For a wingman who later moved back into midfield, his strike rate was a respectable one, but overall he will be remembered as a provider of openings, subtly engineered by artistic footwork on either flank.

Bebbington's first season was memorable for his outstanding performances in the FA Cup competition. Witnessed by the biggest Boundary Park crowd of the season – 24,968 – Keith scored twice against mighty opponents Wolves in a rousing 2–2 draw in the third round. He scored again in the replay at Molineux, but Wolves, who won promotion from Division Two that season, ran out comfortable 4–1 winners.

Season 1968–69 was a disaster for the Latics, who finished rock bottom of Division Three. The season had hardly kicked-off when manager Jimmy McIlroy resigned. New manager Jack Rowley inherited a side at the foot of the table with only one win in 10 matches and a goal record of five for and 23 against. In the uphill struggle that followed, Bebbington was the season's outstanding player, finishing as leading goalscorer with 12 League and one FA Cup goal.

These were dismal times for Athletic and another dreadful start in Division Four – two wins in the first 15 matches – eventually led to another change at the helm. Jimmy Frizzell was appointed caretaker manager on 30 December 1969 and had 22 matches left in which to perform a miracle. The corner was turned on a snow-covered Boundary Park on 14 February. In probably his best ever performance for the club, Bebbington inspired the Latics to a 5–0 victory over Notts County, having a hand in all the goals and scoring two himself.

In the following vintage season, promotion from Division Four was secured. An attacking extravaganza by the tangerine-shirted Latics featured 24 goals by Jim Fryatt, 23 by David Shaw and 10 each from Bebbington and Tommy Bryceland. An additional bonus was the £70,000 prize money from the Ford Sporting League, which enabled a new stand to be erected on the Broadway side of the ground.

Bebbington left Athletic at the close of the following season, having appeared in all but five of the season's matches. His short move to Rochdale brought Ronnie Blair back to Boundary Park for a second spell.

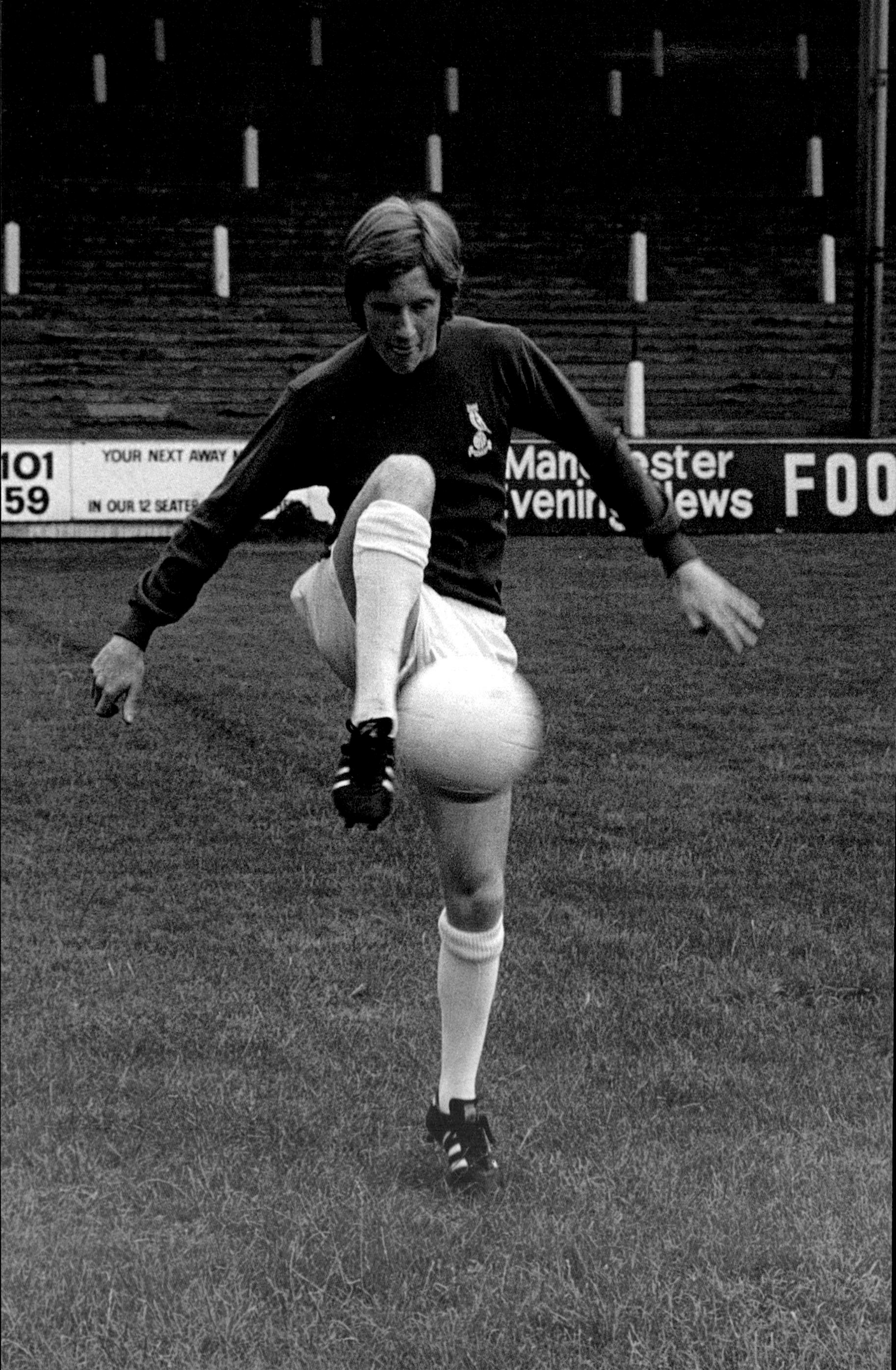
101
59
YOUR NEXT AWAY
IN OUR 12 SEATER

Graham Bell

Date of birth: 30 March 1955, Middleton

Oldham Athletic record:
Appearances: League 166(4), FA Cup 7(1), League Cup 9
Goals: League 9
Debut: Bristol Rovers (h) 31 August 1974

Also played for: Chadderton FC, Preston North End, Huddersfield Town on loan, Carlisle United, Bolton Wanderers, Tranmere Rovers, Hyde United, Mossley, Horwich RMI

A former apprentice coach builder, Graham Bell joined Athletic on amateur forms as a 17-year-old. He followed in his father's footsteps when he signed professional forms with the Latics in December 1973. While Tommy Bell made his mark in League football as a full-back, Graham starred in midfield for six different League clubs, amassing a total of 446(17) appearances.

Flame-haired and enthusiastic, Bell began locally with Chadderton FC and made his way through Athletic's junior sides to make his senior debut in 1974–75, the season that marked a return to Division Two after an interval of 40 years. Although lightly built at 5ft 9in and 10st 6lb, he was extremely mobile. He tackled well and his composure on the ball was coupled with superb distribution skills. His outstanding early form brought him to the attention of England manager Don Revie, but despite being capped at Youth level he failed to capitalise on his meteoric start.

Although Bell gained valuable senior experience at a relatively tender age, Athletic were, at that time, treading water in Division Two – their best finish during his stay being eighth. They were, in fact, fortunate to avoid immediate relegation. The season opened with much hope and anticipation, but the team proved to be poor travellers, with all of the season's 10 League victories being achieved at Boundary Park.

The team finished in 18th position in the table, with a three-point advantage over Cardiff City, who were relegated along with Sheffield Wednesday. Bell made 32(3) League appearances in his first season at senior level. He was absent only twice in 1975–76 and opened his goalscoring account at Carlisle United on 4 November in a 2–1 defeat. His first goal at Boundary Park, scored against the eventual Champions of Division Two, gave Athletic a share of the points against Sunderland on 20 March.

Something of a topsy-turvy season followed. Seven consecutive League victories during December and January raised hopes, but in February and March eight matches without a victory ended any thoughts of promotion. Steve Taylor was the star of the season with 20 League goals in 32 matches. The team finished in eighth position, and Bell missed six matches due to injury and was absent when the new season opened at Luton Town in August 1978. Luton's players must have had the most effective pep talk of all time from manager David Pleat. Athletic led 1–0 at half-time, but things went decidedly pear-shaped thereafter as Luton scored six in the second half. Bell returned to action in the 1–1 draw against Stoke City on 2 September. He substituted for Mike Bernard, whose injury-plagued spell at Boundary Park ended shortly after this latest set-back, along with his League career.

In March of the same season, around the time of the transfer deadline, Bell made the first of his many subsequent moves when Preston North End's manager Nobby Stiles recruited him for a fee of £80,000. He completed 140(3) League appearances and scored nine goals for North End, who were relegated into Division Three in 1981.

A return to Division Two with Carlisle United proved unrewarding as Bell played in only 11(3) League matches during his stay at Brunton Park. This ended when Bolton Wanderers signed him in February 1984. In his last game for the Wanderers he appeared as a substitute at Wembley in the 1986 Freight Rover Trophy Final against Bristol City. Three months later he joined Tranmere Rovers, his last League club. Outside of the game he variously owned a general store in Oldham, worked in the insurance industry and operated as a customer services manager for Group 4 Security.

Tommy Bell

Date of birth: 30 December 1923, Heyside
Died: 21 November 1988, Chadderton

Oldham Athletic record:
Appearances: League 170, FA Cup 11
Goals: 0
Debut: Doncaster Rovers, FA Cup 2 (h) 14 December 1946, lost 1–2

Also played for: Mossley, Stockport County, Halifax Town, Ashton United

Tommy Bell joined Athletic at the mid-point of the first season of League football after World War Two. The 1946–47 season opened with a team unrecognisable from the one that had contested the final season of peacetime football, with Tommy Butler, Bill Hayes and Tommy Williamson being the only familiar faces.

Manager Frank Womack, the former Birmingham full-back and captain, fielded a side with eight new players for the opening fixture against Carlisle United at Boundary Park. A lack of cohesion was perhaps to be expected, and Carlisle, thanks to an outstanding display by player-manager Ivor Broadis, ran out comfortable winners at 2–0.

In early October, in the local derby match against Stockport County at Boundary Park, Athletic lost both their full-backs – Jerry Boothman and Dick Whittam – and finished the match with only nine men. Manager Womack moved quickly to provide extra cover, but his £500 offer to Mossley FC for Dick Threlfall, the ex-Bolton Wanderers right full-back, ended in failure when the player decided that he was happy to remain with the Cheshire League club.

In the following month Athletic spent their £500 on recently demobilised Tommy Bell, Mossley's 23-year-old left full-back, who was only too happy to move up into Football League circles. Replacing Jerry Boothman on his debut, Bell was given a severe examination by the outstanding team in the Division Doncaster Rovers, who went on to win the Championship of the Northern Section that season with a record 72 points and 123 League goals scored.

In a determined display, Bell revealed excellent mobility, he also tackled hard and his measured clearances along the left flank were the source of several attacking runs by Jack Ormandy. Athletic were narrowly beaten 2–1, but centre-forward Bill Waite missed a wonderful opportunity to equalise, his 85th-minute penalty-kick clearing the crossbar to the dismay of the 18,100 Boundary Park crowd.

Bell retained his first-team place through to the end of the season, but a change of management – Billy Wootton replacing Frank Womack – saw him initially out of favour, but in 1948–49 he formed an excellent partnership with Bill Pickering, Bell switching to right-back in order to accommodate the former Sheffield Wednesday left full-back.

In 1950–51, when player-manager George Hardwick, England's former captain, replaced Billy Wootton, Bell was the only player to make maximum appearances during the season. He was similarly impressive in 1951–52 with 42 League appearances, when an excellent start to the season – six wins and three draws in the opening nine matches – gave Athletic an early lead in the table. They finished in fourth place, and in April Bell's six years of sterling service were rewarded with a benefit match. The 7,449 spectators who attended were treated to a feast of goals, the All Stars XI beating Tommy's XI by 9–2. Internationals who played included Jimmy Hagan, Tom Finney, Frank Swift, Tommy Docherty and Roy Clarke.

Bell remained in the Northern Section of Division Three with Stockport County and finally Halifax Town, where he scored his one and only League goal against Workington at The Shay on 29 January 1955. He made his final appearance at Boundary Park in Halifax Town's colours on 27 December 1955 and assisted his team to a 3–1 win.

During his time with Athletic, Bell spent summer months as an extremely effective early order batsman with Crompton Cricket Club. A personal memory surrounds his carrying, along with his equipment, a small canvas bag which, more often than not, was filled with the loose change collected around the ground after he had scored a 50.

Ronnie Blair

Date of birth: 26 September 1949, Coleraine, Northern Ireland

Oldham Athletic record:
Appearances: League 359(13), FA Cup 15, League Cup 16(2)
Goals: League 22, League Cup 1
Debut: Shrewsbury Town (a) 21 January 1967, lost 1–3

Also played for: Coleraine, Rochdale (two spells), Caribous (US), Blackpool. Northern Ireland (5 caps)

One of Athletic's most versatile and accomplished players and a great crowd favourite during his two spells at Boundary Park, Ronnie Blair combined dash, determination and good constructive ideas in both midfield and defensive roles. Recruited during the Jimmy McIlroy era, initially on amateur forms, he was a talented junior having represented his country at both School and Youth levels. He was the first of the youthful Irish contingent to break through into Athletic's first team, swiftly followed by Allan Hunter, the classy, ball-playing centre-half, who was quickly snapped up by Blackburn Rovers.

In the early days one had the impression that Blair had tremendous potential, but that he was capable of starting an argument in an empty room! For whatever reasons, his first spell at Boundary Park was not distinguished, and when he departed to Rochdale in April 1970, having made just nine appearances in that season, it could have been the end of the story.

Jimmy Frizzell was instrumental in bringing Blair back to Boundary Park in a straight swap for Keith Bebbington in August 1972. As he was to say at the time, 'The best thing about my move to Rochdale was that I met my future wife, Hilary.' Certainly he seemed delighted to be back, and his professionalism and versatility went on to serve Athletic unswervingly for the next nine seasons.

In the 1973–74 Championship-winning season Blair appeared in 41 of the League matches, scored 11 vital goals and was the deserved recipient of the Player of the Year award. His influence on the side during the season was enormous, providing steel and bite in defence and an unexpected eye for goal.

It would be difficult to calculate just how many different positions Blair played in, but he certainly occupied both full-back berths, centre-back, across midfield and even led the attack, never giving less that 100 percent effort. One had the feeling that if he had been asked to play in goal he would most probably have made a good job of it.

The upward move into Second Division football saw Blair gain the first of his five prized Irish caps. His breakthrough came in October 1974, when he first came on as a substitute in Northern Ireland's 2–0 win against Sweden in Stockholm. It was in the same season that he scored the 'goal' that never was. A press photograph of the day showed clearly that his shot against Manchester United at Boundary Park on 28 December 1974 had clearly entered the net. It struck the angled stanchion support bar, bounced straight out to goalkeeper Alex Stepney, who promptly cleared the ball up field, and to everybody's amazement the referee waved play on! Fortunately, the result of the match was not affected, the Latics gaining a famous 1–0 victory thanks to a fiercely-struck penalty-kick by Maurice Whittle.

Blair was awarded a testimonial, and an All Ireland International Select XI provided the opposition to an Athletic XI. On a bitterly cold Tuesday evening in November 1974, an entertaining match ended 3–3. Athletic's scorers in the match were Paul Heaton, Vic Halom and Simon Stainrod. Bryan Hamilton scored two for the Irish XI and Kenny Clements scored a 90th-minute own-goal to level the scores.

Blair left Boundary Park for the last time in August 1981 to sign for Blackpool. Typically, he had appeared in every match of his final season, by this time operating at left full-back. He scored on his debut for Blackpool in a 2–0 win against Stockport County on 29 August and completed 42(1) League and Cup appearances (three goals), before rejoining Rochdale in August 1982. Increasing business commitments cut short his second spell at Spotland, and his League career was wound up with aggregate figures of 462(29) appearances and 29 goals.

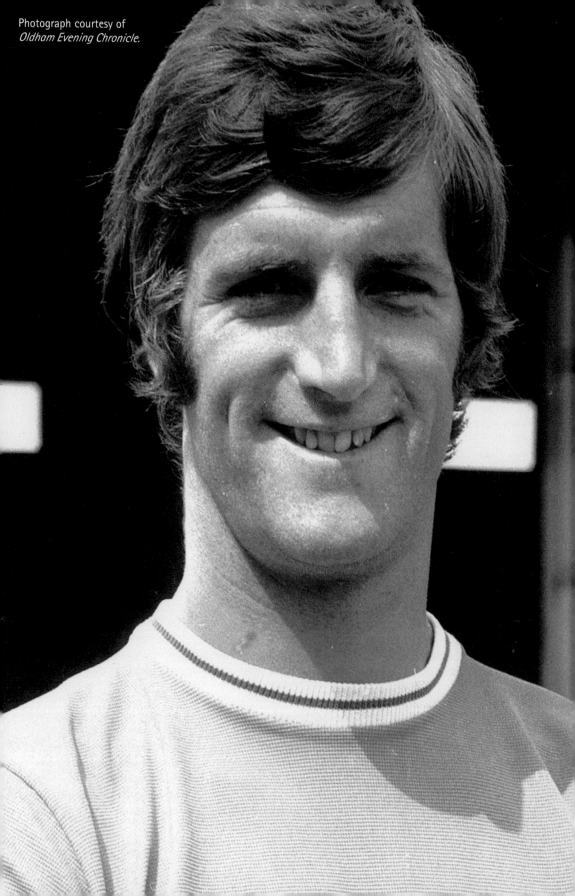

Photograph courtesy of
Oldham Evening Chronicle.

Jim Bowie

Date of birth: 11 October 1941, Howwood, Renfrewshire

Oldham Athletic record:
Appearances: League 331(3), FA Cup 18(1), League Cup 12
Goals: League 37, FA Cup 2, League Cup 3
Debut: Newport County (a) 20 August 1962, drawn 0–0

Also played for: Neilston Waverley, Third Lanark amateur, Arthurlie Juniors, Rochdale

Considering his lengthy stay in Lancashire, 'Big Jim' – as he was popularly known – had initially shown a marked reluctance to leave his native Scotland. He was working in the offices of a Glasgow insurance company when he was first spotted by Athletic, playing in a Scottish Junior Cup tie at Blairgowrie for Arthurlie Juniors. He did not take up Athletic's offer of a contract until six months later, but when he arrived he quickly settled in and became a firm favourite at Boundary Park for the next 10 years. At 6ft 3in and 11st 7lb, the young Scot was built like a lamp-post, but his height enabled him to win most aerial encounters.

In the earliest days as an inside-right, and occupying the same berth as the Scottish maestro Bobby Johnstone, opportunities in his first season were naturally limited. Nevertheless, his five goals in 14 League matches were considered a very useful contribution. Bowie scored his first League goal against Newport County at Boundary Park on his second appearance. This was on 29 August 1962, and the fact that his goal was the winner in a 3–2 victory made it all the more satisfying. In March and early April of the same season he struck a purple patch, scoring in consecutive matches against Doncaster Rovers, Stockport County, Chester and Southport.

From the outset, Bowie's style of play could almost be described as languid, his eye for the open space giving him time and room to manoeuvre with an apparent lack of effort. In true Scottish style, he preferred to play the ball along the ground, and when switched to inside-left in 1963–64 he formed an excellent wing partnership with Colin Whitaker, and later with Tony Bartley.

In the club's first season back in Division Three, Bowie scored against Queen's Park Rangers in the opening fixture at Boundary Park, a match won by 2–1. Despite losing his place late in the season to new signing Bobby Craig, he completed 29 League and Cup matches and scored 10 goals, six coming in League matches and a further two each in the season's FA and League Cup ties.

It was in the late stages of season 1964–65 when manager Les McDowall first tried Bowie in the role of wing half-back, and it was in this position that he spent much of the remainder of his career. This was despite the fact that a managerial merry-go-round marked much of the mid-60s to early 70s. Jimmy McIlroy stretched his versatility to the limit in his final full season in charge – 1967–68 – fielding him in both inside-forward berths, both wing half-back positions and at right and left full-back.

Both Jack Rowley and Jimmy Frizzell recognised Bowie's best position in the middle line, and in 1970–71, when Athletic finished third in Division Four and won promotion, he played in every match during the season. Apart from a worrying dip in form during March – only one win in seven matches – it proved to be a vintage season spearheaded by Jim Fryatt and David Shaw, who between them scored 47 of the team's 88 League goals. Older supporters will recall the usual line up with some relish: Dowd, Wood, Whittle, McNeil, Cranston, Bowie, Heath, Shaw, Fryatt, Bryceland and Bebbington.

Bowie's final season was spent in Division Three, and he played in 40 of the season's League and Cup matches. He scored his last goal against Bournemouth at Boundary Park on 21 March 1972, a match won by 3–1. He departed in the close season and spent a brief trial period with Rochdale. He played in three matches, two as substitute, but refused to extend his trial period when invited to do so.

A keen and accomplished amateur golfer at the local Saddleworth Club, after retiring from football Bowie worked as a representative for an American company who manufactured golf equipment.

Ken Branagan

Date of birth: 27 July 1930, Salford

Oldham Athletic record:
Appearances: League 177, FA Cup 14, League Cup 4
Goals: League 5
Debut: York City (h) 1 October 1960, won 3–1

Also played for: Manchester United amateur, Manchester City

The month of October in 1960 proved pivotal in the fortunes of the Latics. Languishing at the foot of soccer's basement after making a dreadful start to the season, manager Jack Rowley entered into the transfer market with a vengeance. On the first of the month a double swoop on Manchester City brought in Ken Branagan and Bert Lister, for a combined fee of £10,000. On the fourth of the month winger Bob Rackley arrived from Bristol Rovers, and one week later the former Manchester City and Scotland international Bobby Johnstone was signed from Hibernian. The final piece of significant business followed when full-back John McCue, who was on a month's trial, was signed for the remainder of the season.

While Bobby Johnstone was the name on everybody's lips, with hindsight the capture of Ken Branagan and Bert Lister was an equally significant stroke of business.

Branagan played at both inside and outside-right for Lancashire and England Schoolboys, and only became a full-back when covering for an injured teammate. He did so well in his new position that he remained in the role for the rest of his long career.

Although he began as an amateur on Manchester United's books, Branagan spent 12 years with Manchester City, making 208 League and Cup appearances. He was the 12th man for City in the 1955 FA Cup Final against Newcastle United. Had substitutes been allowed in those days, he would have played, as City were reduced to 10 men when full-back Jimmy Meadows was seriously injured, and he would have been the ideal replacement, but in the event he didn't even get a medal.

Branagan was 30 years old when he arrived at Boundary Park, and his full-back partner John McCue was 38, having already appeared in 502 League matches for Stoke City. Nevertheless, the veteran pair did much to tighten Athletic's defensive lines as the Bobby Johnstone-inspired attack lifted the Latics from the doldrums. His debut – in the 13th League match of the season – was the first time that the team had won at Boundary Park. Scorers in the overdue 3–1 victory were Bert Lister, Brian Birch and Peter Phoenix with a penalty. Later in the season Branagan took over as penalty taker and scored his first goal from the spot against Peterborough United – the eventual Champions – in a 1–1 draw that attracted a crowd of 27,888 to Boundary Park. He was on the mark again against Mansfield Town on 31 March, but blotted his copybook one day later when, with the chance to equalise, he shot wide from the spot at Crystal Palace, who won 2–1.

In the promotion season of 1962–63, Branagan was one of five players to appear in every League match. Amazingly enough, during a board meeting at Boundary Park on 1 May 1963 the board voted 6–4 to dismiss manager Jack Rowley, whose three-year contract was due to end in July, even though it had been such a successful season. From Branagan's point of view, this change meant that he was once again playing under his former Manchester City manager Les McDowall. In Athletic's biggest victory since the demolition of Southport by 11–0 on Boxing Day 1962, he was among the scorers in the 7–3 win against Bristol Rovers on 28 October 1964.

Branagan was released on a free transfer in May 1966, but returned to Boundary Park in August 1973 as reserve-team trainer and youth coach. His son Jim, also a full-back, began with the Latics and was signed as a professional in July 1973. He found few opportunities with the Latics but enjoyed nine seasons with Blackburn Rovers, recording 333(40) appearances in all competitions.

Ken Brierley

Date of birth: 3 April 1926, Ashton-under-Lyne
Died: February 2002, Blackpool

Oldham Athletic record:
Appearances: League 125, FA Cup 9
Goals: League 10, FA Cup 1
Debut: Southport, FA Cup 1 (a) 17 November 1945, won 2–1

Also played for: Range Boilers FC, Liverpool, Stalybridge Celtic, Mossley, Wigan Athletic

On 21 April 1945, inside-left Ken Brierley made his first appearance for the Latics in a 2–1 win at Rochdale. With VE Day less than a month away, 19-year-old Brierley was a 'Bevin Boy', working in a Pontefract colliery, and only able to get home every third week. He was unavailable for the return match against Rochdale in the following week, but played in both of the season's concluding matches against Liverpool. He scored his first goal in the 2–3 defeat at Anfield, and three years later Liverpool paid the then significant sum of £7,000 for his signature.

When normal League football resumed in the 1946–47 season, not a lot had changed for Brierley who was still spending his nights in the pit, which didn't make football any easier for him. It says much for the resilience of youth that, despite his tough schedule, he was outstanding in a struggling side. Taking over at inside-left from Jack Bowden, he was subsequently switched to left half-back, where he stayed for much of the remainder of the season.

A change of manager in the close season – Billy Wootton replacing Frank Womack – saw Brierley first tried at outside-left at New Brighton in a 2–2 draw at the Tower Ground on 11 October 1947. Despite being only 11 matches into the season, no fewer than four players had been tried on the left wing.

Brierley proved to be a mobile wingman with subtle ball skills and a natural body swerve. Although not a great goalscorer, his forte was the accurately measured centre from the left wing. That said, he did score in his final appearance prior to his move to Anfield. This was at Gateshead on 21 February 1948, Athletic winning a rousing encounter by 5–3. The game marked the debut of Billy Jessop, who scored twice, as did Billy Blackshaw, with Brierley netting the fifth. It was probably the only time that the Latics had scored five goals in an away match, with all the goals being headers.

Earlier in the season, the Latics had beaten Liverpool at Anfield in a second-round Lancashire Senior Cup tie. They had, incidentally, beaten Manchester United after a replay in the first round. In subsequent years the competition aroused little interest, the Liverpool team beaten 2–0 by Athletic contained eight men with first-team experience. Brierley had starred in the match and doubtlessly impressed Liverpool's management, who signed him in late February 1948.

Brierley was no less a performer than Billy Liddell, who was moved to outside-right to accommodate him on his Liverpool debut when Huddersfield Town were beaten 4–0, centre-forward Albert Stubbins scoring all four goals. Brierley opened his scoring account in March of the same season in a Merseyside derby against Everton, won 4–0 by the Reds before an attendance of 55,035 spectators.

In the season that Brierley returned to Boundary Park (1952–53), he had played most of his Liverpool matches at left-half, and it was in this position that he helped steer Athletic through the final two months of the season. With player-manager George Hardwick out through injury, it was Brierley and Billy McGlen – another late-season capture – who provided the experience in a nail-biting finale that ran to the final match of the season at Bradford City.

Player-manager Hardwick returned to action and was chaired from the field by enthusiastic Athletic supporters at the end of the match, a goalless draw that was sufficient to seal the Third Division North Championship. The Athletic team that clinched the club's first-ever Championship, lined up as follows: Burnett, McGlen, Hardwick, Smith, Whyte, Brierley, Harris, Lowrie, Clarke, McIlvenny and Ormond.

Brierley left Athletic at the end of season 1954–55. In his retirement he lived at Freckleton near Preston.

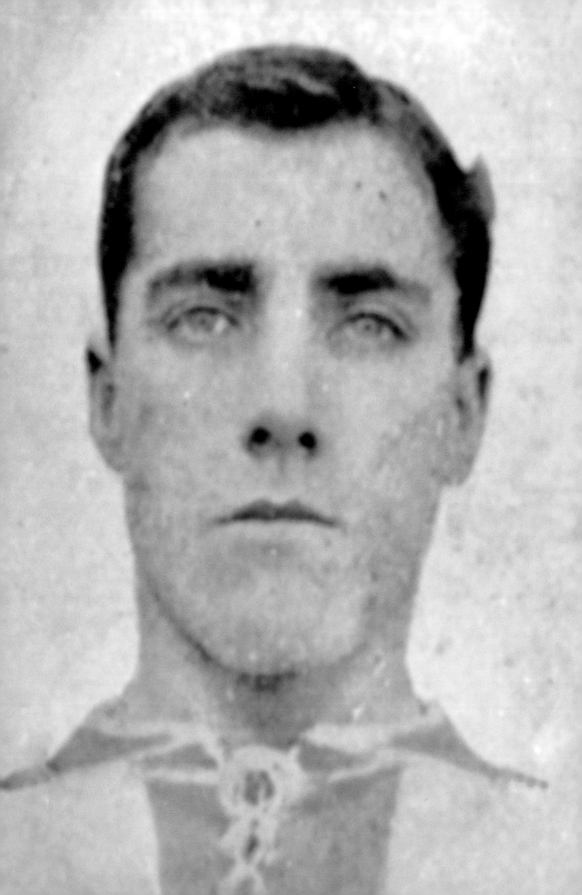

Tommy Broad

Date of birth: 31 July 1887, Stalybridge
Died: October 1966, Barton Irwell

Oldham Athletic record:
Appearances: League 96, FA Cup 8
Goals: League 9
Debut: 4 September 1909 v Birmingham (a) drawn 2–2

Also played for: Redgate Albion, Denton Wanderers, Openshaw Lads' Club, West Bromwich Albion, Chesterfield Town, Bristol City, Manchester City, Stoke, Southampton, Weymouth, Rhyl Athletic, England Junior international versus Scotland, April 1906, Football League representative versus Irish League, October 1910

The son of a former Manchester City trainer who won many prizes on the running track, it was perhaps unsurprising that the younger Broad could show his heels to nine out of 10 of the backs that he encountered. When his speed was utilised to the full, he was one of the most dangerous wingman in the country. All necks at Boundary Park were craned, and a great shout invariably went up as, with an amazing burst of acceleration, he appeared to be in full stride within a couple of paces.

Notable among his early clubs, Openshaw Lads went through an entire season in the Heaton Park and District League without losing a match. At the age of 16 Broad was given a trial by Manchester City, but was told that he was 'too little'. Two years later he was with West Bromwich Albion, but he arrived at Oldham via Chesterfield Town, who failed to gain re-election to the Football League in 1909. Despite interest from several top-flight clubs, manager David Ashworth secured his services in return for a fee of £250 and immediately installed him in the first team.

In three years at Boundary Park Broad was never in any danger of losing his place, following an outstanding first season when the Latics won promotion to the First Division. In what was only the club's third season of life in the Football League, the 1909–10 campaign began falteringly. Two draws and three defeats in the opening five matches was anything but promotion form, but things were to take a dramatic upturn. On 1 January 1910, Broad's goal against Glossop at Boundary Park proved sufficient to take maximum points. In a sequence unlikely to be bettered, the side then went through to the end of the season with the following record: Played 20, Won 15, Drawn 4, Lost 1, For 58, Against 14, Points 34. In the summer, the bottom bank of the ground was raised, the stands renovated, and the dressing rooms considerably extended. Despite elevation to the top flight, the directors announced that the prices of members' cards would not be increased. Match-day prices in those far-off days ranging from 6d to 2 shillings.

Life in Division One began with a trip to Aston Villa and a hard fought 1–1 draw, Villa equalising six minutes from time despite being reduced to 10 men in the second half. The first victory of the new campaign came at the end of September, with goals from Alf Toward and Broad sending the 30,000 Boundary Park crowd home heartened by a 2–0 victory against Tottenham Hotspur. Athletic finished their first season in the top flight in a very satisfactory seventh place.

Broad left Boundary Park upon his return from the club's summer tour to Austria in 1911. Fourteen players plus trainer Hanson and three officials left Hull on 25 May, with a busy schedule taking in six matches. His final outing on the Latics' right wing came on 5 June in a 1–0 victory against the Wiener Sporting Club in Vienna. He was transferred to Bristol City for £600 within days of disembarking, but after World War One he joined Manchester City for a fee reported to be 'less than £200'. However, his value had increased significantly by May 1921, when he joined Stoke for £500. Three years later he joined Southampton and was still in top-class football at the age of 38.

In September 1925 Broad stepped down into non-League football with Weymouth, ending his career with Rhyl Athletic, retiring to take over the licence of the Dudley Arms Hotel in the town. His brother Jimmy was a hard-shooting forward who assisted the Latics from August 1913 until the outbreak of World War One. He played in all four Divisions of the Football League and also sampled Scottish, Welsh and Southern League fare. Continuing the family theme, a team of 'Broads' played a team of 'Wilds' in a charity match at Manchester City's ground in 1908.

Lewis Brook

Date of birth: 27 July 1918, Halifax
Died: July 1996, Halifax

Oldham Athletic record:
Appearances: League 189, FA Cup 7
Goals: League 14
Debut: Lincoln City (h) 13 March 1948, drawn 0–0

Also played for: Northowram FC, Halifax Town amateur, Huddersfield Town (World War Two guest player with Aldershot, Bournemouth and Boscombe Athletic, Heart of Midlothian, Watford, Halifax Town)

Lewis Brook began in League football with Huddersfield Town in Division One at the age of 19. His debut was at inside-left against Middlesbrough (h) on 27 November 1937, with Town winning by 3–0. He played in only four matches in his first season, scoring his first goal against Everton on 5 February 1938. In 1938–39 he played in eight League matches – all at centre-forward – and scored four goals. In the first season of regional football a highlight was his four goals against Darlington in an 8–2 victory at Leeds Road on 25 May 1940. Military Service took him away from Yorkshire, and when he returned to score a hat-trick against Middlesbrough on 6 October 1945, it was his first Town appearance for almost five years. He played in only six first-team matches for Huddersfield in post-war football and was one of several players who crossed the Pennines to team up with the Latics at about this time, with defender Bill Naylor following him in the same month, March 1948.

Dark-haired and swarthy, Brook introduced much needed bustle and speed to Athletic's front line. He also proved alive to every opportunity when nearing goal, ending the season with six strikes in the final five matches, including four against Barrow in two matches, a 2–1 home win followed by a 4–2 victory at Holker Street.

A team featuring four new signings lost the opening fixture of 1948–49, Rotherham United winning 3–1 at Boundary Park. Five days later, at Hull City, Athletic went under by 6–0. After 10 matches, only one had been won, and wholesale changes were the order of the day. Brook lost his centre-forward spot to Eric Gemmell and spent the greater part of the season in the Lancashire Combination side, where he rediscovered his scoring touch with 19 in 22 matches.

Later in the following season, Brook reappeared in the first team at right half-back and scored in consecutive matches against Stockport County and Doncaster Rovers. He also scored the only goal of the match in the Manchester Senior Cup semi-final against Manchester United, who fielded 10 players with League experience. In the last match of the season Athletic beat Manchester City 2–1 to win the Senior Cup, a game attended by 8,321 spectators.

Rather like Matt Gray of an earlier era, Brook was probably too versatile for his own good, able to occupy any position on the field without becoming a fixture in any one role. He did in fact appear in every outfield position during his long spell at Boundary Park. However, he did hold down the right full-back position, in partnership with player-manager George Hardwick, in the 1952–53 season when the Third Division North Championship was won. By this time approaching the veteran stage at 34 years of age, he was far from a spent force. Accomplished displays throughout the season confirmed that he had finally found his niche in the team.

Brook played in 38 League and Cup matches in his final season. He scored his last goal against Hull City in the 3–1 defeat at Boundary Park on 28 February 1957, and on the 30th of the following month he made his final appearance in a high-scoring 4–4 draw at Wrexham. He was 38 years of age and very much the senior professional in a side that lined up as follows: Torrance, Brook, Fawley, Hobson, Murphy, Thompson, Bazley, Wright, Murray, Travis and Betts. He retired in the close season to take up a position in Halifax, unconnected with the game. Always a cheery character, he would rank among the very best of Athletic's club men in post-war years.

Frank Bunn

Date of birth: 6 November 1962, Birmingham

Oldham Athletic record:
Appearances: League 75(3), FA Cup 2, League Cup 8
Goals: League 26, FA Cup 1, League Cup 8
Debut: AFC Bournemouth (a) 5 December 1987, drawn 2–2

Also played for: Luton Town, Hull City, Stalybridge Celtic

Athletic were certainly in need of a lift in early December 1987. A lengthy injury list and a record of only one goal in the previous six League games – this scored by full-back Denis Irwin – had left the team third from the foot of Division Two.

The signing of £90,000 Frank Bunn from Hull City was expected to lift an attack that appeared capable of creating goalscoring chances, yet was incapable of taking them. Athletic ended a six-match losing sequence at Bournemouth and were disappointed to concede an equaliser, just two minutes from time. Bunn was both hero and villain on his debut as he gave away the penalty that provided the equaliser but had earlier won the spot-kick that should have given his side victory.

Bunn opened the scoring at Stoke City with a blistering 25-yard half-volley and, for the second game running, earned a penalty. Skipper Tony Henry successfully converted the award, but another late equaliser gave Stoke a share of the points. Athletic's first double of the season came at the expense of Sheffield United, Bunn scoring twice in a 5–0 scoring spree at Bramall Lane. The humiliated Blades manager Billy McEwan resigned shortly after the final whistle. Two goals in the last minute against Reading in early February gave Athletic a sensational 4–2 victory and a fifth successive League win. Athletic scored 27 goals in 12 matches following Bunn's signing, and their improved form was maintained. Bunn ended his first season at Boundary Park with nine League goals in 21 matches.

The main highlight of the following season was Roger Palmer's feat of smashing the club's all-time record for League goals. He extended his total to 113 by the end of the season. Bunn, despite an injury-hit campaign, scored 13 in 28 outings.

The 1989–90 campaign got off to a slow start, and after missing much of the pre-season build up due to injury Bunn wrote a page in the record books on 25 October. The normally quiet and unassuming striker had every right to feel cock-a-hoop after scoring six goals against Scarborough in a Littlewoods Cup tie at Boundary Park. He had never previously scored a hat-trick in a competitive match, but he came very near to equalling Eric Gemmell's individual scoring record of seven against Chester in 1952. He had seven chances and took six of them. He was chasing a record after scoring five in 32 minutes during the first half. Andy Ritchie scored goal number six after 53 minutes, Bunn completing the scoring with his sixth in the 89th minute. His double hat-trick set an individual record in the competition, previously shared by four players who had all scored five. The reward for the victory was a home draw against mighty League Champions Arsenal and another memorable night as the illustrious visitors were comprehensively beaten by 3–1.

A wonderful season for the club saw them reach the semi-final of the FA Cup and the Final of the Littlewoods Cup, but Bunn was kept out for three months from the turn of the year by a knee injury. His two goals in the 3–0 win against West Ham United on 21 April lifted Athletic's Play-off hopes and their prospects of success at Wembley in the following week. Sadly, his Wembley appearance proved to be his last in senior football. A reoccurrence of his knee injury saw him replaced by Roger Palmer after 67 minutes. Despite major surgery and a 19-month battle to regain fitness, he was unable to continue at top level. It was a sad day for everyone when the popular striker announced his retirement. Manager Joe Royle, whose career ended in a similar fashion, paid warm tribute to him, whom he credited with the turnaround of the club's fortunes.

George Burnett

Date of birth: 11 February 1920, Birkenhead
Died: 29 April 1985, Birkenhead

Oldham Athletic record:
Appearances: League 100, FA Cup 5
Goals: 0
Debut: Accrington Stanley (a) 6 October 1951, won 2–1

Also played for: Everton (World War Two guest player with Millwall, Wrexham, Tranmere Rovers, Manchester United), South Liverpool (loan), Ellesmere Port

George Burnett represented Liverpool Schools and joined Everton from Litherland Boys' Club, initially as an amateur, in May 1938. He was only 18 when he became a professional at Goodison Park. Like countless others of his generation, the outbreak of World War Two disrupted his career. He did, however, establish himself in Everton's first team in wartime competitions and was ever present for three seasons leading to the resumption of normal League football in 1946–47.

It was Burnett's misfortune to be at Everton at the same time as their celebrated England international Ted Sagar, whose Goodison career spanned an amazing 24 years and a total of 495 senior appearances. The highlights of Burnett's career were his appearance for Everton in the FA Cup semi-final of 1950 and his Third Division North Championship medal, won with the Latics in season 1952–53.

In the season prior to his move to Boundary Park, Burnett was on Everton's transfer list at £7,500 – a considerable sum for a goalkeeper at that time. He joined Athletic as cover for Fred Ogden, who had suffered a broken collarbone at Bradford City in September 1951. Athletic had made a splendid start to the 1951–52 season, remaining undefeated until the end of September, and their defensive lines were in no way weakened by his introduction as only five goals were conceded in his first 10 appearances.

At all times appearing cool, calm and collected, Burnett was a brave goalkeeper who, despite his modest build – he stood 5ft 10in tall – was outstanding in his handling of high crosses and was more than able to look after himself. This point was vividly illustrated in his first season at Boundary Park. A Stockport County centre-forward of the time was noted for his bruising tactics, particularly against opposing goalkeepers. He had probably never encountered Burnett before, and the first time that he rushed in to challenge he finished in a heap in the goalmouth and took several minutes to recover. Needless to say, he kept his distance thereafter!

In 1952–53 the Latics won their first-ever Championship in League football, sealing the Third Division North crown with a last-gasp 0–0 draw at Bradford City. It was an edgy display, but thanks to starring performances by Burnett and player-manager George Hardwick, a hard-fought draw resulted, ensuring that Second Division football would be played at Boundary Park in 1953–54. It had been a very close run thing, however, with Port Vale finishing as runners-up, one point adrift and with a better goal average.

With virtually the same team, apart from a newcomer at outside-right in Rex Adams from Blackpool, it quickly became obvious that further investment was required to strengthen the team for Second Division football. Sadly, the signing of new wingmen Harry McShane and Tommy Walker came too late to avoid relegation.

By a strange coincidence, Everton were the visitors for the final match of the season, and they required only a point to regain their First Division status. The 30,072 spectators who packed into Boundary Park saw Burnett endure a torrid first half that ended with Everton 4–0 ahead. There was no further scoring in the second half, but Everton had already achieved their goal of promotion.

Burnett remained a life-long Everton supporter and, after retiring from the game, ran a public house at Moreton.

Les Chapman

Date of birth: 27 September 1948, Oldham

Oldham Athletic record:
Appearances: League 261(2), FA Cup 10, League Cup 16
Goals: League 20, FA Cup 1, League Cup 2
Debut: Bristol Rovers (a) 11 February 1967, lost 1–2

Also played for: Huddersfield Town as an amateur, Oldham Athletic, Huddersfield Town (again), Oldham Athletic
                (again), San Jose Earthquakes, US, Stockport County, Bradford City, Rochdale

Les Chapman was born at the Boundary Park Hospital, just a goal-kick away from the Latics ground. He was a pupil at Chadderton Grammar School and first worked as a trainee accountant in the Borough Treasurer's Department of Middleton town hall.

His footballing prowess was first 'spotted' by Ian Greaves, who was at that time a coach with Huddersfield Town. The youthful wingman spent a trial period at Leeds Road but was not considered sufficiently impressive to be offered a professional contract. Returning to Oldham, he almost abandoned thoughts of a career in football altogether, but was then recommended to the Latics by a scout who had seen him play for the Town Hall team. Quickly signed on amateur forms, he became a professional within three months and in a matter of weeks won a place in the first team.

In the early days as an outside-left with boundless energy and enthusiasm, Chapman's turn of pace enabled him to run the legs off most Division Three full-backs. After making a most promising start – he appeared in 15 of the final 17 matches of the 1966–67 season – he lost out to Keith Bebbington for the number-11 shirt in 1967–68. He came back strongly, however, with a run of 41 consecutive League outings in 1968–69, but, in the season that Jack Rowley replaced Jimmy McIlroy as manager, Athletic were relegated to Division Four.

Nine matches into the following term Chapman crossed the Pennines, returning to where he had started. On this occasion, however, he cost Huddersfield Town a fee of £35,000, with inside-forward David Shaw moving to Boundary Park in a part exchange. It was a hefty investment for the Terriers, considering that he could have been signed for nothing some four years earlier.

It was in mid-season 1974–75 when, in an exchange deal that took Colin Garwood to Leeds Road, Chapman returned to Boundary Park for a second spell. By this time operating in midfield, he joined a side struggling to come to terms with life in Division Two, following their Championship success in the previous season. In the month of his return, and playing in a team without a League victory for 11 matches, a packed Boundary Park witnessed the highlight of the season. Visiting neighbours Manchester United were defeated by the only goal of the match, a typically thunderous penalty-kick converted by Maurice Whittle. It was the Latics first meeting with United since a third-round FA Cup tie at Old Trafford some 24 years earlier, and the first League fixture between the sides for almost 40 years.

In his second spell at Boundary Park, Chapman missed only five League matches in four and a half seasons, never giving less than 100 percent effort. In addition to his quite remarkable work rate, his tackling and cool use of the ball, even under the most severe pressure, were the outstanding features of his play.

Somewhat surprisingly released at the close of the 1978–79 season – in which he was one of only two players to make maximum appearances – Chapman was quickly snapped up by Stockport County. Before he finally retired as a player at the age of 39, he amassed a total of 747 League appearances (including 22 as substitute) and scored 36 goals.

It was during his playing spell with Rochdale that Chapman was given the role of caretaker manager, following the resignation of Jimmy Greenhoff in March 1984. He spent the following season as player-assistant manager, working alongside another former Latics favourite, Vic Halom. Subsequent managerial posts included spells as Stockport County's player-manager from July 1985, Preston North End player-assistant manager from August 1986 and then manager from June 1990 to September 1992.

Johnny Colquhoun

Date of birth: 3 June 1940, Stirling
Died: June 1996, Stirling

Oldham Athletic record:
Appearances: League 231(2), FA Cup 16, League Cup 6
Goals: League 39, FA Cup 11, League Cup 1
Debut: Colchester United (h) 26 August 1961, drawn 2–2

Also played for: Maryhill Harps, Scunthorpe United, Ashton United

On the recommendation of chief Scottish scout Billy Dennis, Athletic signed outside-left Johnny Colquhoun from Stirling Albion on 25 August 1961 for a fee of £6,000. Stirling's manager at this time was Danny McLennan, who had left Berwick Rangers to manage Athletic in May 1960, but he returned to Scotland a month later, having received a better offer from Stirling Albion.

Athletic were two matches into their season when Colquhoun made his debut, and, apart from just one game, he appeared in the remainder of the season's League and Cup matches. He scored his first goals in League football at Crewe Alexandra on 21 October, netting twice in Athletic's 5–3 victory. In his first season he was leading scorer in FA Cup ties with six goals scored in as many matches. Athletic reached round four and he scored against Liverpool at Boundary Park, a match unluckily lost 2–1 but with the compensation of an attendance of 41,733 spectators.

In the 1962–63 promotion season that followed, Colquhoun switched to inside-left when Colin Whitaker was signed from Rochdale in October, and the pair made a very effective partnership. Whitaker scored 18 goals and Colquhoun, who did not miss a single match all season, scored 15.

A change of manager in the close season, Les McDowall taking over from Jack Rowley, saw the side off to a bright start in Division Three. The promotion push faded, however, but ninth place in the League was still a reasonable placing. Colquhoun clocked up his 100th League appearance at Mansfield Town on 23 November and celebrated by scoring Athletic's goal in the 1–1 draw.

Colquhoun left Athletic for the first time in the close of season 1964–65, when he was transferred to Scunthorpe United in June 1965. The highlight of his last season was a hat-trick against Hereford United in the first round of the FA Cup in a 4–0 victory. A measure of his consistency was his record of averaging 45 matches per season over four years, his goal tally at this point being 44.

Colquhoun returned to Boundary Park with his new teammates on 2 October 1965 and scored Scunthorpe's last goal in their 3–1 victory. During his three and a half years at the Old Show Ground, he totalled 172 League and Cup appearances and scored 24 goals, appearing alongside future England internationals Kevin Keegan and Ray Clemence.

When Jack Rowley was induced to return to the Boundary Park managerial chair in October 1968, he inherited a side at the bottom of Division Three. He lost no time in recruiting Colquhoun for a second spell with Athletic, and although some improvement in results ensued, the side's dreadful start to the campaign left them with too much to do and relegation to Division Four resulted. Now operating in a midfield role, he had appeared in all of the remaining matches of the ill-fated season, scoring three goals in 29 matches. He enjoyed another consistent season in 1969–70, the term when Jimmy Frizzell took over from Jack Rowley. He appeared in 39(2) League matches and scored three goals. He also scored against Grantham in the 3–1 win in the first round of the FA Cup at Boundary Park on 15 November. He left Boundary Park for the last time in the close season and was quickly fixed up in non-League football with Ashton United.

Colquhoun's son, John Mark, followed in his father's footsteps when he signed with Stirling Albion in July 1980. Aside from two seasons in English football with Millwall and Sunderland, John junior spent the majority of his career in Scottish football, most notably in two separate spells with Heart of Midlothian (345 Scottish League appearances and 64 goals). He was capped by Scotland against Saudi Arabia at Riyadh in February 1988, thereby emulating his father whose three Scotland caps were awarded at Youth level.

Billy Cook

Date of birth: 16 January 1881, Preston
Died: 18 December 1947, Burnley

Oldham Athletic record:
Appearances: League 157, FA Cup 14
Goals: League 16
Debut: Lincoln City (a) 8 February 1908, won 2–0

Also played for: Preston North End, Ashton Town, Rossendale United (World War One guest player with Burnley), Football League representative, 1 appearance

Billy Cook was one of six brothers whose father was professional and also a groundsman at Preston Cricket Club. Of the brothers, Billy and 'Lol' played in county cricket for Lancashire and both played in League football. 'Lol' – actually Lawrence – played for Gainsborough Trinity in Division Two in 1907–08.

Cook began his football career with Preston North End at 19. He first encountered manager David Ashworth in May 1904, when he signed him from Ashton Town for Rossendale United, and some four years later the pair linked up again at Athletic. He cost Athletic £200, with £175 going to Rossendale and £25 to Preston North End, who had retained him on their League list.

At 5ft 8in and a strapping 13st 4lb, Cook was very much in the mould of full-backs of his era. Despite his build, he was reported to show splendid powers of recovery, and, needless to say, he kicked with tremendous power, clearing his lines in the approved manner of the day. He favoured a robust approach, and his first brush with authority led to a two-month suspension. This followed his sending off at Glossop on 27 December 1910, for a foul charge on H.S. Stapley. When he was again available, the team had embarked on an amazing run of form that won them promotion to Division One. Unable to regain his place, he finished the promotion season with 18 League appearances and three goals.

Cook's two-month suspension paled into insignificance when, in April 1915, he was ordered off the field at Middlesbrough for a foul on Jack Carr after 59 minutes. Convinced of his innocence, the balding Latics full-back refused to leave the field, leaving referee Mr H. Smith no alternative but to abandon the match. The Latics were 4–1 down at the time, and the FA ruled that the result should stand, and Cook was handed a 12-month suspension. He had played in 29 matches in the season, and some felt that the Championship slipped away when the team faced their final two matches without their stalwart defender. Needing two points from their last two games, both at Boundary Park, they lost 1–2 to Burnley and then went down 0–2 to Liverpool four days later.

When normal League football resumed in season 1919–20, Cook was 37 years of age, but, nevertheless, he began in sterling form and was rewarded with a place in the Football League XI that opposed the Irish League at Anfield on 19 November 1919. Sadly, he sustained a severe ankle injury during the match, and although he returned to Athletic's first team in the New Year, he failed to recapture the form that had characterised his early season play.

Cook made his final appearance for Athletic on 26 April 1920 in a 1–0 win at Sheffield Wednesday. He was placed on the transfer list in the close season and appealed to the Football League to give him a free transfer, which was granted. In August he rejoined Rossendale United of the Lancashire Combination.

In the cricket season Cook was a right-arm fast medium bowler and lower order batsman. He enjoyed a very long and successful career as a professional in both the Lancashire and Central Lancashire Leagues. In 1930, at the age of 39, he was professional with Colne C.C. He shared the opening pace attack along with my late father, Sidney Dykes. Both took 58 wickets during the season, my father heading the bowling averages of both Colne and the Lancashire League, with an average of 9.53 per wicket.

When Athletic played Burnley at Turf Moor on 16 October 1943, a welcome visitor to their dressing room was Cook, at that time aged 62 and working as a blacksmith's striker!

Tommy Davis

Date of birth: 3 February 1911, Dublin

Oldham Athletic record:
Appearances: League 72, FA Cup 7
Goals: League 51, FA Cup 4
Debut: New Brighton (h) 9 November 1935, won 6–0 (scored one goal)

Also played for: Midland Athletic, Shelbourne, Cork City, Exeter City trial, Boston Town, Torquay United, New Brighton, FC de Metz (France), Tranmere Rovers, Cork City, Workington (World War Two guest player with Dundalk, Drumcondra, Shelbourne, Distillery), manager-coach of VVV (Venlo) Holland from August 1947, Irish international (3 caps)

Considering his excellent record as a marksman, Tommy Davis's career had a faltering start, as he was released on a free transfer after spending a season in the reserve side of Torquay United. A move to New Brighton – in those days a League side operating in the Northern Section of Division Three – kick started his career. Although at times lacking support, he scored 24 goals in his first season and 26 in 1934–35, twice netting four goals in a match.

Davis broke his contract with the French side FC de Metz to sign for the Latics in June 1936 and as a result was suspended by the Football Association for three months, effective from 31 August 1936. The ban was lifted in late October after Athletic agreed to pay the French club a small sum in compensation. Given a first run out in the reserves, he scored the only goal of the match against Huddersfield Town Reserves at Leeds Road. In the following week he made his first-team debut against his former club New Brighton. Within the space of half an hour into the second half, the Latics rattled in six goals, Davis scoring one of them.

Davis's favoured position of centre-forward was occupied in 1935–36 by Billy Walsh who had a vintage season, scoring 32 League goals, two in the FA Cup and three in the Third Division North Cup. So, Davis played most of his matches at inside-right and scored nine League and Cup goals in 19 matches. More than one contemporary player spoke in later years of the animosity between the pair, which might in part explain Billy Walsh's close-season departure to Heart of Midlothian. Davis certainly prospered in the centre-forward position in 1936–37, with very few centre-halves able to stop him scoring. His 33 League goals included hat-tricks against Port Vale, Rotherham United (both at home and away) and Rochdale, and he also scored three against Barrow in the first round of the Third Division North Cup.

In May 1937, at the conclusion of his most successful season, Davis was placed on the transfer list, at his own request. He nevertheless lined up with Athletic in the pre-season 'Blues v Reds' trial matches, and he scored twice in the first match but was injured after 35 minutes of play in the second. He was out until 9 October, when he returned for the Reserves at Horwich R.M.I. and scored in a 1–3 defeat. Immediately reinstated into the first team, he scored twice against York City in a 6–2 victory at Boundary Park.

In what proved to be his last season, Davis made 17 consecutive League appearances, scoring 11 goals, and on 24 February was transferred to Tranmere Rovers. Two days later he scored twice on his debut against Gateshead in a 4–2 victory. His second outing brought him back to Boundary Park and an attendance figure of 21,548 reflected the great interest in the return of the popular Irishman, the previous home match having attracted little over 12,000 spectators. Athletic managed to keep him quiet, and two goals from Matt Gray earned a 2–1 victory.

From 26 March to the end of the season Tranmere remained unbeaten, and they clinched the Championship of the Northern Section by the slender margin of two points over Doncaster Rovers. Davis added two further Irish caps to build on the one that he earned while on Athletic's books, but he left Tranmere after the briefest of stays and returned homeward to sign with Cork City.

Seventy years on, his individual scoring record for the Latics – 33 League goals in 1936–37 – has yet to be beaten. One feels that it is likely to stand for many more years to come, unless there is a radical change from 4–5–1 formations, and the like, to something a little more adventurous.

Willie Donachie

Date of birth: 5 October 1951, Castlemilk, Glasgow

Oldham Athletic record:
Appearances: League 158(11), FA Cup 5(1), League Cup 13(2)
Goals: League 3
Debut: Birmingham City (h) 25 August 1984, lost 0–1

Also played for: Glasgow United, Celtic (ground staff), Manchester City, Portland Timbers (US), Norwich City, Burnley, Scotland International (35 caps)

Willie Donachie was an amateur on Manchester City's books at 17 and signed as a professional four months later. One year on, he made his debut in the First Division, his first outing from the bench coming on 7 February 1970 in a 1–1 draw against Nottingham Forest at Maine Road.

City won the League Cup in Donachie's debut season, beating West Bromwich Albion 2–1 at Wembley. The young Scotsman's Cup exploits during the season were on a more modest level. His first encounter with the Latics came in the Lancashire Senior Cup second round, when three matches were needed to obtain a result. After two 1–1 draws, Athletic won 3–0 at Boundary Park, later losing to Burnley in the semi-final.

Donachie began with City in midfield but was converted to left full-back, a position in which he succeeded Glyn Pardoe in season 1971–72. For seven seasons he remained an automatic choice, he was ever present in 1973–74 and 1976–77 and played in two League Cup Finals, being a winner in 1976.

In international football, Donachie was capped twice at Under-23 level and was a full international at 21 years of age. Between 1972 and 1978 he appeared regularly for Scotland, played in the 1978 World Cup Finals and won a total of 35 caps.

After 408(3) League and Cup appearances, Donachie signed for Portland Timbers for £200,000 in March 1980. He joined Norwich City for an identical amount in September 1981 and assisted the Canaries to promotion from Division Two. A second spell with Portland Timbers preceded a return to England to sign for Burnley in November 1982.

The Clarets were relegated from Division Two in his first season, having saved their best form for Cup ties. They reached the semi-final of the League Cup and round six of the FA Cup, but League form was uninspired, despite a mid-season change of manager, with Frank Casper replacing Brian Miller.

Donachie arrived at Boundary Park in July 1984 and was appointed player-coach in July 1985, three months short of his 34th birthday. He made his Athletic debut in the opening League fixture of season 1984–85; the visitors to Boundary Park were Birmingham City, who had been relegated from Division One in the previous season. It was a bruising encounter, settled by a single own-goal from Kenny Clements. Athletic's line up also included another newcomer in 18-year-old Andy Barlow.

In various capacities Donachie remained with Athletic for the next 10 years. Always supremely fit, he was an influential figure in the team's defence, his vast experience enabling him to read the game well and react accordingly. In his first four seasons he played in a total of 135(1) League matches. Thereafter, he was an infrequent member of the first team, although he deservedly qualified for a medal in 1990–91 with 12(5) League appearances when the Division Two Championship was won.

Donachie finally, and very reluctantly, retired from playing at the age of 42, having been named as substitute on a number of occasions in 1991–92 and 1992–93 without actually getting onto the pitch. His final League appearance, from the bench, came – fittingly for a Scot – on New Year's Day 1991 in a 1–1 draw against Newcastle United at Boundary Park, with Donachie replacing Paul Moulden after 45 minutes. Former Latics centre-forward Mick Quinn scored for Newcastle, Athletic then sharing the points courtesy of a 90th-minute own-goal by Newcastle full-back Mark Stimson.

Donachie, along with manager Joe Royle, departed Boundary Park in November 1994 to join Everton, marooned at the foot of the Premier League. In the best possible start, their first game in charge produced a 2–0 victory against Liverpool. With relegation avoided, their first season was crowned by victory against Manchester United in the FA Cup Final.

Joe Donnachie

Date of birth: c.1885, Kilwinning, Ayrshire
Died: Unknown

Oldham Athletic record:
Appearances: League 216, FA Cup 22
Goals: League 19, FA Cup 2
Debut: Birmingham (h) 17 October 1908, won 2–0

Also played for: Rutherglen Glencairn, Albion Rovers, Greenock Morton, Newcastle United, Everton, Glasgow Rangers, Blackpool, Chester (player-manager), Scotland (3 caps)

Startling acceleration and quite dazzling footwork were features of Joe Donnachie's play; his electric runs along the touchline thrilled the Boundary Park crowd and first attracted the Scottish selectors in 1913. Although far from a prolific marksman by his own account, he provided many goals for others with his well-timed centres and accurate corner-kicks.

Donnachie began as a youngster with that famous Scottish nursery club Rutherglen Glencairn and first crossed the border in June 1905 to join Newcastle United. His stay was not prolonged as he failed to settle with the Tynesiders, who transferred him to Everton in the February of his first season at St James' Park.

As understudy to Jack Sharp, the England football and cricket international (two Soccer caps and three Test Match appearances), Donnachie found limited first-team opportunities. His move to Boundary Park, however, was a success from the outset. A goal in his second appearance, a 4–1 away victory at Gainsborough Trinity, was the prelude to a run of improved results that ultimately lifted the side to sixth position in Division Two.

On the eve of the following season, Donnachie, Frank Newton and Herbert Butterworth were all suspended by the club for refusing to resign their membership from the newly-formed Players' Union. Several other League clubs also suspended players for membership of the Union, an organisation that found little initial favour with the game's authorities.

All seemed to be resolved following an FA intervention, but Donnachie had his least successful season. He lost his first-team place in the promotion-winning side to Stanley Miller, the amateur outside-left, who combined football with his employment as a yarn salesman with a Preston agency.

In May 1910 Donnachie agreed terms and signed on for the new season, Athletic's debut in the First Division. In the following month the club's directors decided to proceed immediately with the construction of a new stand on the Sheepfoot Lane side of the ground.

In the five seasons preceding suspension of League football during World War One, Donnachie showed consistently good form and gained well-deserved recognition from the Scotland selectors. Underlining his versatility, the first of his three caps against England at Stamford Bridge in April 1913 was made at outside-right. A further two caps followed in 1913–14. Restored to his more familiar role on the left wing, he scored Scotland's goal in their 1–1 draw against Ireland at Windsor Park, Belfast. In the following month he also assisted Scotland to a 3–1 victory against England at Hampden Park.

Donnachie was awarded a benefit with a guarantee of £300, the game against his former club Everton on New Year's Day 1914 being set aside for him. Athletic missed a penalty but won 2–0 to complete a very successful holiday programme that also featured a win and a draw against West Bromwich Albion and a win against Bolton Wanderers.

A homeward move took Donnachie to Glasgow Rangers in March 1919, making him one of very few Roman Catholics to be associated with the Ibrox club. Five months later he rejoined Everton, moving to Blackpool after one season. He retired from the game after a spell with Chester – a non-League club at that time – and took over the licence of a local hostelry, the Mariner's Arms.

Lee Duxbury

Date of birth: 7 October 1969, Skipton, Yorkshire

Oldham Athletic record:
Appearances: League 222(26), FA Cup 16(2), League Cup 12
Goals: League 32, FA Cup 5, League Cup 1
Debut: Manchester City (a) 8 March 1997, lost 0–1

Also played for: Bradford City, Rochdale (loan), Huddersfield Town, Bradford City (again), Bury, Farsley Celtic, Glentoran

A natural leader on the field, fair haired Lee Duxbury captained every side that he played for, first leading Bradford City at the age of 20. An extremely hard-working, fierce-tackling midfielder with energy to spare, he also had the priceless knack of scoring vital goals – finishing as Athletic's leading scorer in League matches during 1998–99 with eight goals, plus a further two in Cup ties.

Duxbury began as a trainee with Bradford City and signed his first professional form in July 1988. Huddersfield Town's manager Neil Warnock paid £250,000 for him in December 1994, and he successfully captained the Terriers to promotion from Division Two, via a Wembley Play-off victory against Bristol Rovers in May of the same season. Twelve months later he was at Wembley again for a repeat performance, this time in the colours of Bradford City – who he rejoined in November 1995. The Bantams beat Notts County 2–0 in the Play-off Final.

When Neil Warnock replaced Graeme Sharp as Athletic's manager in February 1997, he lost no time in recruiting Duxbury, who was pitched straight into a desperate relegation battle. Hopes were raised when a 3–2 home victory against the Wolves lifted the side off the bottom of the table, but they managed only a further couple of wins before the end of the campaign and were relegated from Division One.

The following season saw player-assistant manager Andy Ritchie score his 107th and final goal for the club, and a disappointing campaign in Division Two ended with the team in 13th place. Ritchie took over as manager in May 1998, but his first season in charge almost ended in disaster. Wins in the last two matches of the season took the side to 20th, one point above the relegation place.

Two mid-table seasons followed, with Duxbury enjoying an excellent season in 2000–01, scoring 10 League and Cup goals. In the space of a fortnight during March he scored two against Rotherham United and both goals in the 2–1 win against Northampton Town.

Duxbury made his customary 40 League appearances in 2001–02, scoring four League and two FA Cup goals. The side led the table in early October but won only twice in March and April to finish in ninth place. Mick Wadsworth resigned in early July, having been offered a seat on the board to go along with his duties as head coach just a month before.

Assistant manager Ian Dowie was promoted and handed the team captaincy to Matty Appleby. Duxbury, now 32 years old and the previous club skipper, was told that he would be available to leave on a free transfer if any offers materialised. In the event, he remained involved in the first-team squad all season, although 18 of his 34 appearances were made from the bench. In February he, along with John Sheridan, took over training responsibilities for the reserve and youth teams, their appointments coming in the wake of the departures of David Cross and long serving Bill Urmston.

Uncertainty about the future of the club itself surfaced in the close season, when players and staff were told that owner Chris Moore was planning to suspend all payments for the month of June. Losses were reported to be running at £200,000 per month, and key players were attracting interest as the vultures began to circle. Funds from outside the club enabled a shortened pre-season tour to Northern Ireland to take place, and Duxbury was included in the party. He flew back early from the tour and became the sixth player to join the exodus from Boundary Park, having been offered a contract from Bury. Although loathed to leave, he revealed that he had not been paid for six weeks. This was a sad outcome for the club's senior professional, whose final aggregate career figures totalled an impressive 631(36) League and Cup appearances and 75 goals.

In early June 2006, following the appointment of John Sheridan as Athletic's new manager, Duxbury was brought back to Boundary Park as reserve-team manager.

David Eyres

Date of birth: 26 February 1964, Liverpool

Oldham Athletic record:
Appearances: League 185(21), FA Cup 15(2), League Cup 8
Goals: League 34, FA Cup 5, League Cup 2
Debut: Swindon Town (h) 14 October 2000, won 1–0

Also played for: Morecambe, Southport, Rhyl, Blackpool, Burnley, Preston North End

David Eyres was a late starter in League football, signing for Blackpool in August 1989 at the age of 25. His outstanding record in non-League circles began in Sunday League football and progressed to higher levels with Morecambe, Southport and Rhyl. As a goalscoring wingman there were few to match his record, in excess of a century of goals for his three non-League clubs. He took a drop in wages to turn professional with Blackpool, leaving his job at Ford Motor's Halewood plant to do so. He made his League debut in a League Cup first-round tie, drawn 2–2 against Burnley (h), on 22 August 1989. He was quickly established, playing in 38(2) matches in his first season and scoring nine goals. In the following season his two goals in the Play-off semi-finals helped take Blackpool to Wembley, but they lost to Torquay United in the final, after extra-time and penalties. Twelve months on and another Wembley penalty shoot-out saw them promoted at the expense of Scunthorpe United.

In July 1993 Eyres was reunited with his former Blackpool manager Jimmy Mullen, who paid £90,000 to take the 29-year-old wingman to Burnley. In a splendid first season at Turf Moor he scored 26 League and Cup goals, and he also scored in what was his third Wembley Play-off Final in four years, with Burnley beating Stockport County 2–1 and winning promotion to Division One. In October 1997 Preston North End paid £80,000 to take him to Deepdale. A third promotion and a Championship medal followed in 1999–2000 when North End topped Division Two by a margin of seven points over Eyres's former employers Burnley. During the successful season, Preston North End beat the Latics three times, twice in the League and also in the third round of the FA Cup. All of this had not gone unnoticed at Boundary Park, and when he was made available on a free transfer Athletic manager Andy Ritchie was swiftly in to secure his services.

Athletic were struggling in 23rd place in Division Two, but Eyres's arrival, along with Tony Carss from Carlisle United, proved to be the season's turning point, with the side recovering to finish in mid-table. In his first full season the evergreen wingman swept the board with the most goals (12), most appearances (47 plus 5 as sub) and the Player of the Year award. He additionally scored twice for the reserves in the 3–2 Manchester Senior Cup Final victory against Manchester City on 22 April, and all of this against a background of managerial upheaval, with Andy Ritchie being sacked, Mick Wadsworth arriving (for a brief stay), and leaving Ian Dowie in charge.

A deal to take Eyres beyond his 40th birthday was tabled in May 2003. It followed a heartache season when Athletic lost in the Play-offs to Queen's Park Rangers. Despite being the oldest winger in town, he retained his title as leading scorer. His trusty left foot struck 16 times, the majority from set pieces. It was the best return since Sean McCarthy netted 18 in 1994–95. The withdrawal of financial support by chairman Chris Moore resulted in a circling of vultures around the pick of Athletic's promising squad of players – Wayne Andrews, Chris Armstrong, Fitz Hall, Clint Hill, Tony Carss and Lee Duxbury all departed in July. Veteran coach John Sheridan signed non-contract forms on the eve of the new season, which opened with a 1–3 home defeat by Brighton & Hove Albion. Very much the patched-up underdogs, Athletic nevertheless survived the season despite losing manager Dowie mid-term. Eyres was appointed assistant to caretaker manager John Sheridan, and despite an ankle injury he appeared in half of the season's matches. Of his three goals for the season, his last against Plymouth Argyle was particularly memorable, a trademark long-range free-kick in the 4–1 home win in April.

Despite another season of turmoil and a 19th-place finish in Division Two, Eyres enjoyed another excellent season, missing only four of the League fixtures. He again stepped in as joint caretaker manager with Tony Philliskirk following Brian Talbot's dismissal in March. For the first time since his arrival, the League's oldest outfield player did not feature regularly in 2005–06. Fittingly, however, he signed off with a goal in his last appearance against Scunthorpe United at Boundary Park in the season's final fixture. A 'Latics Legends XI' played a 'Celebrity XI' for his benefit match on 1 May 2006. It would not be surprising if the remarkably fit and greatly admired Eyres – a true 'Latics Legend' – was to continue playing for another season or two, at least.

Jimmy Fay

Date of birth: 29 March 1884, Southport
Died: 4 March 1957, Southport

Oldham Athletic record:
Appearances: League 154, FA Cup 21
Goals: League 37, FA Cup 3
Debut: Ashton Town, FA Cup 1 (h) 7 October 1905, won 2–1

Also played for: Chorley, Oswaldtwistle Rovers, Bolton Wanderers (World War One guest player and team manager of Southport Vulcan, Southport FC, Hesketh Park)

Jimmy Fay began in Southport junior football. His early clubs were Southport Crescent and Southport Working Lads, and during his time with the latter they won the Championship of the Southport and District League. He then spent a season with Chorley – who paid him 10 shillings per week – playing in every match throughout 1903–04. In the following season he joined Oswaldtwistle Rovers, for a 100 percent increase in wages – £1 per week – and played in every match but one, missing the game against Blackpool Reserves due to influenza.

Fay joined Athletic in May 1905, when they played at Hudson Fold, and he certainly helped the club to popularise the Association game in what was very much a Rugby stronghold. His first contract provided wages of 30 shillings (£1.50p) per week in the playing season plus travelling expenses. Three years later he was earning £4 per week both in the playing season and during the summer months, reflecting the rapid advancement of himself and the team in the intervening years.

In addition to the appearance figures quoted above, Fay played in all 38 Lancashire Combination fixtures in 1905–06 with 38 appearances (five goals) and 37 matches (one goal) in 1906–07. Singularly enough, the match he missed was against the same club – Blackpool Reserves – as when he was playing for Oswaldtwistle.

Athletic won the Championship of the Lancashire Combination in 1906–07, gained entry into Division Two of the Football League and finished in third place in their first season in higher company. After finishing sixth in 1908–09, the following term started in a disappointing fashion. In an effort to introduce more firepower into the attack, Fay was switched from right-half to inside-right. He was an instantaneous success, scoring 26 goals in 38 matches and taking Athletic into Division One as runners-up to Manchester City. At the end of the following season one correspondent noted 'One thing that may be said about Fay is that he never shirked his work.' He was, of course, referring to his outstanding record of having missed only two League matches in six seasons.

Fay shared a benefit match with Jimmy Hodson against Liverpool on 3 December 1910, and in October of the following year he was transferred to Bolton Wanderers for a fee of £750. At either side of World War One, he served the Wanderers with great distinction, representing the Football League on three occasions. His final match, against the Scottish League at Ibrox, was billed a 'Victory Match', and it attracted a crowd of 70,000 spectators. Jimmy was 35 years old at the time.

It was during his lengthy spell with the Wanderers that Fay first became a committee member of the Players' Union. He was elected chairman in 1922 and served as secretary from 1929 to 1952. Without his energy and enthusiasm the organisation would not have become the very live force that it is today. They came very close to folding after fighting the 'retain and transfer' system, using an Aston Villa player called Kingsbury as a test case. The Union lost, and heavily in debt they struggled throughout the period of World War One to find the money to keep themselves afloat.

Following Fay's death at the age of 72 in Southport, Sir Stanley Rous, secretary of the Football Association, penned the following tribute: 'Whenever I met Mr Fay, I admired his quiet, efficient manner of dealing with problems, and I am sure that many thousands of players are continuing to benefit from his wisdom and foresight in matters affecting their welfare.'

Athletic's secretary, Mr Bob Mellor, whose association with the Latics had commenced in 1906, wrote: 'James Fay was one of the finest type of players whom one could wish to meet and was an inspiration to any young player. He was a gentleman on and off the field.'

Reg Freeman

Date of birth: 20 December 1897, Birkenhead
Died: 4 August 1955, Wickersley, near Rotherham

Oldham Athletic record:
Appearances: League 101, FA Cup 3
Goals: 0
Debut: Bolton Wanderers (h) 15 January 1921, drawn 0–0

Also played for: Wallasey Rovers, Harrowby, Yorkshire Amateurs, Northern Nomads, Middlesbrough, Rotherham United
Managed: Rotherham United, Sheffield United

After a grim and determined struggle, Athletic succeeded in maintaining their First Division status in season 1920–21. By the way in which the team commenced the season, hopes of a successful campaign were raised, yet, sadly, it was a case of flattering to deceive. The opening game was played against Middlesbrough on a hot August afternoon, and the team played their best football of the season to win 2–1. When they appeared before their own supporters on the following Monday, Athletic recorded their second victory of 1–0 against Blackburn Rovers.

The return game against Middlesbrough was a six-goal thriller, Athletic sharing the points thanks to two goals on his debut by A. F. 'Sandy' Campbell and one from centre-half Elliot Pilkington. Liverpool were the first team to beat Athletic – by 5–2 at Anfield. At the interval the scores were level, but in the space of 15 minutes in the second half the Reds ran riot and scored four goals. A point was taken from Liverpool at Boundary Park, but when meeting Blackburn Rovers at Ewood Park, Athletic's defence again capitulated five times.

In just four matches 19 goals were conceded in November, and despite numerous changes in both defence and attack, the team collected only 13 points during the first half of the season. The arrival of Reg Freeman in January marked a long overdue upturn in Athletic's fortunes. A six-match unbeaten run commenced against Bolton Wanderers in a goalless draw at Boundary Park. Despite stepping straight out of amateur football into the highest circles, Athletic's new left-back acquitted himself with great credit. As the local correspondent enthused, 'About all his work there is a touch of class, his anticipation being intelligent and his kicking clean and sure.'

February proved to be the best month of the season with seven points taken out of a possible 10. A late equaliser from George Wall earned a point at Derby County in a 3–3 draw. Arsenal then visited Boundary Park and took away a point in a 1–1 draw. Following this, the return match with Derby County was played, and a rare goal from full-back Ernie Braidwood seven minutes from time proved to be the winner in a 2–1 victory. A visit to London for the return match at Arsenal yielded another point in a 2–2 draw. The successful month ended with a 2–0 victory against local rivals Manchester City, with Vince Foweather, in his third appearance, scoring Athletic's first goal. The biggest crowd of the season, 27,846 spectators, paid record receipts of £1,576.

A late season double against Bradford City ensured Athletic's escape from the threat of relegation, but manager Herbert Bamlett resigned in May 1921 and was replaced by Charlie Roberts two months later. Despite four successive victories early in the season – home and away against Cardiff City and West Bromwich Albion – for the third successive season Athletic endured another fight against relegation. Despite the Boxing Day attendance of 32,814 for the visit of Bolton Wanderers and record receipts of £1,855, gate receipts overall were down over £4,000, a prolonged trade depression having some bearing. Twenty-five players were called upon during the season, Reg Freeman being the only one who did not miss a match.

Although the first five games of 1922–23 yielded three wins and a draw, the club suffered from a lack of forwards who could find the net, with 23 of the season's matches – more than half the number played – ending goalless. Freeman's run of 92 consecutive appearances ended on 10 February when he was unfit for the match at Birmingham. With two games of the season remaining, Athletic recouped some of the losses of the relegation season when they transferred Freeman to Middlesbrough for £4,000. He spent seven years at Ayresome Park and won two Second Division Championships before joining Rotherham United in September 1930. As their manager, he won the Third Division North Championship in 1951 and led Sheffield United to the Second Division Championship in 1952–53, his first season in charge.

Jimmy Frizzell

Date of birth: 16 February 1937, Greenock

Oldham Athletic record:
Appearances: League 308(9), FA Cup 22, League Cup 11
Goals: League 56, FA Cup 1, League Cup 1
Debut: Northampton Town (h) 20 August 1960, lost 1–2

Also played for: Greenock Belair, Largs Thistle, Greenock Morton
Managed: Manchester City

Despite his outstanding playing record with Athletic, totalling 350 League and Cup appearances spanning nine years, mention of Jimmy Frizzell's name will, most probably, bring initially to mind his outstanding 12-year stint as the Latics manager. Quite simply, however, he filled both roles with equal faculty.

As a player, Frizzell represented West of Scotland Schoolboys and graduated through junior ranks to join his home-town club, Greenock Morton, in 1955. He had turned down an offer from Portsmouth before accepting Athletic's terms in May 1960. He cost a modest £1,500, and considering his subsequent achievements during 22 years as player and then manager, he can rightly be considered the club's all-time bargain buy.

Athletic's team on his debut lined up against Northampton Town as follows: Rollo, Beswick, West, Spurdle, Ferguson, Jarvis, Pheonix, Frizzell, McCurley, Stringfellow, O'Loughlin. In addition to Frizzell, goalkeeper Rollo and centre-forward McCurley were also making their first appearances. Athletic lost 1–2, the unfortunate McCurley being carried off the field after 43 minutes on what proved to be his only first-team appearance. He scored 10 goals in 40 League matches in his first season, notable for the arrival of Scottish international Bobby Johnstone from Hibernian.

In 1961–62 Frizzell netted his first goals of the season, a hat-trick against Millwall in a 4–2 home win on 30 September. Thereafter, he hardly stopped scoring. Totalling 24 League goals in 41 matches, his final record might have been even better had the unfortunate Accrington Stanley not resigned during the season. In Athletic's first League match, staged under the new Boundary Park floodlights on 11 October 1961, they beat Stanley 5–0. Frizzell scored two and Bert Lister three, but the match was subsequently declared void when Accrington resigned.

The promotion season of 1962–63 opened with a 2–1 home win against Bradford City, with Athletic parading three new signings in Bill Marshall, Peter McCall and Bob Ledger. In the 2–1 win at Tranmere Rovers one week later, Frizzell scored Athletic's first goal but was injured and spent the second half as a limping passenger on the right wing. He was in the wars again at Brentford on 8 December and missed the 11-goal romp against Southport on Boxing Day. He was restricted to 22 League matches during the successful campaign, scoring five goals.

New manager Les McDowall was the first to select Frizzell as a wing-half, although in 1964–65 he reverted for a spell as inside-forward and led the goalscorers with 10 in 42 League matches. It was Jimmy McIlroy who first tried him as a full-back, but he made his final appearance at left-half in a 1–2 defeat at Newport County on 6 October 1969. It was during this season that Frizzell's managerial career commenced, initially as caretaker from 30 December and then as manager from 25 March.

In his first full season in charge, Athletic won promotion from Division Four and scooped the £70,000 prize money from the Ford Motor Company Sporting League, enabling a new stand to be built on the Broadway side of Boundary Park. Steady and continued progress saw the side crowned as Third Division Champions in 1973–74. Life in Division Two proved more exacting, but at the time of his sensational dismissal he had guided the club from re-election trouble in Division Four to respectability in Division Two. As Southampton's manager, Lawrie McMenemy was to say at the time 'Not only can Jimmy Frizzell make a silk purse out of a sow's ear, he can fill that purse with money with the ridiculous profits he makes in his transfer dealings.'

Until his sacking, Frizzell was the second longest serving manager in the Football League. After a year out of work he was appointed assistant manager at Manchester City, remaining in various capacities until May 2001.

Jim Fryatt

Date of birth: 2 September 1940, Swaythling near Southampton

Oldham Athletic record:
Appearances: League 76, FA Cup 1, League Cup 2
Goals: League 40, League Cup 2
Debut: York City (a) 21 February 1970, drawn 0–0

Also played for: Charlton Athletic, Southend United, Bradford PA, Southport, Torquay United, Stockport County, Blackburn Rovers, Southport (a second spell), Philadelphia Atoms (US), Stockport County (a second spell), Torquay United (a second spell), Chorley, Hartford Bi-Centennials (US), Philadelphia Atoms (US) (a second spell)
Managed: Las Vegas Quicksilver (US)

Anyone who supported the Latics in the early 1970s is unlikely to ever forget Jim Fryatt; a barrel-chested, balding centre-forward with Dickensian sideboards and an intermittent penchant for a drooping moustache. The strongly-built leader of the attack had a fierce shot in either foot, but it was his headwork that was his strongest asset. Whether soaring at the back post or diving parallel to the ground to convert a low centre, the tangerine-shirted striker was a defender's nightmare.

Fryatt was certainly an inspired first signing by Athletic's then caretaker manager Jimmy Frizzell in February 1970. He paid £8,000 to bring the experienced centre-forward to Boundary Park, thus ending his days of obscurity in the reserve team of Blackburn Rovers. At 27 years of age, he had already scored 124 League goals in a nomadic career that commenced 10 years earlier, when he signed his first professional form with Charlton Athletic while serving an apprenticeship as a draughtsman.

Fryatt joined an Athletic team in deep trouble in February 1970, who had parted company with manager Jack Rowley after five consecutive defeats in December 1969. He opened his scoring account in his third appearance, against one of his former clubs Southend United, in a 3–0 home win on 3 March. He also scored one of the two goals by which Athletic secured their second away win of the season, 2–0 at Exeter City. When League leaders and eventual Champions Chesterfield were beaten 1–0 on 14 March, it was his third goal within the space of four matches that secured the points.

The highlight of the season came on 28 March when Chester were the visitors to a muddy and rain-swept Boundary Park. Fryatt opened the scoring with a penalty after 20 minutes, and Reg Blore added a second before half-time. Fryatt notched a further three goals within the space of 16 second-half minutes to wrap up a stunning 5–0 victory. A further three home wins against Brentford (4–1), Peterborough United (4–2) and Crewe Alexandra (2–1) lifted Athletic away from the foot of the table.

Season 1970–71 would probably qualify as the most entertaining Athletic campaign on record, although the opening League fixture, featuring four new signings in Short, Cranston, Heath and Hartle, resulted in a hugely disappointing 4–1 defeat at Grimsby Town. It was in this season that the forward partnership of Fryatt and David Shaw came into full fruition. Each player made 48 appearances, and in the month of September the lightning-quick Shaw scored four goals against Brentford and a hat-trick against Aldershot. Fryatt commenced with five goals in the season's first four matches and in November registered a hat-trick against Lincoln City in the 4–2 home win. Between them, the pair scored 47 of the team's 88 League goals during the season, which ended in promotion from Division Four.

In November of the following season Fryatt was transferred to Southport. It was his second spell with the Haig Avenue club, and he assisted them to win the Championship of Division Four in season 1972–73, scoring 13 League goals in 37(2) matches. His total included four goals and a 10-minute hat-trick against Darlington in a 7–0 victory on 6 January 1973.

Fryatt played his final Football League match for Torquay United against Newport County on 21 December 1974. His final career aggregate figures were 189 League goals for eight different clubs in 489(10) matches. His tally included a goal within four seconds of the kick-off for Bradford Park Avenue against Tranmere Rovers in April 1964, officially credited as the fastest scored in a Football League match.

Having spent some summer months playing American football, he later settled in Las Vegas, where he worked as a slot machine repair mechanic in the Las Vegas casinos. His son Edward starred in a different sport, becoming a professional golfer.

Arthur Gee

Date of birth: October 1892, Earlestown, near Warrington
Died: 6 August 1959, Werneth, Oldham

Oldham Athletic record:
Appearances: League 112, FA Cup 7
Goals: League 43, FA Cup 3
Debut: West Bromwich Albion (a) 29 April 1912, drawn 0–0

Also played for: Earlestown FC (World War One guest player with Everton and Liverpool), Stalybridge Celtic, Rochdale, Ashton National, Crewe Alexandra, Nuneaton Town, Ferranti's FC, Mossley, Witton Albion

As a member of St John's School side at Earlestown, Arthur Gee had trials for England Schoolboys, and it was often said that he was born to play the game. He was the sixth child in a family of 10, and as a youngster was rarely seen without a ball at his feet. He was still a teenager and an amateur on Earlestown's books when Athletic's manager, David Ashworth, heard of his ability and made arrangements to see him play against Eccles Borough in a Lancashire Combination Division Two match. He scored four goals that day and booked his passage to a professional career.

Aware of Athletic's interest, Earlestown were quick to sign Gee on professional forms, so that they could collect a transfer fee of £30. A modest enough sum by today's standards, but in those pre-World War One days Gee's terms on signing for Athletic – then a First Division team – were £4 in the first team and £2 in the reserves.

Gee's first season at Boundary Park was spent in the reserves, apart from one outing in the first team against West Bromwich Albion in the season's final fixture. Season 1912–13 marked his breakthrough when he was first introduced against Sheffield United at Boundary Park on 28 December 1912, following a 7–1 defeat at Aston Villa two days earlier. In his first season of real involvement at senior level (15 League appearances), his predatory instincts before goal brought him two in a 3–1 win against Liverpool at home, two against Everton at Goodison, and one against Derby County.

It was in the FA Cup competition, however, that Gee found glory. First introduced in the third-round replay against Manchester United at Old Trafford on 26 February – the teams had drawn 0–0 at Boundary Park four days earlier – he marked his debut in the competition by opening the scoring after 53 minutes. Enoch West equalised for United, but Alf Toward scored the winner to earn a fourth-round tie at Everton.

In later years, Gee recalled the match as the best in which he had ever played. He opened the scoring with what turned out to be the winning goal after six minutes. For the remainder of the game, Everton threw all they had at Athletic's defence, but they were unable to beat the man who Gee considered 'the prince of goalkeepers' – Athletic's Howard Matthews. Special training at Lytham St Annes did not prove sufficient to take Athletic to the Final, as a single goal by Clem Stephenson took Aston Villa to Crystal Palace where they beat Sunderland 1–0.

In 1914–15 Gee shared the role of centre-forward with Arthur Cashmore, when the team failed to win their last two games and failed by one point to win the Football League Championship. Athletic were due to pay their players a bonus of £25 each for finishing as runners-up, which they did, in weekly instalments in the following season!

Gee received £350 as his share of benefit money when transferred to Stalybridge Celtic, founder members of Division Three North in season 1921–22. Despite injury problems he scored 11 goals in 28 matches, and wound up his League career at Rochdale. In a 1948 interview, when asked for his opinion on today's players, he replied 'Craft has been sacrificed for speed.'

Eric Gemmell

Date of birth: 7 April 1921, Prestwich, Manchester

Oldham Athletic record:
Appearances: League 195, FA Cup 23
Goals: League 109, FA Cup 11
Debut: Rotherham United (h) 26 August 1947, lost 1–4 (scored)

Also played for: Manchester United as an amateur, Goslings FC, Manchester City, Ashton United on loan, Crewe Alexandra, Rochdale, Buxton, Nantile Vale (player-manager)

Tall, lithe and with a prematurely receding hair line, 30-year-old centre-forward Eric Gemmell entered the record books on a snowy day at Boundary Park on 19 January 1952. The visitors were Chester, and among the Latics faithful – 13,252 attended the match – the pre-match topic of conversation surrounded Chester's outstanding performances in the previous week against First Division Chelsea. Chester had drawn 2–2 at Stamford Bridge in the third round of the FA Cup on the previous Saturday and had then taken the Pensioners to extra-time in the replay before going under by 3–2 midweek.

Worst fears seemed to be almost realised when, with four minutes gone, Gemmell missed an absolute 'sitter' from 10 yards out. On a pitch resembling a frozen waste, Chester opened the scoring from the penalty spot. After missing another golden opportunity by dribbling round Chester's goalkeeper Harry Threadgold, Gemmell equalised on 20 minutes, but Chester were back in front five minutes later.

Syd Goodfellow's equaliser after 30 minutes was the first of five Oldham goals in the next 15 minutes, Gemmell netting his second goal a minute before half-time. Despite a 6–2 half-time lead, there was little to suggest that the game would develop into a personal triumph for him. In the second half, however, he went on to score five goals in succession. Gemmell, who lost count of the score, was to recall that Peter Greenwood, Chester's inside-left and a Lancashire County cricketer, aware of the whip-round practice for high-scoring batsman, told him that he needed only two more for a collection!

The game also brought to Gemmell's mind memories of wartime Navy service and a knock-out competition at Archangel with a midnight kick-off. It had been strange soccer in the land of the midnight sun against Russians who were military allies but sworn enemies on the pitch. He recalled that two officers were selected as 'passengers' on the wings to ensure that the game did not develop into a roughhouse. Perhaps there was nothing in it, but the scene of his greatest triumph in the 11–2 victory was played out on a typical Archangel pitch – deep in snow.

Gemmell's seven goals was the best individual scoring performance in a League match since Joe Payne, who scored 10 for Luton Town against Bristol Rovers in April 1936. Extensive newspaper coverage at the time included an interview with a very proud Mrs Gemmell, who revealed that, aside from his sporting prowess, her husband smoked only four or five cigarettes a day and helped with the washing up!

In the 1952–53 season that followed, Athletic won the Championship of the Third Division North. Although injuries restricted him to only 27 of the season's League matches, Gemmell was leading scorer with 23 goals, his total including hat-tricks against Darlington, Hartlepools United and Tranmere Rovers.

Despite being one of Athletic's scorers in the opening Division Two fixture at Luton Town in August 1953, Gemmell appeared infrequently and in February was transferred to Crewe Alexandra, ending his League career with Rochdale in the following season. Maintaining his eye for goal throughout, Gemmell's career aggregate figures totalled 274 League appearances and 146 goals. For many years his total of 109 League goals was the highest aggregate by an Oldham Athletic player, until his record was finally overtaken by Roger Palmer. The club brought together their two top marksmen in April 1989, when Gemmell was invited to make an on-field presentation of an inscribed statuette to Palmer to mark his achievement.

Ted Goodier

Date of birth:	15 October 1902, Little Hulton, Lancashire
Died:	4 November 1967, Farnworth, Lancashire

Oldham Athletic record:

Appearances:	League 113, FA Cup 3
Goals:	League 2, FA Cup 1
Debut:	Fulham (a) 23 January 1926, lost 1–2

Also played for:	Bolton Wanderers as an amateur, Huddersfield Town, Lancaster Town, Queen's Park Rangers, Watford, Crewe Alexandra, Rochdale
Managed:	Oldham Athletic (1956–58), Rochdale, Birmingham, Wigan Athletic

Ted Goodier played in 18 matches for Bolton Wanderers A Team before Huddersfield Town signed him as a professional in May 1922. He broke an ankle in a Central League match, lost form and confidence and was given a free transfer for the only time in his football career. He then spent a season as captain of Lancaster Town before being transferred to the Latics in June 1925.

The club was in the Second Division at that time and Jimmy Naylor was Athletic's star left-half. Goodier had a lengthy wait for a first-team place, recording only 11 League appearances in his first three seasons. His patience was finally rewarded when Naylor moved onwards and upwards to First Division Huddersfield Town in November 1928.

Goodier made his first appearance of the season against Stoke City on 24 November, and the 1–1 draw ended a sequence of eight straight defeats in away matches. Some drastic team changes by manager Andrew Wilson saw the introduction of Bill Hasson, 'Tiny' Stafford, Matt Gray, Freddie Worrall and Stewart Littlewood, all of whom made their club debuts during the second half of the season.

When the new season opened, the manager had blended together the best side to represent the Latics in the inter-war period. It lined up as follows: Hacking, Ivill, Porter, Adlam, King, Goodier, Worrall, Dyson or Cumming, Littlewood, Gray and Hasson. The team carried all before them until two late-season defeats by Blackpool and one by Barnsley lost them the chance of promotion to the First Division.

An eventful, if brief, FA Cup adventure also coloured the season. Wolverhampton Wanderers were the visitors in round three, and there was no scoring until a few minutes before full-time. Athletic won a corner-kick that Freddie Worrall swung over from the right. The Wolves goalkeeper only managed to fist it out to the edge of the penalty area where the in-rushing Goodier took the ball on the volley and it flashed into the top corner of the net. The reward was another home draw against the season's League Champions, Sheffield Wednesday. The ground record was made that day, with 46,471 spectators paying £3,116 in total at the gate. With 14 minutes left to play, the Latics were 3–2 ahead when centre-forward Littlewood broke through and scored what Goodier considered 'one of the best goals I ever saw.' Sadly, the referee did not agree, ruled out the goal and effectively gave the visitors renewed hope. They scored two goals in the last 10 minutes to win by 4–3.

Goodier's most unfortunate game as an Athletic player was against Blackpool. Ramsay, the Blackpool full-back, broke an arm and was turned out on the field again with his arm in splints, resuming at outside-right. Every time Goodier went near him to tackle the crowd roared their disapproval, and he quite justifiably felt that it was unfair of Blackpool to have let the unfortunate player resume at all.

In November 1931 Goodier was transferred to Queen's Park Rangers, along with Les Adlam, for a combined fee of £1,500. During his spell in London he played for a 'Rest of London' XI against Arsenal at the White City in 1933. The game was played by floodlight and he recalled 'The ball was as visible all the time as though it had been a perfectly clear day.'

First introduced to management during his lengthy spell with Rochdale, Goodier succeeded George Hardwick at Boundary Park in May 1956. Sadly, he was unable to halt his old team's alarming slide into soccer's basement, as founding members of Division Four.

Andy Goram

Date of birth: 13 April 1964, Bury

Oldham Athletic record:
Appearances: League 195, FA Cup 7, League Cup 10
Goals: 0
Debut: Charlton Athletic (h) 4 May 1982, won 1–0

Also played for: West Bromwich Albion, Hibernian, Glasgow Rangers, Notts County, Sheffield United, Motherwell, Manchester United, Boreham Wood, Hamilton Academical trial, Blackpool trial, Coventry City, Queen of the South, Scotland international (43 caps)

Although born in Lancashire, Andy Goram qualified for Scotland by parentage, his father Lewis Goram – also a goalkeeper – played for Third Lanark, Hibernian and Bury in the 1950s. After representing both Bury and Manchester Schoolboys, he became an apprentice at West Bromwich Albion in June 1980. In the following year he was brought to Boundary Park by Athletic's chief scout Colin McDonald – himself a former England goalkeeper – and his accomplished displays at junior and reserve-team level earned him a League debut at 18 years of age. Athletic won 1–0 on his debut and four days later drew 1–1 against Derby County. They wound up the season with a convincing 3–0 victory against already relegated Orient at Brisbane Road.

In the close season, Athletic released their only experienced goalkeeper Peter McDonnell and took Martin Hodge on loan from Everton. A permanent deal was being considered when Hodge was sidelined with a chest problem that required surgery. Promoted from the reserves, Goram took his opportunity with outstanding success, being called up into the England Under-21 squad and additionally elected Player of the Year by the Latics Supporters Club.

Ankle and shoulder injuries restricted Goram to just 22 League appearances in 1983–84 and relegation was only narrowly avoided by virtue of three wins in the last four matches of the season. In 1985–86 England's policy of playing over-age goalkeepers in their Under-21 sides led to Goram being approached to represent Scotland. Having been involved in England Under-21 squads without actually playing, he felt that he had a better chance of international football with Scotland. He won his first cap on 16 October 1985 against East Germany at Hampden Park, and, six months later, he became the first player in Athletic's history to win a World Cup place when named in Scotland's squad for Mexico.

In 1986–87 Goram helped the Latics to the brink of Division One. The team finished third in the table, having conceded only 44 goals in 42 matches. It was the best defensive performance since season 1910–11. By the narrowest of margins – defeat on the away-goals rule after extra-time – Leeds United won the Play-off semi-final.

Nine matches into the following season, Goram was transferred to Hibernian for a £325,000 fee. Although considered by many people in the game to lack height for his position – he stood a fraction under 5ft 11in – his perceived lack of inches was countered by his great reflexes, good timing and a tremendous, spring-heeled leap.

In the summer of 1989, Goram became a double international when he represented Scotland at cricket in a Nat West Trophy match against Yorkshire. In October 1987 he was transferred to Rangers for a £1 million fee, and in the following year he won his 25th Scotland cap, for which he was awarded a silver medal to mark the milestone.

Seven seasons of outstanding success with Rangers included five Scottish League Championship medals, three Scottish Cup and two League Cup-winners' medals. Goram's international career, however, ended in controversial circumstances in 1998. He walked out of the Scotland camp in New Jersey, US, during warm-up preparations for the World Cup Finals in France, blaming media intrusion into his private life.

In March 2002 Goram responded to an emergency call from the Latics and signed a short-term deal. He played in four matches and was immediately on the receiving end of a seven-goal blitz by Cardiff City at Boundary Park. Despite the decidedly shaky start, he signed off in more a familiar form, maintaining a 'clean sheet' at Huddersfield Town in his final appearance on 1 April 2002.

Matt Gray

Date of birth: 18 April 1907, Westhoughton
Died: 18 September 1985, Oldham

Oldham Athletic record:
Appearances: League 289, FA Cup 11
Goals: League 58
Debut: Bradford Park Avenue (a) 22 December 1928, lost 0–2

Also played for: Hindley Green Athletic, Tranmere Rovers amateur, Atherton FC

'If in doubt play Matt Gray'. This appeared to be the policy throughout much of the 17-year career of Gray at Boundary Park. When any position in the side presented a problem, he could be relied upon to provide the solution. This facet was never better illustrated than in season 1932–33 when he settled in to the position of centre-half, having been an inside-forward throughout his time at the club, up to that season.

Gray's signing in May 1928 brought the Latics' playing strength up to 27 professionals. He cost no more than a £10 signing-on fee when recruited from Atherton, a Lancashire Combination club, for whom he had scored 17 goals in the previous season. Earlier he had assisted Hindley Green Celtic and had been an amateur with Tranmere Rovers without appearing at senior level.

A former coal miner, Gray was employed as a steam-roller driver when he arrived at Boundary Park. For some time afterwards he continued his roadwork and operated in Athletic's third team. In a very short time, however, his outstanding form led to his promotion to the Second Division side.

In his first full season – 1929–30 – Gray was a key member of potent attack that took the club to third position in Division Two. There have been few front lines in the club's long history to match that season's usual selection. League goals scored are given in brackets: Worrall (7), Cumming (11), Littlewood (27), Gray (19), Hasson (10). Reserve forward Joe Taylor lacked first-team opportunities despite scoring six goals in just 10 League matches.

For the best part of five seasons Gray was rarely absent, but he missed a large part of season 1933–34 after being injured in the season's first League match against Bolton Wanderers. By the time he was fit enough to resume in mid-January, the side had lost 10 of their previous 12 Second Division matches. The first, and only, back-to-back wins of the season came on 23 February – a 3–1 win against Manchester United – and on 2 March when local rivals Bury were comprehensively defeated 7–2 with Gray and Billy Walsh each registering hat-tricks.

Despite some improvement in results, when the final home match of the season against Newcastle United was contested on 27 April relegation was already a certainty. Only 3,638 spectators bothered to turn up, but despite being a goal behind after only two minutes, and 2–1 down at half-time, goals by Gray and Billy Walsh rounded off the Boundary Park season on a winning note.

Four seasons in the Northern Section of Division Three wound up League football, and in the final term, prior to the outbreak of war, Gray missed much of the season due to a knee injury that required surgery. He was not retained in the close season, but that was far from the end of the story.

Gray lived near to Boundary Park, and in April 1941 – one day after his 34th birthday – he was called upon to help out for a match at Blackpool. Although he admitted that he could hardly walk in the following week, he remained a fixture in the side until season 1944–45. He pulled on a Latics shirt for the last time on 10 March 1945 at Manchester City, completing a total of 105 wartime appearances. Generally at centre-half throughout, he scored just four goals, although a double against Bury in October 1941 ensured a share of the points in a typical wartime encounter that ended 5–5.

Gray died aged 78 in September 1985. At that time his widow, Nell, revealed that her late husband had undergone cartilage operations on both knees and later suffered from arthritis as a result. At the age of 40, a scan revealed that his brain had suffered damage due to many years of heading heavy footballs. Mrs Gray fought hard but with only moderate success to win compensation for his injuries.

Alan Groves

Date of birth: 24 October 1948, Ainsdale, Southport
Died: 15 June 1978, Royton

Oldham Athletic record:
Appearances: League 136(4), FA Cup 3(1), League Cup 9
Goals: League 12, League Cup 1
Debut: Aldershot (h) 23 February 1974, won 2-0 (scored one)

Also played for: Southport, Chester, Shrewsbury Town, AFC Bournemouth, Blackpool

Alan Groves began in League football with Southport and made his League debut at Northampton Town on 11 March 1969. Very much a local product, he lived in Haig Avenue and his father had supported the club since their earliest days in the Football League.

Groves made the first of his many subsequent moves when Chester signed him in July 1970, but his stay at Sealand Road lasted for less than a season, Shrewsbury Town paying £5,000 to take him to Gay Meadow in February 1971. In April of the same season he scored against Mansfield Town, Aston Villa, and twice against Halifax Town to round off his first season in Division Three in sparkling form.

Groves completed 76 League appearances, scoring 11 goals for Shrewsbury Town, and when he joined Bournemouth in October 1972 his value had risen to £40,000. He enjoyed the best possible start at Dean Court, scoring twice on his debut in a 7-2 win against Rotherham United, but he fell out of favour in 1973-74. Although he commenced in the first team, he lost his place after the opening 3-0 defeat by Bristol Rovers. He was not the only casualty, as manager Trevor Hartley made no less than 11 team changes (five positional) for the visit to Brighton in the following week!

His signing by Athletic, for a bargain fee of £10,000 in February 1974, was seen as something of a gamble by manager Jimmy Frizzell when considering Groves's lack of first-team football in the current season (six League matches and four of them from the bench). Any doubts, however, were quickly dispelled when, in a stunning debut, he scored Athletic's second goal in the 2-0 victory against Aldershot. His scoring streak continued with the winner, two minutes from time, at Blackburn Rovers on 2 March, and on the following Tuesday he was again on the mark in the 6-1 thrashing of Cambridge United. A further two victories against Walsall and York City followed to conclude an outstanding sequence of 10 consecutive League victories as Athletic stepped up the pressure on League leaders Bristol Rovers.

Groves missed only one match in the run-in to the Championship and promotion, and he remained an automatic choice throughout his stay at Boundary Park. Powerful, aggressive and fleet footed, he was the type of player always likely to turn any match with a flash of dazzling footwork. Certainly one of Athletic's best wingman in the post-war period, he was a natural footballer with an aptitude for doing the unexpected.

Though not a prolific goalscorer, Groves contributed greatly to the team's success, and the fact that he had his most productive spell in football with Athletic reflects great credit on manager Jimmy Frizzell, who skilfully harnessed his somewhat maverick talents into the team's formation.

Life in Division Two proved far from easy, but after an absence of 21 years Athletic entertained Sheffield Wednesday on their return to higher company on 10 August 1974. They opened with a 2-1 win after being 1-0 down at half-time. Alan McNeil and Colin Garwood scored for Athletic, who lined up as follows: Chris Ogden, Wood, Whittle, Mulvaney, Hicks, Bailey, McNeil, Garwood, Lochhead (sub Robins), Blair and Groves.

In successive seasons the side finished 18th, 17th and 13th, gradually finding their feet in Division Two. In November 1977, after completing 12 League appearances and one as a substitute plus four League Cup ties, Groves was transferred to Blackpool. Two months later he was back at Boundary Park in Blackpool's colours, and 15,308 spectators turned up to see his return – the highest gate of the season. Tragically, in June of the same year, he died as a result of a massive heart attack at the untimely age of 29, leaving the youngest of widows, Debbie, aged just 16. In the following month, on 29 July, Athletic played Blackpool at Boundary Park in a benefit match for his widow.

Harry Grundy

Date of birth: 18 September 1893, Little Hulton
Died: 15 April 1979, Bolton

Oldham Athletic record:
Appearances: League 279, FA Cup 10
Goals: 0
Debut: Notts County (a) 23 January 1915, lost 1–2

Also played for: Wharton Lads, Little Lever Colliery, Rothwell's Athletic

In their long history the Latics have possessed many great club players, perhaps not to international standard, but men of strength and no mean ability who put the club first and foremost all the time. Harry Grundy was a typical example. As a Lancashire lad and an Oldham Athletic player his one ambition was to serve the club, and this he did with great distinction for a period of 16 years.

Once the goalkeeper of the Wharton Lads Club in Little Hulton, Grundy held the position for a season and a half until a new player, also a goalkeeper, joined the club. As two men could not keep goal, Grundy volunteered to play right-back, and a defender he remained ever after. It proved to be a good move for both players as the goalkeeper, Ted Sidlow, went on to play for Bolton Wanderers.

It seems likely that Athletic's trainer, Jimmy Hanson, himself a Little Hulton native, would have had something to do with Grundy arriving at Boundary Park in August 1914, at the age of 21. At that time, the stalwart pairing of Hodson and Cook were the first-team backs, and for a season Grundy was in the reserve team. His senior debut, at Notts County, came in the midst of an injury crisis, and he was paired at full-back with Hugh Lester, whose League debut also proved to be his solitary senior outing for the club. The World War One period found him ordered back to the pit as a miner, where he spent the next four years, although he managed to fit in 99 matches for the Latics in wartime football.

In the first season of post-war football Grundy suffered the one serious accident of his career, a broken ankle on Boxing Day 1919 against Chelsea at Stamford Bridge. The injury brought about a premature end to his season. Still some way from concert pitch in 1920–21, it was not until 1921–22 that he embarked on a run of five seasons in which he missed only a handful of matches.

Grundy was awarded a benefit match in 1923–24 with a guarantee of £500. In the same season, which was their first in Division Two since 1909–10, Athletic were drawn at home to play Sunderland in the first round of the FA Cup. A 24,726 strong crowd packed into Boundary Park, and in a game that remained forever in Grundy's memory, the mighty Wearsiders were defeated by 2–1. Amateur centre-forward Johnny Blair opened the scoring after just nine minutes, with Chris Staniforth adding a second, seven minutes before half-time. Sunderland, however, were not a team to be pinned down, and 15 minutes from the end Sunderland's famous international Charlie Buchan pulled one back. Some strong tackling by Grundy and Sammy Wynne, and some clean handling by goalkeeper Howard Matthews, helped Athletic weather a late siege on their goal and claim a famous victory.

In the next round, Athletic themselves were victims of a giant-killing, going out 0–2 to Swindon Town of the Third Division South. Sunderland, meanwhile, left to concentrate on the League, finished third in Division One.

Despite the fact that Grundy was first employed in a cotton mill as a 'half-timer' at the age of 12, his parents were initially set against his ambition to become a professional footballer. From early youth, however, his heart was in the game, and his career was a long and rewarding one, ending in a well-earned retirement at the age of 37 in 1930. As one contemporary journalist wrote, 'A fine back, who has done equally good service on either flank; a resolute, broad-shouldered clean player who has, all his days, been a credit to himself and to the club.'

A nephew, Arthur Grundy, signed amateur forms with the Latics in February 1939. He played twice for the Northern Midweek team at right full-back and once for the reserves at centre-half. Despite playing in a trio of victories, he was not offered a re-engagement.

Jack Hacking

Date of birth: 22 December 1898, Blackburn
Died: 1 June 1955, Accrington

Oldham Athletic record:
Appearances: League 223, FA Cup 11
Goals: 0
Debut: 30 October 1926 v Southampton (h), drawn 1–1

Also played for: Blackburn Rovers A Team, Blackpool, Wigan Borough (trial), Manchester United, Accrington Stanley (player-manager), England international (3 caps)
Managed: Barrow

Jack Hacking represented Blackburn Schools at the age of 11 and a half and at 13 began work as an apprentice grocer with Blackburn Co-operative stores while playing for their team in the Blackburn Thursday League. In 1917 he was called up into the forces, serving until 1919 with the Royal Garrison Artillery. A few months after demobilisation he was offered a trial by Blackpool, who were then a Second Division side. He quickly gained a Central League Championship medal but found few opportunities of first-team football and was given a free transfer in 1925.

Hacking joined Fleetwood as a part-time professional while still living in Blackpool and working in a grocery store. A three-man deputation from the Latics arrived at his door in 1926 to offer him a professional contract, at which point he strongly recommended his great friend and Fleetwood teammate Billy Porter. Before Hacking's terms had been accepted, Billy Porter and his father were sent for and both players were signed.

The pair were destined to serve the Latics with great distinction. Never a goalkeeper to favour any form of showmanship, Hacking succeeded at the highest level without playing to the gallery by making simple saves look difficult. In 1948 he recalled that his most thrilling moment in football did not occur on the field of play. He was actually at Preston North End's ground to watch a match when Jasper Kerr, a Preston full-back, recognised him. Shaking his hand, he said 'Congratulations Jack'. On enquiring why, Kerr replied 'Haven't you seen the paper? You have been selected to play for England at Hampden Park.'

Sadly, Hacking was beaten in the most important game of his life by a corner-kick in the last second of the Scotland versus England international in 1929. Inside-right Alex Cheyne, then of Aberdeen and later of Chelsea, hurriedly placed the ball at the corner flag. With thousands of spectators streaming from the ground, the referee looking at his watch and journalists on the telephone to their newspapers to give the score as 0–0, the ball came over, high and fast. As it reached the goalmouth, swerve took effect and it sailed into the far corner of the net.

Hacking grieved over that goal for a very long time, but his overall career was greatly distinguished. Aside from three full international caps and two inter-League honours, his contribution at club level – particularly in season 1929–30 – kept the Latics on course for promotion to Division One. The three most vital games of the campaign were at Easter, against Blackpool twice, with Bristol City in between. Sadly, a severe bout of 'flu kept Jack out from all three games, and they lost twice to the Seasiders and only managed to draw against Bristol City. As a result, they were two points short of going up, with Blackpool and Chelsea being promoted.

When Hacking joined Manchester United in March 1934, they were in grave danger of relegation to Division Three, as right to the very last match of the season their fate was in doubt. They then had to meet Millwall, who themselves required only one point to avoid the drop. A United victory was essential, and a wonderful display in the art of goalkeeping by Hacking kept the Millwall attack at bay, enabling United to run out eventual winners by 2–0.

Fourteen months after joining United, Hacking took over as player-manager of Accrington Stanley, and he was later Barrow's manager. His son, Jack junior, was also a goalkeeper with Accrington Stanley and Stockport County and appeared as a guest player with Manchester United in season 1943–44 when only 18 years old. In season 1945–46 Hacking deputised for his son when he was unfit to play. At the age of 47, Jack senior became the oldest player to appear in a League match that season.

Ray Haddington

Date of birth: 18 November 1923, Scarborough
Died: 26 July 1994, Adelaide, Australia

Oldham Athletic record:
Appearances: League 117, FA Cup 9
Goals: League 63, FA Cup 10
Debut: Tranmere Rovers (h) 20 September 1947, lost 0–1

Also played for: Bradford PA amateur (World War Two guest player with Bradford City, Halifax Town, York City, Plymouth Argyle, Portsmouth, Exeter City), Manchester City, Stockport County, Bournemouth and Boscombe Athletic, Rochdale, Halifax Town, Bedford Town, Juventus (Australia)

In his second appearance for the Latics, Ray Haddington was the star performer in a result that shook the football world. Without a win in their first eight League matches, rock bottom Athletic travelled north to Darlington on 27 September 1947 and against all expectations won 6–0. The stockily-built and explosive-shooting inside-right opened his Athletic scoring account with a hat-trick. Centre-forward Jack Fryer scored two and outside-right Billy Blackshaw went on to score number six after 73 minutes.

Athletic ended the season occupying 11th place in the Third Division North. Only Haddington and Billy Blackshaw reached double figures in the scoring charts, each with 17 in League and Cup ties. Sadly, the shooting power shown in away matches was not duplicated at Boundary Park. Only two clubs in the Division scored fewer goals at home than Athletic's 25, yet the side's away record of 38 was exceeded only by Rotherham United who scored 39.

After the customary abysmal start to the new season – one point from the first eight matches – a season of high scoring and excellent attendance figures was memorable for Haddington's return of 23 goals, a figure achieved despite the fact that he had scored only once in the League before Christmas. Thereafter, he hardly knew failure, with goals raining in from improbable distances and angles. Acknowledged in his day as the strongest hitter of a dead ball in the Northern Section, one had the feeling that he did not always know his own strength. It was not unusual for him to hit an intended cross-field pass some feet above the wingman's head, the ball finishing in row Z of the stand!

Eventual progress to round three of the FA Cup in 1948–49 began at Wrexham with a 3–0 victory, despite Athletic finishing with 10 men after Albert Watson suffered a fractured rib. The draw for the second round took the Latics to non-League amateurs Walthamstowe Avenue, who fully deserved their 2–2 draw after extra-time. The replay at Boundary Park attracted 26,048 spectators and two goals from Haddington, with one more from Eric Gemmell, clinched a 3–1 victory. By his own admission, one of his goals – a header – was something of a collector's item. The Cup run ended at Boundary Park in round three, Second Division Cardiff City winning 3–2, with both Haddington and Eric Gemmell again scoring for Athletic. The highest attendance of the season witnessed the match: 28,991 spectators paying £2,546 at the gate.

Season 1949–50 was chiefly memorable for Haddington's 24 goals in 46 League and Cup matches and another run in the FA Cup that brought First Division Newcastle United to Boundary Park in round three. Earlier, two goals from Athletic's ace marksman helped despatch non-League Stockton in the first round, and another two, including a penalty, finally accounted for Crewe Alexandra at Manchester City's Maine Road, after two previous meetings had ended all square. A crowd of 31,706 packed into Boundary Park for the Magpies visit, and many latecomers missed Newcastle's opener after just two minutes. A typical blockbuster from Haddington after 49 minutes lifted hopes, but he later shot wide from a penalty, and the Magpies ran out deserved 7–2 victors.

Three months into the following season, with his record at that point being 10 goals in 15 matches, Haddington was transferred to Manchester City for a fee of £8,000, where he teamed up with another former Athletic player, Billy Spurdle. He threatened to take Division Two by storm as he scored in each of his first four matches but was dropped after failing to score in his fifth outing. When Don Revie and Ivor Broadis arrived at Maine Road, he requested a transfer. Crewe Alexandra agreed terms but Haddington refused to join them unless he went as player-manager. Stockport County paid £2,500 for him in December 1951, but his best subsequent spell was with Rochdale, scoring 12 League goals in 38 matches.

Haddington emigrated to Australia in 1958, where his scoring exploits for Juventus resulted in his appearing as the subject of a *This is your Life* programme on Australian television.

Gunnar Halle

Date of birth: 11 August 1965, Larvic, Norway

Oldham Athletic record:
Appearances: League 185(3), FA Cup 8, League Cup 16
Goals: League 17, FA Cup 2, League Cup 2
Debut: Port Vale (h) 16 February 1991, won 2–0

Also played for: Nesjar Juniors, Larvik Turn, Lillestrom, Leeds United, Bradford City, Wolverhampton Wanderers on loan, Norway (64 caps)

Norwegian international Gunnar Halle was recommended to Athletic by his compatriot Aage Hareide, a former playing colleague of Boundary Park manager Joe Royle at both Manchester City and Norwich City. While the Norwegian clubs were on their winter break, Lillestrom agreed to allow Halle to join Athletic for trials, with a view to a permanent signing. There was just time for him to appear in one reserve-team match against Scunthorpe United before the Pontins League closed down for the Christmas and New Year break. The trialist scored a spectacular goal on his reserve-team debut and returned to Boundary Park in January 1991 to agree terms for a three-year contract.

Delays in obtaining a work permit ensued, and it was not until mid-February that Halle was able to make his first-team debut. Second-half goals from Neil Redfearn and Richard Jobson gave Athletic a 2–0 victory on his debut against a Port Vale side who lost their goalkeeper, Trevor Wood, after 36 minutes. From right full-back, the £280,000 blond Norwegian linked well with the attack as Athletic took another step towards to the First Division. He soon settled in to life on Athletic's plastic pitch, while setting about the difficult task of replacing the popular Paul Warhurst in the run-up to the Second Division Championship. In the nail-biting climax to the season, he was injured in the first half of the title decider against Sheffield Wednesday. His replacement, Neil Redfearn, seized his opportunity and passed into Athletic folklore by converting a penalty-kick – three minutes into injury time – to clinch a 3–2 win, and with it the Barclays League Eagle trophy.

Halle was in the wars in 1991–92, after sustaining a cracked fibula in the 7–1 demolition of Torquay United in the third-round League Cup tie at Boundary Park on 24 September. He was out of the first-team picture until 28 December, before a second injury at Sheffield Wednesday on New Year's Day brought a premature end to his season. In 1992–93 he enjoyed an injury-free season, recording 41 League appearances and five goals, his total including Athletic's fourth goal in the season's final match – a 4–3 win against Southampton that ensured Premier League survival. Cartilage problems saw him out of commission for a lengthy spell from mid-season in 1993–94, as Athletic's three years in the top flight ended with a whimper, taking only three points from their final eight fixtures.

By this time, Halle was Athletic's most capped player – he won 24 of his 64 awards while at Boundary Park – and in 1994 he took part in the World Cup Finals in America. Two years earlier he had scored a hat-trick for Norway in a 10–0 win against San Marino in a World Cup qualifier. It was perhaps surprising that Athletic managed to retain his services for such a lengthy spell, as he was never short of admirers. Having started as a forward in Norway, later switching to midfield and then full-back, he was versatility personified, and although his best position remained a matter of debate, he could be relied upon to shine anywhere across the back line or in midfield.

Halle finally left Boundary Park when he became a Leeds United player in December 1996. He had actually been on the point of joining the Elland Road club in September, but the deal was shelved when manager Howard Wilkinson was sacked. Incoming replacement George Graham made him his first signing, paying £400,000 for the 31-year-old utility man, who made his debut against Tottenham Hotspur at Elland Road in a 0–0 draw on 14 December. He retained his place through to the end of the season, playing in 22 Premier League matches. He played in the 1998 World Cup Finals in France, taking his total of caps past the 60 mark during his spell at Elland Road. He was offered, and signed, a new two-year contract for Leeds during the 1998–99 season, but in June 1999 manager David O'Leary accepted a £200,000 offer from Bradford City for his services.

Halle bowed out of English football after three seasons at Valley Parade but spent his last three months on loan to Wolverhampton Wanderers, assisting them to a third-place finish in Division One. He was sadly denied a fitting climax to his outstanding career as Wolves lost in the Play-off semi-finals to Norwich City. In the summer, he returned to Norway and signed for Lillestrom.

Jon Hallworth

Date of birth: 26 October 1965, Hazel Grove, Stockport

Oldham Athletic record:
Appearances: League 171(3), FA Cup 20, League Cup 20
Goals: 0
Debut: Watford (h) 4 February 1989, won 3–1

Also played for: Stockport and Greater Manchester Schoolboys, Ipswich Town, Bristol Rovers on loan, Cardiff City

Jon Hallworth was first spotted by Ipswich Town's north-eastern scout while playing in an England Schools trial at Durham. He signed apprentice forms with the Suffolk club, becoming a professional in May 1983. He had some time to wait for his League debut, and when the big day arrived – on 23 November 1985 – 20-year-old Hallworth had a traumatic start at Oxford United's Manor Ground. At one stage 3–0 ahead, Ipswich lost 4–3, with a hat-trick from ace marksman John Aldridge ruining his big day.

At the time of his transfer to Athletic, the 6ft 2in goalkeeper had appeared in 45 League games for Ipswich but was currently out of the first team, having been replaced by the Canadian international Craig Forrest. Initially signed by manager Royle on a month's loan with a view to a £125,000 transfer, the tall, blond, shot-stopper was drafted straight into Athletic's relegation battle. He was introduced in place of Andy Rhodes, who was rested from the firing line after conceding four goals at Barnsley.

At the time of Hallworth's debut, Athletic were fourth from bottom of Division Two and were without a win in 15 League and Cup matches. Visitors Watford, however, were riding high in second place and were through to the fifth round of the FA Cup, having beaten First Division Derby County 2–1 at Vicarage Road on the previous Saturday. Against all the odds, two goals from Andy Ritchie and one from Denis Irwin gave Athletic a most vital and welcome 3–1 victory.

Hallworth followed his winning start by keeping a clean sheet at Stoke City and a fortnight after his arrival was signed on a permanent basis, accepting the offer of a three-year contract. His signing gave Athletic two goalkeepers of great potential and much better cover, as it was apparent that Winston Dubose was not considered first-team material. His introduction sparked an unbeaten run of 10 games and the injury-plagued campaign ended with the team well clear of the relegation zone. They had used four goalkeepers in the various competitions and 31 players overall, with the highlight of the campaign being Roger Palmer's smashing of the club's all-time record for League goals.

In Hallworth's second season the Latics covered themselves with honour in both the FA Cup and the Littlewoods Cup. His appearances were restricted by a mid-season knee injury, and although he played in the FA Cup semi-final and the replay against Manchester United, he missed out on a Wembley appearance against Nottingham Forest when Andy Rhodes, who had been recalled earlier in the month, was selected for the Cup Final. Athletic transferred Andy Rhodes to Dunfermline in the close season and signed John Keeley from Brighton as his replacement. In the championship-winning season that followed, Hallworth was one of three ever-presents, along with Andy Barlow and Earl Barrett, all of whom played in 52 matches.

As Division One football returned to Boundary Park, newspaper speculation linked Watford's England Under-21 goalkeeper David James with a £1 million move to Athletic. Joe Royle denied the story and gave Hallworth a well-deserved vote of confidence. The manager's faith was repaid, with Hallworth playing in all but the final League match of the season. However, the emerging talents of the England Under-21 goalkeeper Paul Gerrard began to loosen Hallworth's grip on the first-team jersey in 1992–93, after he had appeared in the first 16 Premier League matches. Athletic lost their top-flight status in 1993–94, their best form coming in the Cup competitions. Hallworth played all of the season's FA Cup ties, including the semi-final against Manchester United at Wembley Stadium and the replay at Maine Road.

Hallworth played in few first-team matches in his final three seasons, understudying Paul Gerrard and finally Gary Kelly. He was transferred to Cardiff City in August 1997 and in his first season helped The Bluebirds to knock Athletic out of the FA Cup by 1–0 in the third round. In an up-and-down spell at Ninian Park, he experienced two demotions and two promotions before being forced to retire with a knee injury in January 2001. He returned briefly to Boundary Park as a part-time goalkeeping coach in September 2001.

George Hardwick

Date of birth: 2 February 1920, Saltburn
Died: 20 April 2004, Middlesbrough

Oldham Athletic record:
Appearances: League 190, FA Cup 13
Goals: League 14
Debut: Lincoln City (h) 11 November 1950, drawn 0–0

Also played for: South Bank East End, Middlesbrough (World War Two guest player with Nottingham Forest, Birmingham, Chelsea, West Bromwich Albion, Reading), England (13 caps plus 17 wartime appearances)
Managed: Holland (National team manager), PSV Eindhoven (Holland), Sunderland, Gateshead

The former England captain's debut against Lincoln City attracted 21,742 spectators to Boundary Park, and it marked a new and exciting era for the club. George Hardwick was one of the leading personalities in the Third Division North during the early 1950s, as he guided the Latics from 21st position to eventual promotion in season 1952–53.

A full-back of style, grace and outstanding ability, Hardwick wore the England shirt on 30 occasions and captained every team that he played for. A star of the glittering post-war era, 'Gentleman George', of the film star features, captained a star-studded England team with such names as Swift, Matthews, Lawton, Carter, Mannion and Finney – just a handful of the world class players available to the selectors.

Hardwick began as a centre-forward, leading his school team and later Cleveland FC – a team managed by his father and for which his mother knitted stockings and laundered jerseys. At 15 he joined Middlesbrough on amateur forms and was farmed out to their nursery club, South Bank. In 1937 he signed as a professional, yet when war broke out he joined the RAF and was seriously wounded in an attack on his airfield, although thankfully he made a full recovery. He appeared at Wembley as a Chelsea guest player in the War Cup Final victory against Millwall in 1945. Chelsea were very keen to sign him in 1946, but Middlesbrough refused to entertain the idea. At the time of his £15,000 transfer to the Latics, he had played in 166 League and Cup matches for Middlesbrough and scored seven goals.

For Athletic supporters of the day, it was an education to watch Hardwick in action. An assured first touch would bring the ball immediately under control, he would then look around for an unmarked colleague and the most advantageous pass. He actually left the full-back pairing of Tommy Bell and Bill Naylor undisturbed for most of season 1950–51 and took the number-10 shirt, operating in an attacking midfield role. He scored his first goals for Athletic against Southport (h) on 3 February 1951, netting twice in a 4–0 win. By the end of the season he had scored seven goals in 23 League matches.

Athletic first challenged for promotion in 1951–52 when Eric Gemmell scored 28 League goals, Peter McKennan 16 and Bobby McIlvenny 13. They led the table for a time but finished in fourth place, 12 points behind the Champions, Lincoln City. Eric Gemmell scored three hat-tricks and Alf Clarke one in 1952–53, but it was an improved defensive performance that led to the clinching of the title, one point ahead of Port Vale. Despite playing well in their long-awaited return to Division Two, they were held to a 4–4 draw by Luton Town. The side did not win in their opening eight matches and, long before the transfer-deadline signings of Harry McShane and Tommy Walker, the side were doomed to relegation. Hopes of a speedy return were dashed by a poor start to season 1954–55, and Hardwick's final campaign ended with the side in a disappointing 20th position in the Third Division North – almost exactly where they were when he took over some five and a half years earlier.

After leaving Boundary Park, Hardwick held coaching appointments in Germany and Holland, returned to Middlesbrough as coach, and was then manager of Sunderland and Gateshead. In June 1963, when the Latics appointed Leslie McDowell as manager from a short list of two, Hardwick, unfortunately, was the unsuccessful applicant. Long after his retirement from the game, Bobby Robson took an England team to Ayresome Park to play in a testimonial for him and his former Middlesbrough and England colleague Wilf Mannion. If any proof of the pair's enduring popularity with the Teesside public was needed, the 14,000 attendance for the match supplied the answer. In recent years a statue of Hardwick has been erected at The Riverside Stadium. His autobiography *Gentleman George* (Juniper Publishing) is a most interesting and well-written book.

Frank Hargreaves

Date of birth: 16 November 1902, Ashton-under-Lyne
Died: September 1987, Tameside

Oldham Athletic record:
Appearances: League 103, FA Cup 1
Goals: League 17
Debut: Manchester United (h) 6 October 1923, won 3–2

Also played for: Ashton National, Hurst FC, Stalybridge Celtic, Droylsden FC, Manchester North End, Everton, Rochdale, Bournemouth and Boscombe Athletic, Watford

Frank Hargreaves enjoyed a lengthy association with the Latics, initially as a player and later as trainer. He was signed as a professional on 1 October 1923 after playing in a trial match in the reserves against Sheffield United reserves at Boundary Park two days earlier. In an eventful debut, Hargreaves scored in the 2–2 draw and earned praise for keeping his wingman, amateur Herbert Hasty, 'well plied with the ball'. Welsh international goalkeeper Albert Gray broke his thumb after 25 minutes play, and with full-back Ernie Gregory in goal the 10 men did well to earn a point.

Despite having had little time to get acquainted with his new colleagues, Hargreaves was pitched straight in to the first team on the following Saturday for his Football League debut against Manchester United. A crowd of 15,120 spectators witnessed a remarkable match. Latics' burly full-back Sammy Wynne inadvertently scored United's first goal when he put through his own-goal after seven minutes play. On the half-hour mark he atoned for his error when he converted a penalty-kick to level the scores. Billy Howson gave Athletic the lead within 10 minutes of the restart, and Sammy Wynne added another on the hour mark. Latics' accident prone full-back then concluded the scoring with another own-goal, the match ending 3–2 in Athletic's favour. It was quite an eventful debut for Hargreaves, and a piece of soccer history was made, as it was the first time that a player had scored two goals and two own-goals in a League match.

Hargreaves retained his place at inside-left for a run of 33 consecutive matches. Of slight build at 5ft 7in and 10st 3lb, he was a wonderful dribbler, often too elusive for opponents. His clever ball manipulation and ability to see the move beyond the next gave all defenders problems, and while he was an arch provider of openings, he did not score many goals himself. He scored only three in his first season, but Everton were sufficiently impressed to pay £750 for him in May 1924.

Although he began in the first team at Goodison Park, Hargreaves lost out to the challenge of Irish international Bobby Irvine. He played in nine First Division matches, his two goals coming in consecutive games in November 1924, against Arsenal and Aston Villa.

After exactly 12 months away, Hargreaves was welcomed back to Boundary Park for a bargain fee of £250. Other forward recruits in the season included Albert Pynegar, Arthur Ormston and Horace Barnes, and they proved to be a high-scoring trio. Hargreaves was very short of opportunities but rounded off the season with his only hat-trick for the club against Nottingham Forest in the season's final fixture. Only 3,966 spectators turned up at Boundary Park, but the missing thousands missed a treat, Latics winning 8–3 with goals by Albert Pynegar (4), Hargreaves (3) and a penalty by Sammy Wynne.

Hargreaves scored nine League goals in 39 matches in 1926–27 but did not feature in a great deal of first-team football thereafter. He joined Rochdale in August 1930 and scored three goals in nine matches. He subsequently failed to settle with either Bournemouth or Watford and returned homewards in March 1932, linking up with Athletic for the third time. He was appointed reserve-team trainer in August 1933 and three years later was promoted to first-team duties. In 1939 he volunteered to become an army physical training instructor, passed his training course at Aldershot and qualified as a sergeant instructor. He was demobilised after six years of service in August 1945 and resumed his duties at Boundary Park shortly afterwards.

In May 1948 Hargreaves became the landlord of the Gatefield public house at Ashton-under-Lyne and in September of the same year was obliged to resign his post as trainer due to pressure of work.

Nick Henry

Date of birth: 21 February 1969, Liverpool

Oldham Athletic record:
Appearances: League 264(9), FA Cup 21, League Cup 30(4)
Goals: League 19, League Cup 3
Debut: Hull City (a) 19 September 1987, lost 0–1

Also played for: Liverpool Schoolboys, Halmstad (Sweden) on loan, Sheffield United, Walsall, Tranmere Rovers, Scarborough
Managed: Scarborough

When Nick Henry arrived at Boundary Park, a fresh-faced 15-year-old in January 1985, Athletic were, at the mid-point of the season, fourth from the bottom of Division Two. In a busy month they signed experienced midfielder Mick McGuire from Barnsley, beat Brentford 2–1 in the third round of the FA Cup and sold 17-year-old discovery Wayne Harrison to Liverpool for £250,000, immediately borrowing him back for the rest of the season.

Henry, who arrived with boots in hand and asking for a trial, was making excellent progress and pushing for a first-team place when he underwent an operation for a potentially serious illness and was on the sidelines for several months. Thankfully he made a full recovery and made his first senior appearance in a narrow 1–0 defeat at high-flying Hull City. The Tigers goal was scored by defender Peter Skipper, who was later booked for a rash challenge on Henry that brought a premature end to his most promising debut after just 48 minutes. In the summer of 1988, Henry was sent out on loan to Sweden in order to broaden his experience, and he derived considerable benefit from his spell of regular football in the Swedish First Division.

In the second half of the 1988–89 campaign, when Athletic lost only two of their last 20 matches, Henry established himself in midfield alongside fellow all-action battler Mike Milligan. The pair were subsequently nicknamed 'Bush-whackers' and 'Yard Dogs' by tongue-in-cheek manager Joe Royle. Although the descriptions were made in jest, they fitted the pair extremely well as they were a very potent combined force who kept the whole team ticking over. Henry's non-stop running, ferocious tackling and lung-bursting work rate certainly made him a firm favourite with the Latics fans.

In the month before his 21st birthday, in January 1990, Henry picked up the Barclays League Young Eagle regional award – an inscribed salver. The panel's representative Bob Paisley, the former Liverpool manager, described him as 'Very bright with good anticipation, and very industrious with a non-stop involvement'. Two months earlier Nick had registered his first goal in professional football, a 30–yard screamer that pushed Arsenal towards a shock 3–1 defeat in the fourth-round Littlewoods Cup tie at Boundary Park. Manager Joe Royle later quipped 'When we have shooting practice in training, the other players duck when Nick lets fly – but that one screamed in'. In subsequent seasons, Nick's strike rate from midfield improved considerably, but he never scored a better goal than his first against the mighty Arsenal – Football League Champions and First Division leaders.

At the end of a momentous season when the team staged a three-trophy charge but narrowly lost out on all fronts, Henry underwent an exploratory operation on an injured knee. He recovered in time to play a full part in the pre-season programme, and in the Championship season that followed he appeared in 43 matches, scoring four goals. Reunited with midfield partner Mike Milligan, who returned after a disappointing season with Everton, Henry was outstanding in Athletic's first season in Division One, scoring six goals in 42 League matches. As Athletic scrapped to avoid relegation in 1992–93, his winning goal at Aston Villa set up the great escape that was to follow. It also handed Manchester United the Premier League title with two matches of the season still remaining, Aston Villa finishing as runners-up.

Henry struggled with injury in the relegation season of 1993–94 but recovered to play at Wembley in the FA Cup semi-final against Manchester United. Less successful days were ahead, however, as his 1995–96 season ended in October when he sustained a severe back injury that required surgery. In February of the following season, he was transferred to Sheffield United for £500,000 with Australian central-defender Doug Hodgson joining Athletic as part of the deal. He continued to be troubled with back problems at Bramall Lane but completed 106(9) matches for Tranmere Rovers, including a Wembley appearance in the League Cup Final against Leicester City in February 2000.

Tony Henry

Date of birth: 26 November 1957, Houghton-le-Spring

Oldham Athletic record:
Appearances: League 185(5), FA Cup 5, League Cup 12
Goals: League 25, League Cup 2
Debut: Fulham (h) 19 March 1983, won 1–0

Also played for: Durham Schoolboys, Manchester City, Bolton Wanderers, Stoke City, Mazda Hiroshima (Japan), Shrewsbury Town, Hyde United

Equally at home in either defence or midfield, versatile Tony Henry was manager Joe Royle's first cash signing and, at just £21,000, he proved to be an absolute bargain. During his time at Boundary Park, Henry remained an important member of the first-team squad. Voted Player of the Season by supporters in May 1985, his versatility at various times saw him fielded as sweeper, midfield mastermind and, somewhat reluctantly, at right full-back. He actually refused to play in this position against Orient in a third-round FA Cup tie in January 1986 and was dropped, fined and transfer listed. Thankfully, all problems were resolved quickly and within three weeks he was reinstated in his customary midfield role.

Born in the Newcastle district but a Sunderland supporter from childhood, in the earliest days Henry had no shortage of admirers, with Chelsea and Everton being among the clubs chasing his signature. He elected, however, to join Manchester City and signed apprentice forms in July 1974, becoming a professional five months later. He made his first League appearance, from the bench, on 8 September 1976 at his beloved Roker Park in a 2–0 victory against Sunderland, Joe Royle scoring one of City's goals.

Henry had his first experience of regular first-team football towards the end of season 1978–79. He scored his first League goal in the Manchester derby against United on 10 November 1979 in a 2–0 win, but the highlight of his Maine Road career came in the following season. He won an FA Cup medal for his substitute appearance in the Centenary Final against Tottenham Hotspur. He did not, however, feature in the replay, memorably won by Spurs thanks to a wonder goal scored by Argentina international Ricky Villa. In September 1981, Bolton Wanderers paid £125,000 to take Henry to Burnden Park, where he was leading scorer in each of his two seasons, despite making his debut at right full-back. He left the relegation-bound Trotters in March 1983 to join Athletic, having scored 24 goals in 76 matches.

Henry made his Latics debut against fellow promotion-contenders Fulham, the 1–0 victory secured thanks to Roger Palmer's 13th goal of the season and an outstanding display by teenage 'keeper Andy Goram. He scored his first Athletic goal in the final League match of the season, Cambridge United's record run of 12 home matches without conceding a goal coming to an abrupt end in a second-half goal blitz. His goal was the last in an eight-minute spell when Athletic banged in four goals to round off the campaign with a crushing 4–1 victory. In his first full season, Athletic narrowly avoided relegation, late season wins at Barnsley and at home to Grimsby Town finally assuring them of Second Division football in the following term.

Henry appeared in 39(3) League matches in 1983–84 and in exactly 40 in each of the following two seasons. A broken collarbone kept him out for some weeks in 1986–87, restricting him to 35(1) matches, and he had played in 20(1) matches the following season at the time of his mid-season transfer to Stoke City in December 1987. Henry departed in the same month that Frank Bunn arrived at Oldham, after he was signed for £90,000, and Henry scored from a penalty on Bunn's debut at Bournemouth. Two days later, he scored his final goal for Athletic – again from the penalty spot – in a 2–2 draw against Stoke City at Boundary Park. In the same month, Stoke's manager Mick Mills paid £30,000 to take Tony to the Victoria Ground. Although he signed a two-and-a-half year contract, he stayed for only 18 months before being transferred to Mazda Hiroshima, where he had two successful years as leading scorer in both seasons.

Henry returned to England in August 1991 for a final season of League football with Shrewsbury Town, managed at that time by John Bond, his manager for a spell at Manchester City. Shrewsbury won four and drew one of their opening six Division Three fixtures, but the team's form plummeted; they finished 22nd in Division Three and were relegated. He was released in the close season with career aggregate figures of 421(20) League matches and 71 goals.

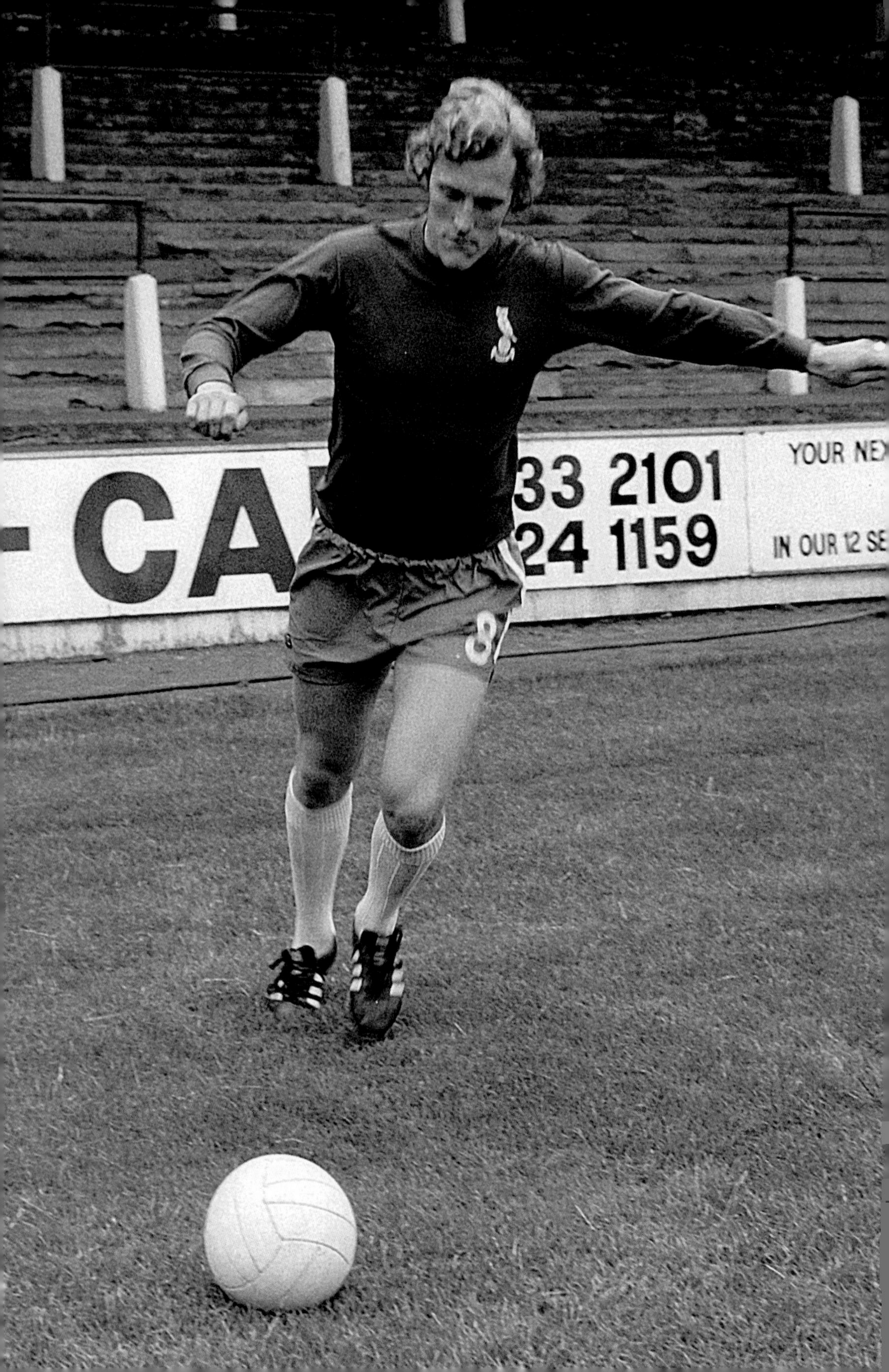

-CA
33 2101
24 1159
YOUR NE
IN OUR 12 SE

Keith Hicks

Date of birth: 9 August 1954, Oldham

Oldham Athletic record:
Appearances: League 240(2), FA Cup 15, League Cup 12
Goals: League 11, League Cup 1
Debut: Plymouth Argyle (a) 3 April 1972, drawn 0–0

Also played for: Hereford United, Rochdale, Hyde United, Mossley, Hyde United, Radcliffe Borough, Bacup Borough, Rossendale United
Managed: Mossley

One of Athletic's best home-produced players, Keith Hicks was originally associated with the club on schoolboy forms at the age of 15. In less than a year he became an apprentice and signed professionally on his 18th birthday in August 1972.

Hicks's name was first traced on a Latics team sheet on 6 September 1969, for a Lancashire League fixture with the A Team against Crewe Alexandra A. Three other youthful members of the line up eventually graduated to senior level. The successful trio were midfielder Micky Lester, who made his first-team debut in 1972 at 18 years of age, Ian Buckley, a left-winger who was the first Athletic player to win an England Youth cap in February 1972, and goalkeeper Chris Ogden, who won a Third Division Championship medal with the Latics in 1974.

After playing regularly for the Reserves in the Cheshire League and for the Youth Team in the FA Youth Cup in 1971–72, Hicks made his first-team debut at left half-back while still an apprentice, as deputy for Bill Cranston at Plymouth Argyle late in the season. Alongside seasoned campaigners Jim Bowie and Dick Mulvaney in the middle line, and a back three of Dowd, Wood and Whittle, his assured display in the 0–0 draw earned him a further two outings in his debut season. He collected his first winning bonus from a heartening finale to the campaign, a 5–1 home victory against Rotherham United, which featured a hat-trick by David Shaw.

In his first taste of senior football, Hicks had proved well up to the job. A six-footer with a physique to match, the fair-haired, lantern-jawed, central defender's robust style featured fearless tackling, exceptional headwork and a maturity beyond his tender years. A busy pre-season programme that opened with the traditional Rose Bowl fixture against Rochdale saw a settled team pattern emerging, with Hicks flanked by Alan McNeill and Bill Cranston in the middle line. The side earned their highest placing for 20 years, finishing fourth in Division Three. He was one of three ever presents during the campaign, and he scored his first League goal against Swansea City in the 2–0 home win on 28 October 1972.

In the Championship season that followed, Hicks completed 52 League and Cup matches, and in the inspired mid-season run of 10 consecutive League victories he scored at Rochdale in a 3–1 win and in the 6–1 home victory against Cambridge United. Athletic, incidentally, played Cambridge on five occasions during the season, with three FA Cup ties commencing with a 2–2 draw at the Abbey Stadium. It was Athletic's first ever Sunday fixture and the 11am kick-off made it the first of four FA Cup ties to be played on the same day.

Hicks played in seven full seasons for Athletic, helping the club establish its place in the Second Division. In addition to defensive duties, his outstanding headwork and physical presence in set-piece situations was seen to best effect in 1975–76, when he scored three League goals and one in the FA Cup. He also scored another four – all in League matches – in 1978–79, his total including a timely second-half double at Millwall on 4 November that gave Athletic the points in a 3–2 win.

Hicks's 10-year association with the Latics ended in September 1980 when he was transferred to Hereford United, at that time a Division Four side. In a five-year stay, he clocked up 201 League appearances before a homeward move brought him to Rochdale in July 1985. In his second season at Spotland a groin injury brought an end to his League career, which concluded with aggregate figures of 473(2) matches and 14 goals. His injury did not prevent him from prolonging his career in local non-League circles, and he also had a spell in management with Mossley. He subsequently returned to Rochdale as the Spotland club's community officer and director of coaching in the club's centre of excellence.

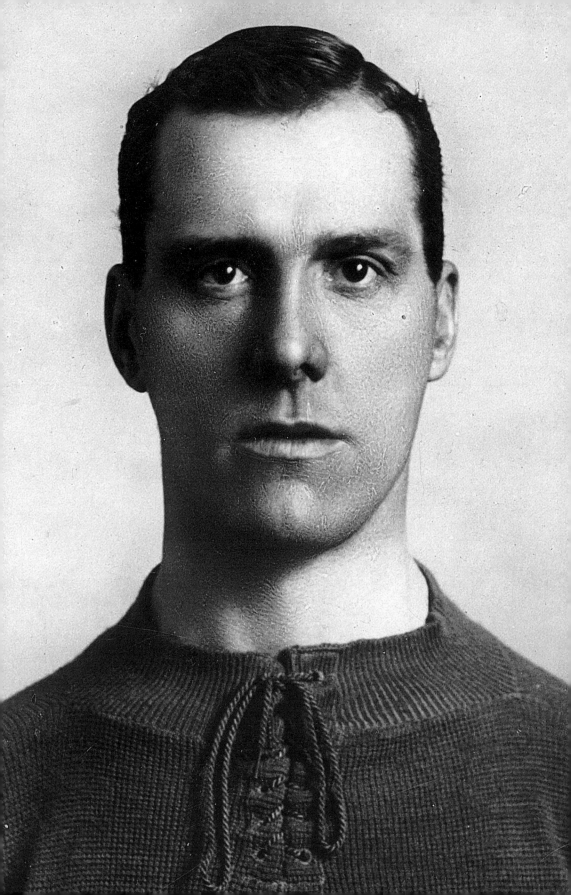

Jimmy Hodson

Date of birth: 5 September 1880, Horwich
Died: February 1938, Holland

Oldham Athletic record:
Appearances: League 252, FA Cup 37
Goals: League 1
Debut: Ashton Town, FA Cup 1, 7 October 1905, won 2–1

Also played for: St Helens Recreation, Bury (World War One guest Southport Vulcan), Belfast Celtic, Brentford
Managed: Guildford United (manager-coach), Berehem Sports Club, Antwerp (manager-coach)

It was over a century ago that Jimmy Hodson joined Athletic, at that time a Lancashire Combination A Division side. They had been promoted from the B Division in the previous season after finishing third in the table behind St Helens Recreation and Barrow. They opened season 1905–06 with a home fixture against Atherton Church House at Hudson Fold and drew 1–1. The local correspondent estimated the crowd to be 'approximately 8,000'.

There were a number of new players in the side but the pair who were destined to make the greatest long-term impact were the two Jimmys – Fay and Hodson. By the time the two qualified for a benefit, in season 1911–12, Athletic had risen to the heady heights of the First Division of the Football League. In the case of Hodson, he stayed with Athletic for 10 years, a spell terminated by World War One, at which time his team proudly stood as runners-up of the First Division Championship.

At 5ft 9in and 13st 4lb, Hodson was built in the manner of most full-backs of his era, but despite his hefty build he combined strength with surprising pace and mobility. He was also remarkably free from injury, his appearance figures accurately reflecting his consistency and fitness levels. In 1914 the *Athletic News* commented 'Hodson is a most assiduous player for attention to training, and will shortly qualify for a second benefit. No player has better merited such an award.'

Hodson's football career began with St Helens Recreation in July 1900. In his first season they finished fifth in the Lancashire Combination A Division, with the first four places in the table occupied by the reserve teams of Liverpool, Everton, Manchester City and Bury. In May 1902 he joined First Division Bury and was reserve full-back for the team that won the FA Cup in 1903 without conceding a goal, and by the record score of 6–0 against Derby County. They additionally won the Lancashire and Manchester Senior Cups in the same season.

Lack of first-team opportunities led to Hodson joining the Latics in June 1905 for the princely sum of £15. He played in all but three of the season's matches in 1905–06 and scored his first goal against his former teammates, Bury Reserves, in a 4–0 home win on 24 April 1906. In the following season he played in every match – 38 Combination and eight FA Cup ties – as the team won the Championship of the Lancashire Combination.

After just three seasons of Second Division football, promotion to Division One was secured in 1910, Hodson appearing in 32 of the season's matches. He scored his solitary League goal in 1911–12, and it was enough to secure the points in a 1–0 win against Sheffield Wednesday on 16 March 1912. As one who rarely stepped over the halfway line in normal circumstances, his goalscoring opportunity came after he had retired injured in the first half. Patched up in the interval, he returned to play on the wing in the second half and seized his unexpected opportunity to register the match-winning goal.

Consistent to the last, Hodson missed just one match in his final season before World War One suspended League football for the duration. He remained on Athletic's books but joined Southern League Brentford in May 1919. In a little short of two seasons, he played in 68 matches before joining Guildford United as coach-manager in February 1922. He then moved to Europe, holding coaching appointments in Belgium and Holland.

Hodson's son, Jimmy junior, a 31-year-old Lance Corporal, called in at Boundary Park just before Christmas in 1942. Although he played for his regiment at outside-left, he admitted that he was a better sprinter than a footballer. When war broke out he was working for an English firm in Belgium, and when the Germans invaded he escaped to England with his mother. His late father was buried in Holland in February 1938 with all the honours the Dutch could muster for the popular Englishman.

Rick Holden

Date of birth: 9 September 1964, Skipton

Oldham Athletic record:
Appearances: League 171(18), FA Cup 20(1), League Cup 18(3)
Goals: League 28, FA Cup 3, League Cup 4
Debut: Blackburn Rovers (a) 19 August 1989, lost 0–1

Also played for: Burnley, Halifax Town, Watford, Manchester City, Blackpool, Peel FC (Isle of Man)

In August 1989 Athletic transferred popular winger Tommy Wright to Leicester City for £650,000. His replacement, Rick Holden, cost just £165,000 from Watford, but he proved an absolute bargain and quickly endeared himself to the Latics faithful. In the three seasons before his £900,000-rated transfer to Manchester City, Holden was one of the best wingers in the country. His style was almost a throwback to the days when all teams fielded speedy and tricky wingmen who made straight for the bye-line and pulled back inviting crosses for their inside men. Quite tall for a wingman and nicely built, he was a real wonder-worker on the left flank. With more than one way of beating a defender, he supplied a stream of inviting crosses, sometimes from seemingly impossible angles. Fielded as an out-and-out winger, his strengths were utilised to the full. In addition to his numerous 'assists' he was a useful marksman by his own account, particularly in his first season, when he scored the first hat-trick of his career against Oxford United in May 1990. As Athletic reached a Wembley final in the Littlewoods Cup and featured in the semi-final of the FA Cup, his telling contribution during the season was nine League and four Cup goals from 64 matches.

Athletic's strength on the wings played a key role in the following season when the Second Division title was won. Holden scored six goals – and supplied many more – in 48 matches, while Neil Adams scored seven in 20 starts and 12 substitute appearances. The team scored 93 goals with 13 players finding the net; leading scorers were Ian Marshall (18), Neil Redfearn (17), Andy Ritchie (15) and Roger Palmer (10). A wonderful season was crowned when Joe Royle was named Second Division Manager of the Year, collecting the prestigious award at the Savoy Hotel in London.

Holden was a scorer in Athletic's first home match in Division One, which was a 3–0 win against Chelsea. In a season when the Latics sought to consolidate their hard won promotion, Holden was again in outstanding form. He played in every top-flight match, scoring five goals, and one in the League Cup against Torquay United. The season's final fixture was against Manchester City at Boundary Park, and the heavy defeat (2–5) served to underline the defensive frailties that had existed throughout the campaign. It was unfortunate that the moves to address the problem involved the departure of Holden in a major transfer deal, rated at £900,000. It took him to Manchester City in exchange for a pair of City players – Neil Pointon and Steve Redmond – plus a cash adjustment of £300,000. He was a regular in his first season at Maine Road, scoring five goals in 48(1) matches, but the appointment of Brian Horton in late August of the following season saw him surplus to the new manager's requirements.

Holden was welcomed back to Boundary Park, but he rejoined a side in serious trouble in 20th place in the Premier League. It was a season when Athletic appeared to reserve their best form for Cup ties; they reached the semi-finals of the FA Cup and round four of the League Cup, but their League form was well below par. In mid-March, three wins and a draw in four matches ended a streak of seven matches without a win and raised hopes, but without a win in their final eight matches Athletic surrendered their Premier League status with a whimper. They totalled just 42 goals in League matches, Holden's total of six in 28(1) matches made him joint-second in the goalscoring list with Darren Beckford.

When Graeme Sharp replaced Joe Royle as Athletic's manager in November 1994, Holden lost his place to Mark Brennan and was almost exclusively used from the bench thereafter. In September 1995, with 20 months still remaining on his contract, Holden requested and was granted a free transfer. Having passed exams to qualify as a chartered physiotherapist, he spent his last season in League football with Blackpool while acting as part-time physio to Bradford Rugby League club.

Holden left Blackpool in June 1996 and moved to the Isle of Man. He linked up with Peel FC on the island and later became head coach of the national team. In March 1999, while on international duty with his team in preparation for the Guinness Cup, he made a nostalgic visit to Maine Road for the Manchester City v Athletic fixture. Who he was supporting was not revealed, but the Latics won 2–1. He is currently reunited with Andy Ritchie at Barnsley as assistant manager and physiotherapist.

Garry Hoolickin

Date of birth: 29 October 1957, Middleton

Oldham Athletic record:
Appearances: League 209(2), FA Cup 7(1), League Cup 23
Goals: League 2, League Cup 1
Debut: Luton Town (h) 14 May 1977, lost 1–2

Also played for: Middleton and Lancashire Schoolboys

Flame-haired Garry Hoolickin began with Middleton Schoolboys, captained Lancashire Schoolboys and joined the Latics as a 16-year-old full-back in April 1974. He was not the first family member to represent the club at senior level, his brother Steve spending three years at Boundary Park, during which time he made eight League appearances as understudy to long-serving right full-back Ian Wood.

While Steve departed Boundary Park to fulfil his potential with Bury, Carlisle United and Hull City, his brother remained a one-club man throughout and eventually succeeded Ian Wood at right-back. He made his debut in the final Division Two fixture of season 1976–77 as deputy for Ronnie Blair, with Ian Wood switching to left-back to allow Hoolickin to take up his usual position on the right flank. Visitors Luton Town took the lead after 12 minutes, Vic Halom equalised on the hour, but John Aston, the former Manchester United outside-left, spoiled Hoolickin's big day when he netted the winner five minutes later.

The full-back pairing on his debut was very much one of youth and experience, as Ian Wood was making his 412th League appearance, and three days later he scored twice in a 3–1 win in his own testimonial match against Manchester City. Ten years and 190 League appearances later, Hoolickin was the beneficiary when Manchester City again provided the opposition in his testimonial match on 9 September 1986. It was his first outing on the new artificial pitch, although he had been a substitute when the first League match was contested on the new surface against Barnsley on 25 August 1986, Athletic winning 2–0 with goals from Roger Palmer and Tony Henry.

Hoolickin played in 21(1) League and Cup matches in 1977–78 when Athletic finished eighth in Division Two, but his progress was cruelly halted in August of the following season. It was a black month for the Latics. The season opened with a benefit match for Debbie Groves, teenage widow of former outside-left Alan who had died from a heart attack at the age of 29. Six days later, in the Anglo-Scottish Cup tie against Sheffield United at Boundary Park, goalkeeper John Platt suffered a broken leg. On the 29th of the month Hoolickin also suffered a broken leg, eight minutes into the League Cup second-round tie against Nottingham Forest at Boundary Park. Just three days earlier he had scored his first League goal in the 3–1 victory at Cardiff City, a game that also marked the successful debut in League football of Jim Steel, who scored the other two Athletic goals.

It was October of the following season when Hoolickin returned to reserve-team action, his reintroduction to the League side being delayed until the final four matches of the season. Nicky Sinclair contested the right-back role with him in 1980–81, but in Jimmy Frizzell's final season in charge (1981–82) Hoolickin's total of 34 League and Cup matches was his best seasonal return. For the next four seasons under Joe Royle, he became a regular, his versatility being usefully employed in either full-back or central-defensive roles. Although defensive duties precluded many attacking forays, his perfectly-placed, delicately-flighted scoring chip shot against Middlesbrough in the 2–1 win at Boundary Park on 15 October 1983 deserved a bigger audience than the decidedly thin gate of 3,994.

Hoolickin made his final first-team appearance at Shrewsbury Town on 5 May 1987 in a game that marked the League debut of Neil Edmonds at left-back. Athletic were third in the table and entertained a faint hope of snatching an automatic promotion spot. Shrewsbury Town were third from bottom and facing relegation, but they hit Athletic with two first-half goals, and the 2–0 defeat kept Shrewsbury up and consigned the Latics to the Play-offs, where they lost to Leeds United. A serious knee injury sustained in a pre-season friendly in the summer of 1987 brought down the curtain on Hoolickin's career. Despite a two-year battle to regain full fitness, the club's longest-serving player was obliged to retire on a specialist's advice. He became a publican and ran the Joiners Arms in Middleton, later working in the building and property trade. His son, Anthony, spent two years at the Latics as a trainee but did not reach senior level.

Fred Howe

Date of birth: 24 September 1912, Bredbury, Cheshire
Died: October 1984, Stockport

Oldham Athletic record:
Appearances: League 30, FA Cup 1
Goals: League 20
Debut: Carlisle United (h) 31 August 1946, lost 0–2

Also played for: Hyde United, Stockport County, Liverpool, Manchester City, Grimsby Town (World War Two guest player with Stockport County, Watford, Ashton United)

Fred Howe joined the Latics in July 1946, on the eve of resumption of normal League football. What was less well known was that he had been on the point of signing for Athletic eight years earlier. Terms had been agreed with Liverpool for his transfer, and Howe had agreed personal terms, yet at the last moment Manchester City stepped in, and so he changed his mind and went to Maine Road.

Howe made his City debut in the season's opening Division Two fixture against Swansea Town and scored one goal in the 5–0 victory. Two days later, at Chesterfield, he scored twice in a 3–0 win. He had scored five goals in six consecutive matches when First Division Grimsby Town moved in to sign him after less than three months at Maine Road.

Howe enjoyed an excellent season with the Mariners; his 15 League goals in 29 matches included four in one game against Leicester City in a 6–1 victory on 17 December 1938. Additionally, he scored six goals in six FA Cup ties, a significant contribution that took his team to the semi-final at Old Trafford, where the ground record attendance was broken, with 76,962 attending. Sadly, Grimsby lost their goalkeeper through injury and the 10 men went under to Wolverhampton Wanderers by 5–0.

At the outset of his career, Howe made just two League appearances for Stockport County and was recommended to Liverpool by their centre-forward 'Tosh' Johnson. In his first full season at Anfield, he scored four goals against Everton in a 6–0 victory on 7 September 1935 and a fortnight later netted a hat-trick against Grimsby Town. He was Liverpool's leading scorer in successive seasons in 1935–36 and 1936–37, recording 36 goals in 89 League matches for the Reds.

Of Athletic's recruits for the resumption of League football, the flame-haired centre-forward was by far the most well known and with a proven pedigree at the highest level. The 1939–40 season, aborted after just three matches due to the outbreak of war, commenced for Athletic with a 3–1 victory against Carlisle United at Boundary Park. The Football League, using the same set of fixtures for 1946–47, matched the same opponents seven years later.

Perhaps unsurprisingly, only one player appeared for Athletic in both matches – Tommy Williamson. The unfamiliar line up fielded on Howe's debut was as follows: Harris, Boothman, Witham, Williamson, Hayes, Horton, W. Blackshaw, Butler, Howe, Bowden and Ormondy.

On a day of blue skies, high clouds and similar expectations, the 7,696 spectators left Boundary Park disappointed after a 2–0 defeat. A point from the midweek visit to Halifax Town lifted spirits, and Athletic's new centre-forward found his scoring touch in his third outing, away at Accrington Stanley. His two goals at Accrington included one from the penalty spot and was a major contribution in the first victory of the season by 3–2. Two days later, in the first post-war 'derby' against Rochdale at Boundary Park, his brilliant hat-trick, which included two goals within the space of one minute in the first half, gave Athletic the points in a rousing 3–2 victory.

In the return fixture at Spotland on 17 September, Howe was again on the mark in the 3–1 win, a match that marked the debuts in League football of Bill Lawton (husband of actress Dora Bryan) and Ken Brierley. At the end of the month, in a repeat of his quick-fire hat-trick against Rochdale, Howe scored all three of Athletic's goals in the 3–1 victory against Lincoln City.

Howe scored 20 goals in 30 League matches in his only season at Boundary Park, all models of coolness and good judgment. His industrious approach and strong left foot made him a forward to be feared. Outside of the game he was a plumber by trade.

Jack Hurst

Date of birth: 27 October 1914, Lever Bridge near Bolton
Died: February 2002, Harrow, Middlesex

Oldham Athletic record:
Appearances: League 98, FA Cup 9
Goals: League 2
Debut: Lincoln City (a) 1 February 1947, won 3–1

Also played for: Bolton Wanderers (World War Two guest player with Swindon Town, York City, Reading, Norwich City), Chelmsford City

A member of Bolton Wanderers' FA Cup semi-final team of 1946, Jack Hurst joined Athletic in February of the following season. His transfer fee of £1,510 was a significant outlay for a player approaching the veteran stage, but he proved an extremely sound investment.

At 6ft 1in and 12st 10lb he was ideally built for his preferred role of centre half-back, and although lacking a yard of pace, he proved a dogged and relentless 'Policeman' with two good feet and a rare gift of anticipation. Although primarily a defensive pivot, he was effective in his exploitation of the long pass out to the wings.

Hurst made his Athletic debut at Lincoln City, where second half goals by Frank Tomlinson (2) and Fred Howe gave the side a welcome away victory. Another player making his first League appearance for the Latics was goalkeeper Malcolm Schofield, while 17-year-old outside-left Dennis Wright was making his second appearance as deputy for a man old enough to be his father, 35-year-old Jack Ormandy.

Hurst had first appeared in League football with Bolton Wanderers, one week before his 20th birthday in October 1934, in a 2–0 win at Hull City. As reserve to Jack Atkinson he made only three League appearances in his first season, in which Bolton won promotion from Division Two and reached the semi-final of the FA Cup.

Having joined the Territorial Army, along with several of his teammates, before the outbreak of World War Two he was quickly drafted into the Royal Artillery as a gunner. He was evacuated from Dunkirk in 1940 and served in the Desert Campaign including El Alamein and Tobruk. Later, he saw action in Italy before demobilisation in October 1945.

On returning to Burnden Park, Hurst appeared in eight rounds of the FA Cup in 1945–46, which included the Burnden disaster match versus Stoke City on 9 March 1946 when 33 spectators lost their lives and many hundreds were injured when crush barriers collapsed on the railway embankment. Play was suspended but eventually resumed and the match ended goalless with Bolton winning 2–0 on aggregate.

Under new manager Billy Wootton in 1947–48, Hurst did not feature for Athletic until mid-season. No fewer than eight new signings made their debuts in the opener at Chester. There were only three familiar faces, Horton, Hayes and Blackshaw, and it was Blackshaw who scored Athletic's goal in the 2–1 defeat. Athletic finished in 11th position in the Third Division North with 41 points from 42 games. They fielded 30 players in League matches, of which 19 made their debuts during the season.

One point from a possible 16 was a dire start to 1948–49, not helped by a spate of injuries. The month of October marked an upturn. Four wins and a draw included a 3–2 victory against Crewe Alexandra in which Hurst scored his first goal, a timely winner in the 79th minute. Athletic finished in sixth position with 45 points from 42 games. They fielded 24 players, and full-back Bill Pickering was the only ever-present, with Hurst playing in 38 League and Cup matches.

Season 1949–50 was Hurst's last as a first-team regular, and it was memorable for the visit of First Division Newcastle United to Boundary Park in the third round of the FA Cup. 31,706 spectators attended the match in which Jackie Milburn scored a hat-trick and Tommy Walker, who later played for the Latics, scored two. In the 7–2 defeat, Spurdle and Haddington scored for Athletic.

Hurst left at the close of season 1950–51 and joined Chelmsford City. On retirement he became a Heywood publican, despite the fact that he was himself a teetotaller.

Denis Irwin

Date of birth: 31 October 1965, Cork, Republic of Ireland

Oldham Athletic record:
Appearances: League 166(1), FA Cup 13, League Cup 19
Goals: League 4, League Cup 3
Debut: Derby County (a) 23 August 1986, won 1–0

Also played for: Leeds United, Manchester United, Wolverhampton Wanderers, Republic of Ireland international (56 caps)

Denis Irwin won Irish Schools honours and his game was developed at Turner Cross College in Cork. He joined Leeds United in February 1982 and made his senior debut in the second replay of a third-round FA Cup tie against Scunthorpe United on 16 January 1964. Despite his tender years, he captained both the Northern Intermediate League and Central League teams at Elland Road before making his senior bow. In season 1984–85 he was established at right-back and on 29 September was a member of the Leeds side that thrashed Athletic 6–0. All of the Leeds scorers that day subsequently starred for the Latics, the quartet were Tommy Wright, Andy Ritchie (who scored a hat-trick), John Sheridan and Andy Linighan. In October 1985 Leeds sacked manager Eddie Gray, replacing him with Billy Bremner, and at the end of the season Irwin was given a free transfer.

In May 1986 Athletic's manager Joe Royle made a speedy return from France, where the Latics youngsters were playing in the European Junior Tournament, in order to snap up the talented 20-year-old defender. He was the second Leeds United player to move to Boundary Park in fairly short order, following Andy Linighan's move some five months earlier. Irwin was probably seen as a suitable replacement for 34-year-old player-coach Willie Donachie, although the Scottish international proved to be anything but a spent force as he did not retire as a player for another eight years!

Irwin got off to a winning start at Derby County's Baseball Ground. The newly promoted Rams were hoping to celebrate their return to Division Two in style, but a Ron Futcher header in the 19th minute was enough to give Athletic the points. Comfortable on the ball and with a surprising turn of pace, he enjoyed a truly eye-catching debut. He missed only one out of 50 possible appearances in his first season. Derby County ended the campaign as Champions, and although Athletic were never out of the top three all season they fell in the Play-off semi-finals to his old team, Leeds United. For the second season in succession – 1987–88 – Irwin and Roger Palmer appeared in more of Athletic's matches (49 of a possible 51) than any other players. He also chipped in with three goals in the League Cup, including one against his former team, Leeds United, in the 4–2 third-round replay at Boundary Park.

Despite a 1988–89 season spent battling the threat of relegation, Irwin caught the eye of the Eire Under-23 selectors, and in April 1989 he received rave reviews for his display in Eire's 3–0 win against Northern Ireland Under-23 in Dublin. Mike Milligan also enjoyed a sound game, but it was Irwin who stole the show, scoring his first international goal with a 30-yard drive, five minutes after Mick McCarthy had put Eire in front. In what proved to be his last season at Boundary Park, he appeared in the Littlewoods Cup Final against Nottingham Forest and in two rousing semi-final ties in the FA Cup against Manchester United. His faultless displays in both matches impressed United's manager Alex Ferguson so much that he paid £625,000 to take him to Old Trafford. Irwin was quoted as saying 'This is the best day in my life.' Although all at Boundary Park were sad to see him go, the 24-year-old right-back had netted Athletic their record incoming fee, a handsome return for a player who had cost nothing just four years earlier.

Although moving up two Divisions, Irwin enjoyed outstanding success during his 12-year career at Old Trafford and marked St Patrick's Day in 2001 by making his 500th competitive appearance for United. His enviable collection of winners' medals included seven Championships, three FA Cups, one League Cup and two European trophies. On the international front, he was the only player to be capped at six levels with the Republic and won 56 full caps before retiring from international football in January 2000, in order to extend his career at club level. His fondest international memory was the Republic's 1–0 win against red-hot favourites Italy at The Giants Stadium, New York, in the World Cup on 18 June 1994. He ended his long and successful career with two seasons at Wolverhampton Wanderers. He joined them on a free transfer in July 2002 and announced his retirement in May 2004, having completed a total of 895 senior appearances for his three League clubs.

Teddy Ivill

Date of birth: 7 December 1898, Little Hulton
Died: 24 November 1979, Accrington

Oldham Athletic record:
Appearances: League 276, FA Cup 9
Goals: League 2, FA Cup 1
Debut: Southampton (a) 30 August 1924, drawn 0–0

Also played for: Bolton Wanderers amateur, Atherton FC, Wolverhampton Wanderers, Charlton Athletic, Accrington Stanley, Clitheroe FC

Teddy Ivill left school at the age of 12 and began work as a half-timer at the Suez Mill in Little Hulton. At the age of 13 he left the cotton industry and joined his father Sam, who was a well-known Lancashire crown green bowler, at the New Lester Colliery. He first played football at the age of 16 in the Colliery XI at right half-back, leaving after one season to join Williams Temperance of Boothstown, who played in the Leigh and District League.

Ivill was then offered a trial by Bolton Wanderers and was farmed out to Atherton, a nursery club for the Wanderers in those days. He remained with Atherton as captain and centre-half for two seasons and was 26 years old when he joined Athletic after a brief trial in July 1924.

Athletic were almost relegated in his first season, but Ivill featured mainly in reserve, his 11 League appearances producing one goal, which was scored against Stoke in a 2–0 victory at Boundary Park on 4 October 1924. He had fewer first-team opportunities in 1925–26, appearing in only seven League matches as cover for regular backs Sammy Wynne and Harry Grundy.

From 1926–27 onwards, Ivill became the most consistent stalwart of the side, who could be relied upon to pull his weight week in, week out. Embarking on a remarkable sequence of appearances without missing a match, his run began in April 1926 and ended in October 1932, when he was transferred to Wolverhampton Wanderers. His record included five full seasons as an ever present and his run totalled 224 consecutive League matches plus eight FA Cup ties.

It was in the latter competition that Ivill scored the last of his three goals against First Division Huddersfield Town, in the third-round tie at Boundary Park on 9 January 1932. A crowd of 30,607 – around three times the usual number – witnessed a rousing Cup tie in which he gave the Latics an unexpected lead after 32 minutes. Sadly, they were unable to hang on to their hard-won advantage, with Huddersfield's ace marksman David Mangnall equalising two minutes from time. In the replay at Leeds Road on 13 January, the Latics were three down at half-time and went under by 6–0. Mangnall scored four of the goals to continue his remarkable sequence that netted him 33 in 34 League matches and nine in five FA Cup ties in 1931–32.

Ivill was awarded a benefit match against Barnsley on 7 May 1932 and six months later joined Wolverhampton Wanderers for a fee of £1,700. He played in only four First Division matches for Wolves and had hardly had time to unpack his bags when he was transferred after three months to Charlton Athletic. He cost Charlton £1,250 but was unable to save them from relegation from Division Two. He left the Valley at the end of the 1934–35 season having appeared in 35 League and two FA Cup matches.

At this point Ivill had decided to retire to concentrate on a chip potato business in Farnworth. He was, however, coaxed out of the idea of retirement by his old friend Jack Hacking, at that time the newly appointed player-manager of Accrington Stanley. Ivill was very much at the veteran stage when he made his debut for Stanley at Lincoln City on 31 August 1935, but his long experience was put to good use when he was appointed reserve-team coach in August 1936.

Ivill returned to Accrington after the war in Europe had ended to take charge of Stanley's Lancashire Combination team. His brother Sam had trials with the Latics in January 1934 and was on Accrington Stanley's books in season 1935–36. His son Jeffrey, who subsequently achieved high rank in the Police Force, was an amateur on Athletic's books in the 1940s but did not progress to senior level.

Richard Jobson

Date of birth: 9 May 1963, Holderness, Yorkshire

Oldham Athletic record:
Appearances: League 188(1), FA Cup 13, League Cup 19
Goals: League 10, League Cup 1
Debut: Portsmouth (h) 1 September 1990, won 3–1

Also played for: Nottingham and English Universities, Burton Albion, Watford, Hull City, Leeds United, Southend United on loan, Manchester City, Watford on loan, Tranmere Rovers, Rochdale

Richard Jobson began his footballing career with Burton Albion of the Northern Premier League while studying for a degree in civil engineering at Nottingham University. Plucked from non-League obscurity by Watford's manager Graham Taylor as a 19-year-old, he was to enjoy a lengthy and highly-successful 20-year career, retiring as a Rochdale player at the age of 40 in May 2003.

When signed by the Latics for a club record fee of £460,000, manager Joe Royle admitted that he had tried to sign Jobson on several previous occasions, but he had proved to be unaffordable. The outgoing transfers of Mike Milligan to Everton, Denis Irwin to Manchester United and Andy Rhodes to Dunfermline had enabled the manager to secure his services in a spending spree that topped one million pounds. David Currie and John Keeley were the other big-money signings.

Only 48 hours after signing, Jobson was awarded the sponsor's Man of the Match award for his faultless display in the heart of the Latic's defence in the 3–1 victory against Portsmouth, maintaining the side's 100 percent record with a third successive win to remain top of the Division Two table. Despite his signing just after the campaign had commenced, Jobson missed only one match during the promotion-winning season, and this when he was held up in motorway traffic and failed to arrive in time for the kick-off.

Life in Division One got off to a painful start for Jobson, who suffered a fractured cheekbone when playing against Norwich City in the third match of the season. A few weeks later, however, he received a welcome pick-me-up when, along with Earl Barrett, he received a call-up from England manager Graham Taylor. Jobson admitted being 'stunned and delighted' to be drafted into the squad for the European Championship qualifier against Turkey at Wembley. Graham Taylor, who had given him his First Division debut with Watford within six weeks of signing him from Burton Albion, admitted that he had slipped up by not insisting on a sell-on clause when he sold Jobson to Hull City for a bargain fee of £40,000.

With the Latics back in Division One following their relegation from the Premier League in 1994, a £1 million dream move to Leeds United for the 32-year-old defender proved to be more of a nightmare. Injuries denied him the opportunity to make his mark in the Premier League, restricting him to just 26 appearances in two and a half years at Elland Road.

A move to Manchester City, and a link up with his former manager Joe Royle, brought happier times as in season 1999–2000 Jobson – City's oldest player – appeared in 43(1) matches as City won promotion to the Premier League. At the end of season annual Player of the Year function, amid gales of good-natured laughter, it was revealed that he had received a vote for the City Young Player of the Year trophy.

Jobson's playing career ended with Rochdale, but not before he had recorded a further 49 (2) League appearances and scored three goals, to take his overall career record to an impressive 580(8) League matches and 40 goals. As either central-defender or right full-back, he will be fondly remembered by Latics fans as a class performer, whose assured first touch gave him both time and space to use the ball to his advantage. He is best remembered at Boundary Park for his partnership with Earl Barrett at the heart of the Latics defence.

Capped twice by England B in season 1991–92, Jobson was unfortunate to miss out at full international level, probably due to age considerations and his lack of any lengthy experience at Premiership level.

Photograph courtesy o
Oldham Evening Chron

Bobby Johnstone

Date of birth: 7 September 1929, Selkirk
Died: 22 August 2001, Selkirk

Oldham Athletic record:
Appearances: League 143, FA Cup 12, League Cup 3
Goals: League 36, FA Cup 1
Debut: Exeter City (h) 15 October 1960, won 5–2 (scored one)

Also played for: Newtongrange Bluebell, Newtongrange Star, Hibernian, Manchester City, Hibernian (a second spell), Witton Albion, Scotland (17 caps)

Athletic supporters of a certain vintage will have little difficulty in recalling Bobby Johnstone, or his instantaneous impact at Boundary Park. An impish figure on the field with a wayward lock of dark hair falling over his forehead, he was an unlikely looking footballer who appeared a little overweight and rarely appeared to break a sweat. That said, his instinctive ability to control a game from midfield, and his priceless knack of creating goalscoring opportunities with a single, defence-splitting pass, marked him as one of the great inside-forwards of post-war football. Comparable to the likes of Wilf Mannion and Peter Doherty as a schemer and ball artist, his influence on the team's fortunes was quite extraordinary, and he certainly sparked a long-overdue revival at Boundary Park.

Johnstone began as a professional with Hibernian at 17 years of age, made his first-team debut against Partick Thistle at 19 and won his first international cap in April 1951. He scored against England at Wembley in a 3–2 victory on his international debut, went on to win 17 Scotland caps and was additionally honoured when he represented Great Britain against the Rest of Europe in August 1955, a few months after he had joined Manchester City for £22,000. He was one of the 'Famous Five' forward line fielded by Hibernian in the late 40s and early Fifties and was twice a Scottish League Championship winner in 1951 and 1952. He also appeared in the Scottish League Cup Final of 1951.

In his first season at Maine Road Bobby appeared in the FA Cup Final against Newcastle United, having scored the only goal of the semi-final against Tottenham Hotspur. He scored in the Final but finished on the losing side, with Newcastle winning 3–1. 12 months later, City returned to Wembley and Bobby became the first player to score in successive Wembley FA Cup Finals when Birmingham City were beaten 3–1. After scoring 51 goals in 138 League and Cup matches for Manchester City, Bobby was transferred back to Hibernian for £7,000 in September 1959. A little over a year later he was back in Lancashire, this time with Athletic, for an extremely modest fee of £4,000.

Rarely has a player's debut attracted greater attention from the Oldham sporting public, and Bobby was doubtless the Pied Piper who led 17,116 spectators into Boundary Park for his first appearance in the famous old colours of blue and white – the one broad stripe variety. The 'gate' was the highest for six and a half years, and the Athletic team to face visitors Exeter City lined up as follows: Hardie, Branagan, McCue, Phoenix, Greenhall, Hall, Bazley, Johnstone, Birch, Liddell, Rackley. A former Latics favourite, wing-half Jim Thompson was directly opposed to Bobby as Exeter's left-half.

Under new manager Jack Rowley, the Latics had made a faltering start to the 1960–61 campaign, but things were about to improve. Although a number of the players who featured in the match became well-known favourites, it is interesting to reflect that – in terms of Athletic appearances – seven of the team were still in single figures. The 5–2 victory, memorably orchestrated by Bobby, set Athletic on the road to recovery. Eight consecutive victories between December and February were promotion form, but the poor start had left the team with too much to do. Despite this, a crowd of 27,888 gathered for the visit of high-flying newcomers Peterborough United on 11 March, a Ken Branagan penalty giving Athletic a share of the points in a 1–1 draw.

Promotion was finally achieved in season 1962–63, a term remembered for arctic weather conditions and Athletic's record League victory – 11–0 against Southport on Boxing Day. Bobby enjoyed one further vintage season in 1963–64 under new manager Les McDowall, but a troublesome knee injury affected his mobility in 1964–65, restricting him to just 11 League appearances in his final season. Bobby settled in the Hollinwood area for many years after retirement and starred as a crown-green and flat bowler, with many successes in local competitions. In 1998, he auctioned his collection of caps and medals at Christie's which realised £23,000, twice the auctioneer's estimate. Chief Executive Alan Hardy represented Athletic at Bobby's funeral in Selkirk on 27 August 2001.

Gary Kelly

Date of birth: 3 August 1966, Fulwood, near Preston

Oldham Athletic record:
Appearances: League 224(1), FA Cup 19, League Cup 13
Goals: 0
Debut: Sheffield United (h) 7 September 1996, lost 0–2

Also played for: Newcastle United, Blackpool on loan, Bury, Northwich Victoria, Sheffield United, Leigh RMI

Hailing from a family of goalkeepers, Gary Kelly began with Newcastle United straight from school, becoming a professional at St James' Park in June 1984. His father Alan was an Irish goalkeeping legend who played in 447 League matches for Preston North End and won 47 Republic of Ireland caps. His career was ended by injury in September 1973, and he subsequently had a stand at Deepdale named after him.

Kelly's younger brother Alan also began with Preston North End, and the brothers first opposed one another in a League match when Bury met Preston at Gigg Lane on 13 January 1990. It was his first season with Bury and later in the campaign he played for the Republic of Ireland B team against England in April. He also assisted Bury in reaching the Division Three Play-offs, but they lost the two-leg semi-final against Tranmere Rovers 2–0 on aggregate.

Kelly's brother assisted five League clubs, won 34 Republic of Ireland caps and totalled 402 League appearances, while Kelly featured with five League clubs and amassed a career total of 519(1) League matches, but fell just short of full international standard, appearing for the Republic of Ireland at Youth, Under-21, Under-23 and B levels.

Kelly made his League debut for Newcastle United in Division One against Wimbledon on 20 September 1986 in a 1–0 home victory, the Magpies goal being scored by Paul Gascoigne. He took over the first-team spot from Martin Thomas in season 1987–88 but was replaced by Newcastle's record signing – £850,000 Dave Beasant – fresh from his Wembley FA Cup Final triumph with Wimbledon. Kelly had made 60 senior appearances at the time of his £75,000 transfer to Bury in October 1989.

In almost seven years at Gigg Lane, Kelly appeared in 263 League and Cup matches, this despite missing virtually all of the 1993–94 season after he was injured in a League Cup game at Bolton on 17 August. He assisted Bury to promotion from the Third Division in 1995–96 but departed Gigg Lane for Boundary Park in the summer for a very modest fee of £10,000. He quickly replaced John Hallworth as first choice in Athletic's goal and immediately impressed with his excellent technique, awareness and ability to impose himself despite lacking the physical advantage of his 6ft 2in blond predecessor.

In six seasons at Boundary Park, Kelly dominated the goalkeeping position, despite the team's lack of any success during his tenure. Relegation to the Second Division in his first season was a bitter disappointment, despite the fact that no blame could be laid at his door. He did in fact receive the unanimous vote as Player of the Year for his heroic efforts to keep the sinking ship afloat. He found favour with each of the four different managers during his spell at Boundary Park, although he was hardly free from injury during Mick Wadsworth's brief spell in charge. He was first laid aside for a lengthy spell in 1997–98 but returned mid-season and enjoyed an outstanding sequence spanning from December to February, when he conceded just two goals in 10 matches.

In the three seasons that followed, Kelly missed just four League matches. In the opening month of 2001–02, he was Athletic's hero in a remarkable Worthington Cup tie at Stoke City. A fairly uneventful 120 minutes ended goalless, with the high drama occurring in the sudden-death penalty shoot-out. He saved two of Stoke's penalties and with the score on 5–5 he became the match winner when he stepped up to score with a perfect spot-kick, placed inches inside the left-hand post.

In November 2001, when Ian Dowie was installed as Athletic's new first-team coach, it was reported that 35-year-old Kelly had extended his contract for a further two years. In the event, he left to join Northwich Victoria in February 2003 before joining Sheffield United in the following month, where he made his final Football League appearance in a 2–0 defeat at Watford on 4 May 2003.

Seth King

Date of birth: 14 February 1897, Penistone, Yorkshire
Died: 8 February 1958, Leigh, Lancashire

Oldham Athletic record:
Appearances: League 91, FA Cup 5
Goals: 0
Debut: Bury (a) 31 August 1929, won 2–0

Also played for: Huddersfield Town amateur, Penistone FC, Sheffield United, Denaby United

Centre-half Seth King was a seasoned campaigner by the time he reached Boundary Park in May 1929. He had spent eight and a half years with Sheffield United, making a 2–0 winning start on his League debut against Newcastle United in Division One on 16 September 1922. He won an FA Cup medal in 1925, when a single goal by the Blades and England international outside-left Fred Tunstall was sufficient to beat Cardiff City at Wembley Stadium. Throughout the Cup-winning year, King was considered to be one of the outstanding centre half-backs in the country.

At the outset of his career, King was signed on amateur forms by Huddersfield Town and played in many Central League matches. Huddersfield played him at centre-half, but when Sheffield United signed him they played him at right full-back in their reserves, and it was not until an emergency occured that he was first tried at centre-half. When first-team pivot Jimmy Waugh was injured, King grabbed his opportunity in the first team with both hands.

Having avoided almost certain relegation with a brilliant after-Christmas spell in 1928–29, Athletic's new £400 signing King took over the centre-half position for the new season, replacing another Yorkshire man, Jack Armitage. Most shrewd judges agreed that one of the chief factors in the team's excellent start – they won all of the first five matches of the 1929–30 season – was the experience and on-field leadership of King. After just a handful of matches, Jack Hacking sportingly handed over the captaincy of a winning side to their inspirational pivot.

By 23 November the team's record was: Played 15, Won 11, Drawn 3, Lost one, For 38, Against 14, Points 25. In the midst of the run, and despite four enforced team changes due to injuries, Tottenham Hotspur were beaten 2–0 at Boundary Park. In the following month a more familiar looking line up despatched Wolves by 6–0. A lack of reserve strength beat the club's promotion bid in the last few games, but the side that finished third in the League scored 90 League goals in 42 matches, conceding 51. King, Teddy Ivill and Leslie Adlam were the season's ever presents.

King, in fact, did not miss a single League or Cup match in his first two seasons. Despite his modest physique – 5ft 9in and a little over 11st – he was a forceful, attacking pivot whose cross-field passes to either wing effectively kept his forwards on the move.

The season's first away match in 1931–32 was at Barnsley, and it proved a bruising encounter. The Latics finished with nine men, King being one of the casualties, along with goalkeeper Frank Moss who retired with a broken nose. King played little first-team football subsequently and an agreement was reached to cancel his contract in February 1932 to enable him to take over the tenancy of the Castle Inn, Hillsborough, Sheffield. In August 1932 he resumed his career in non-League circles, joining Denaby United, a Midland League club.

As one of four sporting brothers who were well known in the Penistone district for their cricketing prowess, King carried off the League bowling prize for the Netherfield club in 1925. He subsequently shone as a batsman with Barnsley in the Yorkshire Council. During his spell with Athletic, he spent summer months as an all-rounder with Crompton Cricket Club in the Central Lancashire League. The club's professional in 1930 was Tom Smelt, another cricketer-footballer, who spent two years with Athletic as a reserve centre-forward between 1928–30.

At the time of his death, just days away from his 61st birthday, King was running a newsagent's shop in Holden Road, Leigh, Lancashire.

Bob Ledger

Date of birth: 5 October 1937, Craghead, County Durham

Oldham Athletic record:
Appearances: League 221(1), FA Cup 12, League Cup 6
Goals: League 37, FA Cup 1
Debut: Bradford City (h) 18 August 1962, won 2–1 (scored one)

Also played for: Huddersfield Town, Mansfield Town, Barrow, Lancaster City

In his early days Bob Ledger represented Doncaster and District Schoolboys, Yorkshire Schoolboys and first appeared for Huddersfield Town in their Northern Intermediate League side at right half-back. Ray Wilson, England's World Cup-winning full-back, appeared as an inside-forward in the same match.

Always a versatile performer, Ledger first appeared in Huddersfield's first team at left-back, but one week later he lost his place to Ray Wilson. Subsequently appearing on both wings and at centre-forward, he recalled that the most memorable week of his Huddersfield Town career came in March 1958 when he was demobilised from the forces and celebrated by scoring twice from outside-left against West Ham United.

Ledger took the short trip over the Pennines to join the Latics in May 1962, with a fee of around £6,000 being involved. At Boundary Park he initially appeared at outside-right and scored the winning goal on his debut against Bradford City, a curtain-raiser to the season that attracted a crowd of 15,163 spectators.

Season 1962–63 proved to be a memorable one. Despite atrocious weather conditions, the Latics skated to promotion, scoring 95 League goals along the way. A season of many highlights included the 11–0 demolition of Southport on Boxing Day – a record score for Division Four and the Latics' record League victory. Ledger was one of the scorers in the match, which featured six goals by centre-forward Bert Lister, a hat-trick by Colin Whitaker, and singles by Ledger and Johnny Colquhoun. The architect of the victory, Bobby Johnstone, failed to get on to the score sheet, despite all efforts by his teammates to contrive an opening for him to do so.

The League season rounded off with a 6–1 home victory against Hartlepool United, Ledger scoring his eighth League goal of the season from a maximum 46 Division Four appearances. Later in the same month the Manchester Senior Cup Final against Bolton Wanderers was contested at Boundary Park. Both teams fielded what were virtually full strength sides, and the First Division side, Bolton, took the old trophy by 3–1, with Ledger scoring the Latics goal.

In Division Three the following season a satisfactory ninth position was achieved. Ledger's total of 10 League goals from 45 League appearances included a stunning 10-minute hat-trick at Crystal Palace in the final match of the season. A crowd of almost 28,000 spectators attended the match at Selhurst Park and the majority of them must have gone home very disappointed. The 3–1 result in the Latics' favour denied Palace the Championship of Division Three. Coventry City, with the same number of points, went on to take the title on goal average.

It was during Les McDowall's spell in charge that Ledger was asked to take over the right full-back position. He was well settled in the last line of defence when – in early season 1967–68 – he was asked to take the centre-forward position by manager Jimmy McIlroy. Typically, he responded to the call in a positive fashion, scoring a hat-trick against Scunthorpe United in his first match, and went on to find the net in each of his next three starts as attack leader.

A move to Mansfield Town opened another chapter, and in September 1968 he scored twice against his former teammates at Field Mill to give the Stags their best League victory of the season. It was in the FA Cup, however, that the Stags won the attention of the nation, their adventure ending in round six with a narrow 1–0 defeat by Leicester City, the eventual finalists. Earlier 'scalps' included West Ham United – including World Cup heroes Moore, Peters and Hurst – convincingly defeated by 3–0.

Without doubt one of the best utility players ever to represent the Latics, Ledger's League career spanned four clubs, for whom he totalled 351(8) appearances and scored 61 goals.

Photograph courtesy of
Oldham Evening Chronicle.

Bert Lister

Date of birth: 4 October 1939, Miles Platting, Manchester

Oldham Athletic record:
Appearances: League 135, FA Cup 14, League Cup 4
Goals: League 81, FA Cup 10, League Cup 6
Debut: York City (h) 1 October 1960, won 3–1 (scored one)

Also played for: Manchester City, Stockport County, Altrincham, Stalybridge Celtic

Bert Lister captained Manchester Schoolboys and thanks to a strong recommendation from his headmaster, the former Irish international and Manchester City full-back Jimmy Mulligan. He was taken on to Manchester City's staff, initially as an amateur, while serving an electrical apprenticeship. He signed professional forms in November 1957 at the age of 17 and made his League debut at Wolverhampton Wanderers on 11 October 1958 in a 0–2 defeat. Despite scoring freely in the Central League side, he lacked opportunities at first-team level.

Lister was not particularly well built for his role as attack leader, but he was tenacious, hard-working and a superb opportunist. In October 1960 he was part of a double signing from Manchester City by Athletic's manager Jack Rowley, whose first term in the managerial chair had started disastrously with only one win from the first 12 matches of the campaign. For a combined fee of £10,000, the ailing Latics recruited both Lister and the vastly experienced full-back Ken Branagan.

Both players proved to be excellent captures, Ken Branagan stiffening the defensive lines while Lister scored the goals that ultimately lifted Athletic out of Division Four. York City were the visitors on 1 October 1960, and a much improved attendance of 9,284 witnessed a vastly-improved display from their favourites who lined up as follows: Hardie, Branagan, McCue, Phoenix, Greenhall, Hall, West, Frizzell, Birch, Lister, O'Loughlin.

Lister had a bittersweet debut, scoring Athletic's third goal in the 76th minute but injuring himself in the process. The 10 men held on for a heartening 3–1 victory, but Lister was sidelined until the end of the month, when he returned to score both of Athletic's goals in the 2–6 League Cup second-round defeat at Norwich City. By this time, the Scottish international Bobby Johnstone had joined the Boundary Park brigade and the team, for a heady spell in mid-season, won eight consecutive League matches. Lister scored 21 goals, his haul including hat-tricks against Crystal Palace and Accrington Stanley.

In October of the following season, Accrington Stanley were midweek visitors to Boundary Park, and they were put to the sword in a crushing 5–0 defeat. Lister scored a hat-trick and Jimmy Frizzell scored the other two. Sadly, the 11,275 spectators who attended the match were unaware that Accrington's tenure as a Football League club was drawing to a close. On 6 March 1962 the club offered its resignation to the League, and on the 12 March it was accepted. Stanley's record to that point was expunged and with it Lister's hat-trick, which would have given him exactly a century of League and Cup goals for the Latics.

Bradford City were the opponents for the opening fixture of season 1962–63, and Lister netted within two minutes to set up a 2–1 victory, with Bob Ledger, in his first appearance, scoring the winner in the second half. Although Athletic finished three points behind Division Four Champions Brentford, their second place in the table brought automatic promotion and rewarded a vintage season played for a large part in arctic weather conditions.

It was certainly a bitterly cold day on Wednesday 26 December 1962 when Athletic entered the record books on a snow covered Boundary Park with an overwhelming 11–0 victory against Southport. Athletic led 7–0 at half-time and the scoring spree continued, Lister famously bagging a double hat-trick. Later in the season, he scored within 10 seconds of the kick-off against Chesterfield in a 2–1 win and finished the season with 32 League goals from 39 matches and three from two FA Cup ties.

Lister left Athletic in January 1965 to join Rochdale in a £2,250 transfer deal and in a two-year stay netted 16 League goals in 56 appearances. It was with Stockport County, his final League club, that he won a Division Four Championship medal in season 1966–67. He also completed a career century of League goals when he scored the winner against Aldershot at Edgeley Park on 5 May 1967.

Stewart Littlewood

Date of birth: 7 January 1905, Treeton, Rotherham
Died: 2 January 1977, Rotherham

Oldham Athletic record:
Appearances: League 78, FA Cup 3
Goals: League 46, FA Cup 2
Debut: Preston North End (h) 19 January 1929, won 2-1 (scored both goals)

Also played for: Chesterfield amateur, Matlock Town, Sheffield Wednesday, Luton Town, Alfreton Town, Port Vale, Bournemouth and Boscombe Athletic, Altrincham, Northwich Victoria

Athletic made one of their best signings in January 1929 when taking centre-forward Stewart Littlewood from Port Vale, for the well-built 24-year-old had always been a regular goalscorer. It was well in line with previous exploits when he scored both priceless goals by which Athletic beat Preston North End on his debut. He had done exactly the same thing when he made his League debut for Port Vale on Christmas Day 1926, the two goals that won the match against Clapton Orient being scored by him.

At the age of 24, Littlewood had already had a variety of experience. His first senior club was Chesterfield, who signed him in January 1924 from Hardwick Colliery, a Derbyshire Senior League club. However, he had returned to minor football when Sheffield Wednesday signed him a year later. His next move took him to Luton Town in July 1925, but after a season he returned to Derbyshire non-League football with Alfreton Town. It was on the strength of his free scoring with Alfreton that Port Vale negotiated his transfer in November 1926.

At this point, his stock immediately went up with a bound and his development into a capable and highly-effective centre-forward led to Athletic not only paying £1,300 for him, but also throwing in Albert Pynegar as makeweight.

In the remaining 18 matches of the season, Littlewood transformed Athletic's fortunes, his 12 goals doing much to lift the side clear of relegation from the Second Division. He also finished as leading goalscorer, one ahead of Jimmy Dyson who had played in 31 matches.

In the following season, Littlewood enjoyed the most marked success of his career. As spearhead of a formidable forward line, he cashed in to the tune of 27 League goals and two in the FA Cup. His performance left him just one League goal short of Frank Newton's record of 28 in 1907–08 – Athletic's first season in the Football League. An injury over the Easter period, when he missed three vital matches within the space of seven days, denied him the chance of equalling or surpassing the previous record.

Littlewood's absence also cost the team dear, as they took only one point from the three matches and effectively scuppered their chances of promotion from Division Two. A few weeks earlier, he had ended a barren run – two goals in seven matches – by recording a hat-trick against Stoke in a 5-0 victory that took Athletic to the top of the table. Athletic's football correspondent at that time ended his weekly column in the *Green Final* on a jocular note. Under the heading 'A Tonic' he penned the following: 'Son (lying sick in bed): "Father, will you get me the *Green Final* as soon as they are out?" – "Certainly, my lad." Father waits for the first sign of a G.F. and hurriedly takes a copy to his sick son, who is a follower of Athletic. The sequel: So overjoyed with the 5-0 win and Littlewood's hat-trick, the son was up and doing on Sunday, much to his doctor's surprise. Cost of *Green Final* 2d, doctor's fee 3s 6d.'

Despite starting the new season with a home win against Bradford Park Avenue and an away win at Reading, the team did not win another away match all season and finished in 12th position in the table. In March 1931 Littlewood returned to Port Vale for a record fee of £1,550. Immediately, at home, he wrote a page in the history of the club when they recorded their highest ever League victory, a 9-1 home win against Chesterfield on 24 September 1932. He scored six of the goals, but unfortunately underwent a cartilage operation in the following month. His League career wound up with a season at Bournemouth. His aggregate career figures were impressive – 93 goals in 157 matches.

Darron McDonough

Date of birth: 7 November 1962, Antwerp, Belgium

Oldham Athletic record:
Appearances: League 178(5), FA Cup 5, League Cup 12
Goals: League 14, League Cup 3
Debut: Notts County (a) 13 December 1980, won 2–0 (scored one)

Also played for: Luton Town, Newcastle United

One of the most whole-hearted players to pull on an Athletic shirt, Darron McDonough began at Boundary Park as a 15-year-old schoolboy and, one month beyond his 18th birthday, marked his Football League debut by scoring with a spectacular long-range volley against Notts County at Meadow Lane. In the course of exactly 200 matches for the Latics, his aggressive, 100 percent displays and wonderful versatility made him a warm favourite with the Boundary Park faithful.

McDonough made the breakthrough into senior action in 1980–81, replacing Mark Hilton on his debut in a side that had won only one League match in the previous two months. The Athletic team lined up as follows: Platt, Sinclair, Blair, Keegan, Clements, Hurst, Wylde, Futcher, Steel, Palmer (sub Hoolickin), McDonough. Athletic took the lead after 56 minutes when Roger Palmer netted his first goal since his £70,000 signing from Manchester City three weeks earlier. McDonough marked his debut with a second and Notts County – who went on to win promotion – surrendered their hitherto unbeaten home record. He appeared in 13(2) Second Division matches in his first season. On his sixth appearance he scored the only goal of the home game against Bristol Rovers on 7 February, playing alongside teenager Martin Nuttall, another local product to break through into the League side that season.

Under new manager Joe Royle, who was appointed to succeed Jimmy Frizzell, McDonough made his first appearance of 1982–83 on 20 September in brilliant sunshine at Chelsea. Athletic dominated for much of the match but had nothing to show in terms of goals and lost 2–0. On their third visit to the capital, Athletic were back to winning ways. One day before his 20th birthday McDonough netted his first goal of the season – Athletic's third – in the 3–0 victory at Fulham. Usually paired with Rodger Wylde in attack, he scored 10 League goals in 38 matches and netted one in two League Cup ties.

The final game of the season, at Cambridge United, proved memorable. Cambridge had put together a record run of 12 League games without conceding a goal, but, inspired by the powerful 20-year-old, Athletic tore the Cambridge defence apart. Four goals in eight second-half minutes included two by McDonough, his second being a particularly memorable header from a deep cross by John Ryan.

The 1983–84 season opened with a 1–0 home win against Brighton, with Mark Ward scoring on his debut. Veteran striker David Cross was signed in October, but the loss of Rodger Wylde – transferred to Sporting Lisbon in July 1983 – was keenly felt. McDonough's continuing role as a free-running forward lacked service and support, so by mid-season he reverted to a midfield role. His versatility in a variety of positions brought him 42 appearances during the season but only two goals, both scored against Stockport County in the League Cup.

In the final pre-season game of 1984–85, club-captain McDonough suffered a groin strain in the 1–0 home defeat against West Bromwich Albion and missed the first eight matches of the season. His return brought about an immediate improvement, but only 2,815 turned up for the visit of Middlesbrough, who were beaten 2–0. Athletic finished in 14th place in Division Two.

In yet another positional change, McDonough found himself in the role of centre-half in 1985–86. His season was curtailed, however, when he suffered severe ligament damage to his right ankle in the 2–0 defeat at Huddersfield Town on 21 December. The injury required immediate surgery and he missed the remainder of the season. In the close season he turned down Athletic's offer of a new two-year contract and in September completed a £87,000 transfer to First Division Luton Town.

McDonough was a League Cup finalist with Luton Town in 1989 after missing the previous year's final against Arsenal due to injury. He completed 88(17) League appearances and scored five goals for the Hatters, but his £90,000 transfer to Newcastle United in March 1992 was totally ruined by injuries. He had played in only two League matches when he was forced into early retirement following an Achilles tendon injury, sustained in a reserve-team match at Liverpool.

Peter McKennan

Date of birth: 16 July 1918, Airdrie
Died: October 1991, Dundonald, Ayrshire

Oldham Athletic record:
Appearances: League 78, FA Cup 5
Goals: League 28, FA Cup 5
Debut: Southport (a) 18 August 1951, drawn 0–0

Also played for: Partick Thistle (World War Two guest player with Linfield and Glentoran), West Bromwich Albion, Leicester City, Brentford, Middlesbrough, Coleraine

Peter McKennan began with Whitburn Juniors in the Edinburgh League and signed professional forms with Partick Thistle at the age of 17. The youthful but well-built tyro made his senior debut at inside-right in a 1–1 draw on 28 August 1935 at Dunfermline Athletic. He scored his first senior goal against Kilmarnock in a 2–0 victory in the following month. By the following term he was fully established and in the three seasons leading up to World War Two scored successive totals of 20, 20 and 24 Scottish League goals. In September 1937 he was included in the Scottish League XI that defeated the Football League 1–0 at Ibrox Park, Glasgow. One year later, at the same venue, he scored one of the goals by which the Scottish League defeated the Irish League 6–1.

McKennan joined the army in September 1939, first with the Royal Artillery and later with the Royal Welsh Fusiliers. He landed in Normandy two weeks after D-Day, took part in the battle of Caen and finished in Hamburg in February 1946. He was one of only four survivors of his section in one engagement and was mentioned in dispatches for patrol work. Between times, he was a regular member of the BAOR team and played in army international matches. He also had the unique experience of twice appearing for the Northern Ireland Regional League in matches against the League of Ireland in 1941. He scored a hat-trick in his first appearance – an 8–3 victory at Dalymount Park, Dublin – and then scored both goals in the 2–1 victory in the return fixture at Windsor Park, Belfast.

In the immediate post-war period, McKennan seemed to have set his mind on seeing the football world. Having left Firhill – where it is probably true to say that his heart remained – he sampled three Divisions of the Football League in fairly short order and added the Irish League to his colourful record before his career ended.

Athletic's player-manager George Hardwick was well aware of McKennan's abilities, the two having been playing colleagues at Middlesbrough. Signed for a bargain fee of £3,000, he certainly had a major influence in the revival of Athletic's fortunes. A strong and forceful forward with magnificent ball control and a never-say-die spirit, he proved an inspiration to his colleagues. His ability to hold the ball and provide openings for either wingmen or centre-forwards was an added bonus to his own goalscoring abilities. He opened his account in his second outing in the 2–0 victory against Gateshead at Boundary Park on 21 August 1951. He scored 16 League goals in 38 matches, plus three in two FA Cup ties in his first season when Athletic finished fourth in Division Three North.

Despite being increasingly troubled by knee injuries in subsequent seasons, McKennan played a significant role in the 1952–53 Championship campaign with 10 League goals in 32 matches and a further two in three FA Cup ties. Often seen with both knees bandaged and thighs strapped, he was still a class act who used the ball to advantage and frequently confused opponents by doing the unexpected. As Athletic returned to Division Two, after an interval of 19 years, McKennan was the first goalscorer in the season's opener – a 4–4 draw at Luton Town. He played in seven of the first eight matches of the season but then lost his place to Alf Clarke, the former Burnley forward, with wholesale changes being the order of the day in an attempt to lift the side from the foot of the table.

McKennan did not regain his place, and, as Athletic suffered relegation after just one season in Division Two, he left in July 1954 to join Coleraine as player-coach. Having fulfilled his earlier ambition to see much of the footballing world, Peter continued his travels after retiring from the game. News of their former inside-forward appeared in the local Oldham press in January 1960, when it was reported that he was working for an Irish construction company, assisting in the laying of an oil pipeline in Iran. McKennan died at the age of 73 after a long illness but was heartened in his last days when he received letters from Partick Thistle's president, Mr James Aitken, and his former Thistle teammate and Scotland international half-back Jackie Husband.

Alan McNeill

Date of birth: 16 August 1945, Belfast

Oldham Athletic record:
Appearances: League 154(16), FA Cup 9(1), League Cup 5
Goals: League 19
Debut: Aldershot (h) 25 October 1969, won 4-2 (scored one)

Also played for: Crusaders, Glentoran on loan, Middlesbrough, Huddersfield Town, Stockport County, Witton Albion

One of the best attacking midfield players in the lower Divisions, Alan McNeill combined a great flair for creative football with a hard, accurate shot. He began with Crusaders and won an Irish Cup medal in 1967, scoring one goal in the 3-1 victory against Glentoran. He seemed destined to join the beaten finalists when he was invited to join them for their summer tour of America in 1967. Already an Irish amateur international, his progress had been monitored by several English League clubs, and in August 1967 it was Middlesbrough who stepped in smartly, paying £10,000 to take him to Ayresome Park.

It was Middlesbrough's first season in Division Two following promotion, and although they made an uncertain start, they rallied to finish sixth. McNeill had some time to wait for his debut, which came at Aston Villa in a 1-0 win on 10 February 1967. Two weeks later he played in the 1-1 home draw against Charlton Athletic. In the following month he was capped by Northern Ireland at Under-23 level, appearing in the 1-0 win against the Wales Under-23 team at Cardiff. Although McNeill played in the opening 2-1 home win against Preston North End in August 1968, in November he was transferred to Huddersfield Town, ending an unproductive spell in the North East.

McNeill's stay at Leeds Road was equally unrewarding. After two games in 1968-69 (one from the bench), he had not figured at senior level in 1969-70 when he was transferred to Athletic in October 1969. He joined a side in total disarray, having won just two of their first 15 matches in Division Four, with manager Jack Rowley two months away from getting the sack. Nevertheless, spirits were lifted with a welcome 4-2 home win against Aldershot on his debut. Reflecting the team's lack of success, only 3,275 spectators attended the match, and Athletic were quickly two goals in arrears. McNeill registered his first League goal when he scored after 27 minutes, and Jim Bowie equalised 12 minutes later. Second half goals by John Bingham and Jim Bowie secured the points.

Jimmy Frizzell took over as caretaker manager on 30 December 1969 with the team at the foot of the table and with 22 matches of the season remaining. He steered the side to safety with nine wins and six draws and was rewarded with the managership in March 1970. An eventful season concluded with friendly matches against Blackpool and East Fife, plus the Manchester Senior Cup Final against Bury, which Athletic won 4-1, with Jim Fryatt scoring a hat-trick and McNeill netting number four.

A Latics XI with four players making their debuts for the opening Division Four fixture of 1970-71 lined up as follows: Short, Wood, Whittle, Bowie, Thomson, Cranston, Heath, Shaw, Fryatt, Bryceland, Hartle. McNeill was named as substitute. The 4-1 defeat was quickly forgotten when the side, with one change – Bebbington for Hartle at outside-left – won 3-1 at Bury in the first round of the League Cup. After three appearances from the bench, McNeill made the starting line up on 22 September when a David Shaw hat-trick was the highlight in a rousing 5-2 win against Aldershot.

McNeill scored his first League goal of the season on 11 October in another high-scoring 5-3 extravaganza against Crewe Alexandra. Four days earlier the Latics had despatched Great Harwood 9-0 in the first round of the Lancashire Senior Cup. He scored eight goals in 39 League matches as Athletic won promotion from Division Four and scooped the £70,000 prize money for winning the Ford Sporting League, enabling a new stand to be built on the Broadway side of Boundary Park.

McNeill missed very few matches until season 1973-74, when he was injured in the 1-1 draw against Port Vale on 1 September and missed three months of the season. He nevertheless made sufficient appearances – 13 starts and five from the bench – to qualify for a Third Division Championship medal. He joined Stockport County in July 1975 and made 69(2) League appearances in two seasons before moving into non-League circles with Witton Albion. As a reinstated amateur he continued to play in the Huddersfield League until the age of 46, when a series of knee injuries forced his retirement.

Ian Marshall

Date of birth: 20 March 1966, Liverpool

Oldham Athletic record:
Appearances: League 165(5), FA Cup 14, League Cup 17
Goals: League 36, FA Cup 3
Debut: Swindon Town (h) 12 March 1988, won 4–3

Also played for: Everton, Ipswich Town, Leicester City, Bolton Wanderers, Blackpool

Ian Marshall captained Everton's FA Youth Cup-winning team in season 1983–84, but subsequent lack of senior opportunities led him to accept Athletic's offer of a contract following two weeks on loan at Boundary Park in March 1988. In four years at Goodison Park, he had played in only 9(6) League matches; nevertheless he commanded a fee of £100,000 and was drafted straight in to Athletic's team, replacing Andy Linighan, who had been transferred to Norwich City one week earlier.

Marshall's debut in central-defence against Swindon Town also featured the first appearance of goalkeeper Andy Rhodes from Doncaster Rovers. Athletic won 4–3, with Roger Palmer registering his 99th goal in League football. Marshall's arrival coincided with an unbeaten run of nine matches that lifted the side to 10th place.

Marshall scored his first goal from the penalty spot in a 3–1 defeat at Blackburn Rovers and followed up one week later with another from open play in the 4–0 win against Birmingham City. In the same week news came that another Latics centre-half of earlier vintage – Keith Hicks – had been sacked as manager of Mossley and was about to resume his playing career with Hyde United. As Athletic collected the first Barclays League monthly Divisional goalscoring award, their attacking flair and policy of getting players forward was certainly entertaining, but they were prone to being caught out at the back. The signing of seasoned defender Peter Skipper from Hull City saw Marshall switched to sweeper, the first of his positional changes that eventually saw him successfully employed as attack leader.

The tall defender certainly appeared to enjoy his initial run-outs in attack, and the makeshift striker's physical presence and strong running were first in evidence in season 1989–90. Although Athletic's dreams of an amazing Wembley double were shattered, their two meetings with Manchester United in the FA Cup semi-final were widely praised as fine adverts for the game. In the initial 3–3 draw, Marshall netted Athletic's second goal with a volley 'of the kind that Marco Van Basten would have been proud', according to one admiring correspondent. Sadly, he injured his thigh in the replay and failed to recover in time to play at Wembley in the Littlewoods Cup Final against Nottingham Forest.

Marshall's hat-trick at Wolverhampton Wanderers in a 3–2 win on the opening day of season 1990–91 launched Athletic's promotion bid, which commenced with a 16-match unbeaten run in Division Two. Despite being sidelined for lengthy spells during the campaign, Marshall returned for the final two months. Having set the ball rolling against Wolves, his double strike against Ipswich Town at Portman Road on 27 April 1991 sealed Athletic's 2–1 victory and put the club back into the First Division for the first time in 68 years. He also scored in the nail-biting finale to the season, the 3–2 win that clinched the Championship trophy. Despite being restricted to just 25(1) League matches during the season, he scored 17 of the side's 83 League goals to head the scoring chart.

Marshall opened the scoring as First Division soccer returned to Boundary Park, with visitors Chelsea being comprehensively despatched 3–0. He stormed clear of the visitors' defence after 16 minutes to smack a low, left-foot volley past goalkeeper David Beasant from just outside the penalty area. He finished the season with 10 League goals in 41 matches, despite reverting to a defensive role mid-term. Season 1992–93 was his last at Boundary Park, and he was again troubled by injuries that restricted him to just 26(1) League appearances. He had been out for a lengthy spell when introduced as a substitute in the final match of the season, when Athletic completed their 'Great Escape' by beating Southampton 4–3, thereby ensuring Premier League survival.

In August 1993 Marshall joined Ipswich Town in a £750,000 transfer and three years later moved to Leicester City for £875,000. Before retiring due to injury in March 2002, he had spells with Bolton Wanderers and Blackpool. He appeared in successive League Cup Finals with Leicester City, collecting a winners' medal in 2000. Later he assisted Bolton Wanderers into the Premier League in 2000–01.

Howard Matthews

Date of birth: 29 November 1885, Roadend, Worcestershire
Died: 9 February 1963, Oldham

Oldham Athletic record:
Appearances: League 344, FA Cup 24
Goals: 0
Debut: Blackpool (a) 12 September 1908, lost 0–1

Also played for: Oldbury St John's, Langley St Michaels, Burslem Port Vale, Burton United, Port Vale, Halifax Town, Chester, Oswestry Town

A model professional and wonderful ambassador for the club, Howard Matthews began with Athletic in April 1908 and stayed until October 1926 when he returned to Port Vale. He actually appeared in 14 seasons of League football for the Latics and played in a further 122 matches during the World War One period.

Standing at only 5ft 9in, Matthews was blessed with amazing agility and an uncanny positional sense that made goalkeeping look easy. He made his debut in League football with Burslem Port Vale on 1 September 1906, and in January 1930 the veteran shot-stopper was still turning out with Halifax Town in his 45th year, when he was the oldest player in League football.

An all-round sportsman, Matthews played cricket in the Central Lancashire League as a wicket keeper/batsman for Royton, and he also excelled as a tennis player. The son of a well-known amateur goalkeeper, he was promoted to first-team duties with Athletic after just one appearance at reserve-team level. Curiously enough, both matches were away fixtures at Blackpool. The reserve team won 2–0 on 5 September, but the first team lost 0–1 one week later. He played in 36 Second Division matches in his first season and conceded only 41 goals.

Matthews did even better in the following term with 37 appearances and only 38 goals conceded, a major contribution to the team's success in winning promotion to the First Division as runners-up to Manchester City. Ironically, his reward was a season in the reserves in 1910–11, when the former Woolwich Arsenal goalkeeper Hugh McDonald took over as first-team custodian. Three matches into the following season, however, McDonald took great exception to being dropped in favour of Matthews and refused to travel to Everton with the reserve team. He did not play again for Athletic, and Matthews resumed first-team duties, missing only a handful of matches before League football was suspended due to World War One.

Matthews was awarded two benefits by Athletic, with guarantees of £250 in November 1913 and £500 in May 1922. When normal League football recommenced in August 1919, he found very stiff competition from the emerging talents of Ted Taylor, who won the first of eight England caps within four months of his £2,000 transfer to Huddersfield Town in June 1922. He was destined to remain one of the game's best uncapped goalkeepers, his solitary representative honour being an appearance for the Football League against the Irish League, a match played at Boundary Park on 9 October 1909, and won 9–1 by the Football League.

In December 1919, when the senior spot was being contested between Matthews and Ted Taylor, the two goalkeepers each saved a pair of penalty-kicks at Turf Moor. The feat occurred on consecutive Saturdays and at the same goal. Matthews saved two spot-kicks in the reserves 2–0 victory on 6 December. A week later Taylor repeated the feat for the first team, who nevertheless lost 1–2.

Matthews played in 33 matches in Athletic's final season in Division One (1922–23) and missed only two matches in the following season. At this time the evergreen he held off the challenge of Albert Gray, who assisted Wales to win the international championship, conceding just one goal in three matches.

A civil servant by profession, Matthews was a teetotaller and non-smoker. He was also a devoutly religious man, but one of his defensive colleagues was anything but. One week the full-back launched himself at the ball, attempting to cut off a goal-bound shot, but only succeeding in rocketing his header into the back of the net. Grinning sheepishly at the bemused 'keeper, he said cheerfully 'Never mind Howard, even the Salvation Army couldn't have saved that one!'

Mike Milligan

Date of birth: 20 February 1967, Moss Side, Manchester

Oldham Athletic record:
Appearances: League 278(1), FA Cup 21, League Cup 30(1)
Goals: League 23, FA Cup 1, League Cup 2
Debut: As substitute v Liverpool, League Cup 2 (h) 9 October 1985, lost 2–5

Also played for: Manchester City associate schoolboy, Flixton, Everton, Norwich City, Blackpool

Athletic's captain in the Final of the Littlewoods Cup at Wembley in April 1990 earned his first one-year professional contract at the age of 18, with part of his wages being paid by the European Social Fund and Greater Manchester Council. Mike Milligan along with another reserve-team player Brian Marriott, boosted Athletic's list of professionals to 21, thanks to the money from the EEC. Athletic were the first sports club to apply for the grant, and it certainly paved the way for a permanent career for Milligan, although centre-half Brian Marriott failed to graduate to senior level at Boundary Park.

Two years after being released by Manchester City, Milligan was spotted by Athletic scout Jim Cassell while playing for Manchester County Boys against Liverpool. His elder brother, Terry, was at Boundary Park at the time, although he did not graduate to first-team level. With only 14 minutes of first-team action to his name when he came on as a substitute against Liverpool in the Milk Cup defeat in October 1985, 18-year-old Milligan made his League debut at Sheffield United on 12 April 1986. An extended injury list gave him his first opportunity, although his impact with the table-topping reserves in the Central League had earned him his big chance.

Milligan's hopes of a winning debut were lost when Willie Donachie was sent off in a bruising encounter at Bramall Lane, which also saw Roger Palmer and Mick McGuire cautioned, along with two players from the home side. Despite the 2–0 defeat, he enjoyed an outstanding debut, and he held his place for the remaining matches of the season. He scored his first League goal in the season's final fixture, a 2–1 home win against Carlisle United, and Athletic ended with a flourish to finish eighth in the table.

Milligan was fully involved in the following season when Athletic qualified for the Division Two Play-offs, only to lose to Leeds United in the semi-final on the away-goals rule. After six matches, Athletic headed the table with no goals conceded, but the excellent opening was followed by a wayward display at Huddersfield Town. Lacking the suspended Milligan in midfield, the Latics crashed 5–4 in an entertaining but ultimately disappointing display. Athletic's most improved young player was watched in early season by both England and Eire Under-21 representatives, and he took the decision to stake an international claim with the Republic of Ireland.

Milligan was to appear in eight seasons of football for the Latics as a gritty ball-winner and provider from midfield. In season 1988–89 another young midfielder, Nick Henry, emerged in the second half of the campaign, in which Milligan enjoyed his best season to date as a goalscorer with seven. Athletic now had a pair of all-action midfield ball-winners, the equal of any in Division Two. Club skipper Milligan was voted supporters' Player of the Year in May 1990 for his 60 appearances and eight goals in the season when Athletic lost out on all fronts – Littlewoods Cup Final, FA Cup semi-finals, and a Play-off place. His displays in the memorable season, however, earned him an upward move to Everton in August 1990 when he became the first Athletic player to be involved in a £1 million transfer.

A year later, Milligan returned to the newly promoted Latics after a disappointing season with Everton, not helped by an early-season injury that sidelined him for two months. Rejoining Athletic for a record fee of £600,000, he battled hard in midfield for three seasons as the Latics fought to survive in the top flight. Sadly, their relegation in 1994 also saw his departure to Premier League club Norwich City for a tribunal-set fee of £850,000. In six seasons with the Canaries, he totalled 113(11) League appearances and scored five goals. When his Carrow Road contract was up in June 2000, he was linked with a move to Shrewsbury Town as player-coach. He opted, however, to return to Lancashire and joined Blackpool on a free transfer. Injuries restricted him to 24(2) League matches in his first season, and he played little first-team football in the following term, announcing his retirement in March 2002.

Milligan won international recognition with the Republic of Ireland at Under-21, Under-23, B, and full levels – the latter against US in 1992. A lively, enthusiastic character both on and off the pitch, he completed career aggregate figures of 432(16) League appearances and 30 goals.

Hugh Moffat

Date of birth: January 1885, Congleton
Died: 14 November 1952, Macclesfield

Oldham Athletic record:
Appearances: League 162, FA Cup 20
Goals: League 10
Debut: Bury (a) 17 December 1910, drawn 2–2

Also played for: Congleton Town, Burnley, Chesterfield Municipal, Congleton Town (again), England (1 cap)

Hugh Moffat played for three seasons as a full-back with Congleton Town from the age of 16. Joining Burnley, he made his League debut in Division Two as left full-back against Barnsley in a 2–2 draw at Turf Moor on 1 April 1904. Later in the same month an injury to Joe Taylor, the Clarets' long-serving left half-back, saw him drafted into the middle line, and he scored against Lincoln City in a 3–1 home win. He also scored Burnley's first goal in 1904–05, but blotted his copybook in November of the same season when he missed his train connection and arrived too late to play at Chesterfield. Burnley had travelled without a reserve and played with only 10 men, yet the depleted ranks held out for a 1–1 draw.

Moffat remained at Turf Moor for almost six years, completing 214 League and Cup appearances and scoring 13 goals, and in April 1910 he played for the Football League against the Southern League at Stamford Bridge. His final game for the Clarets was the Lancashire Cup Final against Blackburn Rovers at Ewood Park, and three days later, on 15 December 1910, he became an Athletic player, with a fee of £490 securing his signature. In the week before his signing, Latics captain Alex Downie had been suspended for 14 days following misconduct in the match at Nottingham Forest – he was found guilty of kicking Forest's Welsh international Grenville Morris.

Despite having spent the majority of his career as a left-sided defender, Moffat was drafted in at right half-back and did so well that he retained the position for the remainder of the season. His outstanding form was rewarded by a call-up from the Football League as travelling reserve for the Inter-League match against Scotland at Ibrox Park on 4 March 1911.

The Latics finished their first season in the top flight in seventh position and in April accepted an invitation to tour Austria and Hungary. Illness prevented manager David Ashworth from making the trip, and so secretary Bob Mellor took charge. Three directors and trainer Jimmy Hanson also made the trip. Moffat played in all of the six matches contested in Budapest and Vienna, which included two exhibition matches against Blackburn Rovers.

In his second season at Boundary Park, Moffat appeared for the Football League against the Southern League at Old Trafford on 30 September 1912. On 17 March of the same season, he became the second Athletic player to win a full international cap for England when he played in the high-scoring 4–3 victory against Wales, played at Ashton Gate, Bristol.

In the final season before World War Two suspended League Football for the duration, Athletic fielded an all international half-back line of Moffat, Roberts and Wilson. Manager Herbert Bamlett had inherited a fine side from David Ashworth – they had finished fourth in Division One in 1913–14 – and he wisely made few changes.

The season opened with a 3–1 win at Manchester United and was followed by a 5–3 victory against Bolton Wanderers. A 4–1 defeat at Blackburn Rovers proved to be the only setback in the first three months. A match report during the season revealed that 'Moffat did a lot of work, swung a loose leg, and kicked with power and precision.' Sadly, his best efforts during the campaign ended in frustration when Athletic finished as runners-up for the First Division Championship.

After the war, Moffat joined Chesterfield Municipal, where Athletic's wartime secretary Mr Tom Callagan was in charge. His son, Stanley, followed in his footsteps, assisting several League clubs in the inter-war period including Birmingham and Millwall.

Jimmy Naylor

Date of birth: 2 March 1901, High Crompton, Lancashire
Died: 31 August 1983, Shaw, Lancashire

Oldham Athletic record:
Appearances: League 238, FA Cup 11
Goals: League 5, FA Cup 1
Debut: Preston North End (a) 2 December 1922, lost 1–5

Also played for: Shawside FC, Huddersfield Town, Newcastle United, Manchester City, Macclesfield Town, Nelson, Wigan Athletic

Jimmy Naylor was playing for Shaw Parish Church in the Rochdale Sunday School League when, following a donation of £100 by Mr Joe Ridings of Shaw, a new club was formed named Shawside FC. Along with others from the Parish Church side, he transferred his allegiance. Operating at outside-left he secured 10 medals, his club winning the Oldham Amateur League Championship three seasons in succession, while the Oldham Amateur Cup and the Oldham Charity Cup were also lifted.

Naylor first caught the attention of Athletic's representatives when playing for Shawside in a Junior Cup Final at Boundary Park. At 19 years of age he had two outings with Athletic Reserves while training in the evenings at Boundary Park. While still on amateur forms, he played in an emergency at left-half in a third XI match at Altrincham and played so well in his new position that he remained there for the rest of his career.

Naylor signed professional forms in October 1922 and was delighted to get the opportunity as there was a lot of short-time working in his particular job, that of a cop packer at Joseph Clegg's cotton-spinning mill in High Crompton. Athletic were overrun by Preston North End on his debut at Deepdale, but one week later in the return fixture Athletic won 2–1, with both goals being scored by Charlie Wallace, the 37-year-old former England international right-winger. Naylor scored his first League goal when making his fifth appearance against Birmingham in the 2–0 home win on 3 February. One week later the side completed the season's only double when they won 3–2 at St Andrews.

Naylor appeared in 19 out of a possible 26 matches in his debut season, rounding off with Athletic's first goal in the 3–1 win against Cardiff City on the final day. However, the team were already doomed to relegation from the top flight, having failed to score in 23 of their 42 League matches. They totalled only 35 goals, by far the worst return in the First Division.

One of Naylor's greatest attributes was his consistency of form and fitness. Excluding his first season, when he was making the berth his own, he missed just six matches in the following five seasons, four absences occurring when he was injured by one of his own teammates in a pre-season trial match at Boundary Park on 19 August 1924.

When it became known that Athletic were prepared to part with their star half-back, providing a satisfactory price was forthcoming, several First Division clubs expressed an interest. Huddersfield Town were the keenest on the scent and paid £3,750 to take him to Leeds Road, where his polished displays quickly attracted the attention of the international selectors, leading to an appearance for The Rest against England at Hillsborough in February 1929.

An appearance in the 1930 FA Cup Final against Arsenal was the undoubted highlight of Naylor's career, despite the fact that the Gunners, for the first time in their history, won the trophy by 2–0. The Wembley appearance proved to be his last as a Huddersfield Town player. In July 1930 Newcastle United paid £4,000 for him and an early thrill was his appearance in the match against Chelsea in September 1930, which set a ground record attendance of 68,386 at St James' Park.

Injuries blighted Naylor's second season at St James' Park and cost him a place in the 1932 FA Cup Final against Arsenal, won 2–1 by Newcastle. He was the 12th man but did not receive a medal. An undisclosed fee took him to Manchester City in October 1932, and in February 1933 he was loaned to Athletic, giving him the satisfaction of helping his first love to avoid relegation from Division Two. He was housing manager for Crompton Council for 28 years until his retirement in 1967.

Chris Ogden

Date of birth: 3 February 1953, Oldham

Oldham Athletic record:
Appearances: League 128, FA Cup 5, League Cup 10
Goals: 0
Debut: Blackburn Rovers (h) 11 December 1971, drawn 1–1

Also played for: Swindon Town, Rotherham United, Bath City, Cheltenham Town

In common with his father Fred, Chris Ogden had a lengthy association with the Latics and followed family tradition when he won through to senior level, representing his home-town team as the club's last line of defence. Although it could be argued that his father had been thrust into the limelight at too early an age – he was 17 when he first appeared during wartime season 1942–43 – he was not much older at 18 when he made his debut. Both endured the sternest of examinations, Fred conceding 17 goals in his first five outings while Chris fared little better, being beaten 16 times in his first six matches. Happily, both matured into fine 'keepers, ensuring that the Latics' long tradition for good goalkeepers remained in safe hands.

Ogden signed amateur forms at Boundary Park in August 1969 and was A team goalkeeper in the Lancashire League in 1969–70. Professional goalkeepers on the books at that time were Barry Gordine and John Fitton. In the following season, when promotion from Division Four was secured, Harry Dowd, the former Manchester City goalkeeper, replaced Barry Gordine. Dowd made his debut at Northampton Town on 5 December in a 3–1 win and the side immediately embarked on a run of seven wins in eight matches. Almost exactly a year later, a 25th minute injury to Harry Dowd at Blackburn on 4 December saw Maurice Whittle take over as emergency goalkeeper. Despite being reduced to 10 men, the Latics won 1–0. Ogden was selected for his debut one week later, when Blackburn Rovers were the visitors to Boundary Park. He might well have enjoyed a winning start, but the hero of the previous week, Maurice Whittle, had his 78th minute penalty-kick saved by the Rovers goalkeeper Roger Jones. Ogden's six-match run ended on 15 January when Athletic entertained high-flyers Brighton & Hove Albion. The visitors were two goals up inside five minutes and ran out 4–2 winners on their way to promotion from Division Three.

Ogden enjoyed a nine-match run in 1972–73, commencing with a 1–0 away win at Southend United on 9 October. In the following week, the 19-year-old goalkeeper lined up alongside a player old enough to be his father, 41-year-old Bobby Collins, the celebrated Scottish international inside-forward, who was making his first appearance as player-coach in the 2–2 draw at Wrexham. His second spell of senior action saw him involved in some high-scoring encounters – a 7–1 home win against Plymouth Argyle on 4 November which was immediately followed by a 2–6 defeat at Grimsby Town. It was to be in the following season that he wrote his name indelibly into the folklore of the Latics.

The Third Division Championship season began in uneventful fashion with a scoreless encounter at Halifax Town followed by a 1–1 home draw against Port Vale. Harry Dowd commenced the season as first choice, but following four straight League defeats in the month of December he was replaced by Ogden for the visit to Wrexham on 12 January 1974. Despite losing Paul Edwards with an injured ankle after six minutes, his replacement George Jones came off the bench to score both of Athletic's goals in the 2–1 victory. One week later Halifax Town were beaten 3–2, with Tony Bailey – on loan from Derby County – making his debut. Throughout the month of February, Athletic collected maximum points from all four League matches, with three clean sheets by Ogden keeping the run going. March began with a visit to Blackburn Rovers where heroics by Ogden and an 88th minute winner by Alan Groves earned a hard-fought 1–0 victory. A 6–1 demolition of Cambridge United followed, and two wins, each by 2–1 against Walsall and then York City, rewrote the record books with a total of 10 consecutive League wins, Athletic's best-ever sequence.

Ogden retained his position throughout the difficult first season back in Division Two, extending his run to 86 consecutive matches before the emerging John Platt provided stiff competition in his last three seasons at Boundary Park. He joined Swindon Town in August 1978 and shared goalkeeping duties with Jimmy Allan in a season when the Wiltshire club finished fifth in Division Three. In November 1979 he joined Rotherham United, but a brief stay ended in May 1980. Three years later, he assisted Cheltenham Town to the Championship of the Southern League, Midland Division.

Fred Ogden

Date of birth: 3 April 1925, Oldham

Oldham Athletic record:
Appearances: League 156, FA Cup 11
Goals: 0
Debut: Bradford City (h) 10 April 1948, won 3–0

Also played for: Chesterfield, Nelson

Athletic's popular, locally-born goalkeeper of the early post-war period actually began at Boundary Park as a raw 17-year-old in wartime season 1942–43. Fred Ogden was the first of five goalkeepers fielded by the Latics in the 18-match Football League North (First Championship). To give a flavour of the times, on the day prior to the announcement of his selection for the season's opener at Chester, Latics' secretary Bob Mellor had launched an appeal to supporters for 100 clothing coupons! An opportunity had arisen for the purchase of new boots and stockings, and Mr Mellor felt that they would be unlikely to locate any further supplies until the end of the war.

Ogden's height was given at 5ft 9in at the time, and he had been playing for Edge Lane Sunday School. Neither statistic gave much comfort to the war-restricted following of the club, for example, the next fixture at Boundary Park on 5 September attracted only 521 spectators and the receipts totalled £28 11s 9d. Chester won 5–1 on Ogden's first appearance, and it could have been worse as they squandered a penalty in the 88th minute. Athletic were 2–1 up against Chester in the return at Boundary Park, but two late goals by the visitors spoiled his home debut. The youthful custodian was removed from the firing line after five matches, in the course of which he had conceded 17 goals.

Ogden returned to Boundary Park in December 1947 in the season when Brendan McManus was established as first-team goalkeeper. His deputy, Jack Sawbridge, had recently been transferred to Chorley when Ogden made his first Lancashire Combination appearance in the 3–1 win against Netherfield on 27 December. Although not the build of many of today's goalkeepers, by this time he had grown to 5ft 11in and weighed in at 11st 2lb. Although considered rather lightweight for his position – in the days when goalkeepers were offered little protection by referees – his cat-like agility, anticipation and a safe pair of hands effectively compensated for any lack of physical advantage. In late season Ogden was given his first League outing. The 3–0 victory against Bradford City featured two goals from Ray Haddington and one from Lewis Brook, and it also marked the second appearance of Bill Naylor who went on to complete 238 appearances in 11 seasons at Boundary Park. Ogden also played in the final match of the campaign at Halifax Town, the Latics signing off with a stunning 5–1 win – Billy Blackshaw scoring four and Lewis Brook the other.

Athletic transferred their Irish goalkeeper McManus and replaced him with Welshman John Jones, for the start of season 1948–49. Jones held the first-team spot until mid-season before losing out to Ogden, whose return sparked a run of greatly improved results that took the side to sixth place in the table. In late February, during the 1–1 draw against Wrexham at Boundary Park, he sustained a hand injury after 15 minutes of play. Tommy Bell took over in goal and for the remainder of the half Ogden made a remarkably good impression as a fleet-footed outside-right. To the great delight of the 13,776 spectators, on several occasions he showed a clean pair of heels to Wrexham's left-back, Ron Jackson. It was quite an anticlimax when he reappeared as goalkeeper for the second half!

In the following two seasons Ogden missed only four first-team matches. He saved penalty-kicks at New Brighton and Darlington in 1949–50, but was debited with an own-goal in the Manchester Senior Cup Final against Manchester City at Boundary Park on 8 May 1950. Athletic won 2–1 and lifted the trophy thanks to second-half goals by Jimmy Munro and Ray Haddington. The crowd numbered 8,321.

The arrival of George Burnett – an emergency signing from Everton – ended Ogden's domination of the first-team position. Injured in an explosive encounter with Bradford City, in the course of which player-manager Hardwick was sent off for aiming a kick at Bradford's trainer, he then shared senior duties but was unable to dislodge Burnett, who played in 42 League matches in the 1952–53 Championship season. Ogden joined Chesterfield in June 1955 but was back at Boundary Park in March of the same season, his final appearance in the 1–1 draw against Wrexham (h) on 28 April 1956 also marking the last appearance of player-manager George Hardwick. He remained a popular member of the training staff at Boundary Park and his son, Chris, followed the family tradition as Latics' last line of defence.

Roger Palmer

Date of birth: 30 January 1959, Manchester

Oldham Athletic record:
Appearances: League 419(47), FA Cup 19(5), League Cup 34(5)
Goals: League 141, FA Cup 5, League Cup 10
Debut: Orient (h) 22 November 1980, lost 0–1

Also played for: Manchester City

Considering that it is 12 years since Roger Palmer hung up his boots and left Boundary Park, the fact that the Latics faithful continue to include in their musical(?) repertoire the unique terrace chant 'Ooh Roger Palmer' says much about the affection in which the 'black pearl' is still held.

Palmer represented Manchester Schoolboys and his first experience of the big stage came when he was a Wembley ball boy for the 1974 League Cup Final between Manchester City and Wolverhampton Wanderers. One year later he signed apprentice forms at Maine Road and after impressing in the Central League side was given his League debut against Middlesbrough in December 1977. In his early days an orthodox striker, three goals during 4(3) matches in his first League season underlined his undoubted potential. He had advanced his tally to nine goals in 22(9) League appearances when a change of management at Maine Road – John Bond replacing Malcolm Allison – brought a flurry of transfer activity and Palmer was made available for transfer.

Athletic's manager Jimmy Frizzell was also busy in the transfer market. Having sold popular striker Simon Stainrod to Queen's Park Rangers for £250,000, he immediately lined up Palmer as his replacement. Although the £70,000 fee that he commanded when arriving at Boundary Park seemed a substantial outlay, it was made during a period of generally inflated transfer fees. Nevertheless, the wonderfully consistent displays of the silky, clinical marksman made him one of Athletic's all-time best buys. His Latics career commenced with a Second Division match against Orient, and the team's indifferent form continued with a 0–1 defeat. They lined up as follows: John Platt, Garry Hoolickin, Ronnie Blair, Ged Keegan, Kenny Clements, John Hurst, Paul Heaton, Paul Futcher, Steve Gardner, Roger Palmer, Paul Atkinson. The senior professionals at that time were Ronnie Blair, making his 336th League appearance, and John Hurst with his 154th.

Palmer scored his first Athletic goal at Notts County in the 2–0 win on 13 December, the other goal coming from Darren McDonough on his Football League debut. His modest enough start saw him score six goals in 23 League and Cup matches. He reached double figures for the first time in 1981–82 with seven League and three FA Cup goals, but, along with all of his playing colleagues, he had a new manager to impress when Joe Royle took over in June 1982. Many years later, Royle was big enough to admit that his first impressions of Palmer, who he had pigeon-holed as an orthodox striker, were misleading. As a midfield player, however, Palmer soon won over his new manager and remained an essential element of his first-team set up. The manager was once quoted as saying 'Roger has only one trick, he puts the ball into the back of the net.' Not strictly accurate of course, but his scoring rate from midfield was quite phenomenal.

Landmarks in Palmer's 13½ years included his 100th League goal, scored at Birmingham City in a 3–1 victory on 19 March 1988. He was presented with a silver salver from the club before the following week's match against Shrewsbury Town and said 'thank you' by salvaging a point with an injury-time equaliser in the 2–2 draw. He scored 20 goals that season, his best-ever tally, with the total including three hat-tricks. In the following season he smashed the club's all-time goalscoring record, his spectacular diving header in the 4–0 win against Ipswich Town on 4 April 1989 taking him beyond Eric Gemmell's 35-year-old record of 109 League goals.

There can have been few regrets in Palmer's outstanding career, but one must have surrounded the fact that Athletic's glory days arrived just too late for him. One of the biggest disappointments of his career was the Second Division Play-off defeat against Leeds United in season 1986–87; a time when he was at the peak of his powers and would surely have continued to impress at the very top level of the game. The Oldham public turned out in droves to pay tribute to Palmer on the occasion of his testimonial match against Manchester City on 13 May 1991. The game attracted 15,700 spectators – the third highest Boundary Park crowd of the season and well in advance of the 5,707 who turned up to witness his debut in November 1980!

Peter Phoenix

Date of birth: 31 December 1936, Salford

Oldham Athletic record:
Appearances: League 161, FA Cup 12, League Cup 5
Goals: League 27, FA Cup 4
Debut: Bury (a) 8 February 1958, lost 0–4

Also played for: Lostock Gralam, Manchester City amateur, Stoke City amateur, Tamworth, Rochdale, Exeter City, Southport, Stockport County, Wigan Athletic, Witton Albion, Bangor City

In September of the 1960–61 season, the Latics travelled the short distance to Rochdale for the first 'derby' match of the season. They had made an awful start to the campaign, their record prior to kick-off at Spotland being: Played 9, Won 1, Drawn 2, Lost 6, For 11, Against 24, Points 4. Things were to get even worse before Scottish international Bobby Johnstone appeared on the scene in the following month and lifted the side to a respectable halfway spot in Division Four.

I was one of the 7,352 spectators who attended the Tuesday evening match at Rochdale on 20 September and witnessed a most amazing incident in an otherwise immediately forgettable match, which Rochdale won 3–0. With an excellent view from immediately behind the goal at the Sandy Lane end, I saw Pheonix's sweetly-struck penalty-kick arrow into the top corner and rebound off the net stanchion. Rochdale's goalkeeper, Jimmy Jones, caught the ball as it came out and immediately hoofed the ball up field. To the amazement of everyone, the referee waved play on. In the happy days before crowd segregation, there was a mix of hilarity and anguish behind the goal, depending on where your allegiance lay!

The younger brother of Ronnie the Manchester City and Rochdale wing-half, Pheonix also had an early association with Manchester City but opted to complete his apprenticeship as a joiner before entering the professional ranks with the Latics in February 1958. He made an immediate League debut in the outside-left position at Gigg Lane and was plunged straight into a desperate battle to lift Athletic into the top half of the table. Season 1957–58 was the last Third Division campaign to be contested on a regional basis, prior to the inception of Divisions Three and Four in 1958–59. The top 12 teams from the Northern and Southern sections became founder members of the new Third Division, while the bottom 12 became inaugural members of Division Four.

Sadly, Athletic finished 15th and for the next four seasons Pheonix plied his trade in soccer's basement; nevertheless, his impressive approach work on the left flank and useful scoring record served Athletic well in their wilderness years. For their first game in Division Four against York City at home, Athletic fielded two new players, Albert Bourne (Manchester City) and Wally Taylor (Southport). They lost 1–0, with a Bill Naylor own-goal settling the issue. Pheonix was dropped for the midweek win against Coventry City, but his replacement, Ron Clark from Gillingham, lost his place after just four outings. In mid-season, Athletic transferred Jimmy Thompson to Exeter City for £3,000, plus Ray John as a makeweight in the deal. Three wins in the final four matches lifted the side away from the foot of the table to 21st place. Pheonix was leading scorer with 14 goals in 43 matches.

1959–60 opened brightly; Pheonix's inside partner Peter Stringfellow scored in both of the opening two matches, twice within five minutes of the kick-off against Bradford Park Avenue in the 2–0 home win and his goal after 11 minutes won the Monday evening game against Crystal Palace. There then followed a run to test the patience of the keenest supporter – 16 matches without a win. The worst season in the club's long history ended in a re-election application, with the fewest wins (eight) of any Football League team that season. Pheonix scored four goals during the season and survived the end-of-season clear out that saw eight players given free transfers and four made 'open to offers'.

It took some time for new manager Jack Rowley to infuse some of his own fighting spirit into the side, with the season 'taking off' in October. Pheonix scored eight goals in 49 matches, four of his goals coming from the penalty spot. In both 1960–61 and 1961–62 he was increasingly utilised as a wing half-back and remained a fixture in the side during a period of rapid change in playing personnel. It was ironic that he should depart Boundary Park in October 1962 with the side riding high in the table and set for promotion. Nevertheless, his move to Rochdale brought the free-scoring wingman Colin Whitaker in exchange. Pheonix passed quickly through a further four League clubs before retiring, but he continued in amateur circles beyond his 50th birthday, a broken leg finally enforcing his retirement.

Elliot Pilkington

Date of birth: 2 April 1890, Radcliffe
Died: 23 November 1945, Bury

Oldham Athletic record:
Appearances: League 269, FA Cup 11
Goals: League 14, FA Cup 1
Debut: Notts County (h) 2 December 1911, lost 1–2

Also played for: Salford United, Llandudno, Macclesfield Town

As a junior, Elliot Pilkington assisted St Thomas's, Radcliffe and later Salford United in the Manchester League. He began as an inside-forward and was leading scorer in the Manchester League in season 1909–10. At the end of the same season he joined Athletic, who were about to embark on their first season in the top flight.

Pilkington began in the reserve team and made his debut against Blackpool Reserves at Bloomfield Road on 1 September. Later in the month he scored his first goal against Stockport County Reserves. Athletic used 41 players in the 38-match Lancashire Combination tournament, with Pilkington appearing in 34 matches and heading the scoring list. It was a similar story in 1911–12 when Athletic Reserves joined the Central League. He appeared in 29 of the 32 matches and was again leading scorer with 11. In mid-season he made his first appearance at senior level, deputising for Tommy Marrison at inside-right against Notts County at Meadow Lane. Sam Richards opened the scoring for Notts after six minutes play, with Athletic's Welsh international centre-forward Evan Jones equalising two minutes later. On the stroke of half-time, Richards scored again. There was no further scoring in the second half and Notts won by 2–1.

In season 1913–14 Pilkington passed the milestone of 100 appearances for the reserve team, and his patience was about to be rewarded in the following momentous season. By strange coincidence, his first start in 1914–15 was at centre half-back, a position he was to dominate for six seasons after World War One. After just one outing in central-defence, he reverted to his more accustomed inside-right role and scored the winner at Newcastle United in a 2–1 victory on 21 November.

Pilkington held his place for much of the remainder of the season, scoring four goals in 22 League matches and one in four FA Cup ties. At the end of a great but ultimately disappointing season, Athletic finished a good second in the First Division. The season had commenced with World War One already one month old and League football did not recommence until 1919–20.

Post-war football began for Athletic at West Bromwich Albion on 30 August 1919, and the team lined up as follows: Matthews, Goodwin, Stewart, Wolstenholme, Pilkington, Wilson, Jones, Walters, Dougherty, Gee, Wall. It was a radically different team to the pre-war side, with four players making their debuts. Albion won 3–1 and they went on to win the First Division Championship. Athletic finished in 17th place having hovered around the foot of the table for most of the season.

Athletic suffered relegation from the First Division at the end of season 1922–23, mainly due to deficiencies in attack – they scored only 35 goals in 42 matches. The defence, marshalled superbly by 33-year-old Pilkington from centre-half, fought gallantly to the end, conceding only nine goals in the season's final 13 fixtures. Commenting on the disappointing outcome, the local correspondent wondered whether Pilkington – a player of light build and gentlemanly conduct on and off the field – would be able to last out in the hurly-burly of Second Division football. He need not have been concerned as it was 'business as usual' from Athletic's durable veteran, who even moved back to inside-right for much of the 1924–25 season and finished as joint leading scorer.

Pilkington lost out to new signing Albert Pynegar after three matches of season 1925–26. For once the side scored plenty of goals, the new off-side law having some bearing. Later in the season he returned at centre-half in place of Tommy Heaton but he left in the close season to join Llandudno. His benefit match against West Bromwich Albion in March 1921 accurately reflected his popularity with the Oldham public, a crowd of 19,440 attending. After retiring from the game, he was in business as a coal merchant in his native Radcliffe.

Billy Porter

Date of birth: July 1905, Fleetwood
Died: 28 April 1946, Manchester

Oldham Athletic record:
Appearances: League 274, FA Cup 10
Goals: League 1
Debut: Southampton (h) 31 January 1928, won 3–1

Also played for: Windsor Villa, Fleetwood FC, Manchester United (World War Two guest player with Oldham
Athletic, Manchester City, Blackburn Rovers, Accrington Stanley, Newcastle United), Hyde United
(player-manager)

Billy Porter graduated from local junior football and was signed by his home-town team, Fleetwood, in November
1925 at the age of 20. In his only season with the club, they won the Lancashire Combination Cup and finished fourth
in the League table.

In May 1926 the Latics signed Porter and his close friend, goalkeeper Jack Hacking, with all negotiations for the
dual signing taking place at Hacking's home in Fleetwood. Both players began in the Central League, Porter first
appearing at left full-back against Bradford City Reserves (h) in a 4–0 win on 11 September. Later in the same month
tragedy struck when he suffered a broken leg, bringing his season to a premature end.

Porter was eased back into action in a reserve-team friendly match against Northern Nomads on 24 September
1927 after a year on the sidelines. In January of the same season he made his first-team debut at left full-back
against Southampton and made a winning start. Goals from Jack King and Cliff Stanton (2) accounted for the Saints
in a 3–1 victory that maintained the side's excellent home record – undefeated in 13 League matches at that point.

Porter finished with 10 League appearances to his name in 1927–28 but became a regular first-team player in
the following season, taking over from Harry Grundy and commencing with his long partnership at full-back
alongside Teddy Ivill. Never known to venture over the halfway line, he scored his solitary goal from the penalty spot
at Reading on 5 January 1929. There was little cause for celebration, however, as the Latics lost 6–1. Four of
Reading's goals that day were scored by centre-forward Billy Johnstone, who joined the Latics two years later to
become part of an inside-forward trio of Johnson, Johnstone and Johnston – a football historian's nightmare!

Porter missed just one match in season 1929–30 when the Latics came so very near to promotion to the top
flight. Over the next five seasons he missed only six League matches, his consistently polished displays eventually
leading to inevitable interest from bigger clubs.

By a strange coincidence, Porter's final League appearance for the Latics was against Southampton at Boundary
Park on 5 January 1935. The same fixture had marked his club debut, just short of seven years previously. It was
Manchester United who signed him, and in season 1935–36 he assisted them to the Championship of Division Two,
appearing in all 42 League matches during the season.

Well known for his ability and willingness to help younger players, Porter's coaching of the emerging Johnny
Carey was spontaneously rewarded in September 1938 when the 19-year-old Irishman presented Porter with his first
cap. This had been awarded that month for his appearance in the FA of Ireland (Eire) team versus Switzerland at
Dalymount Park, Dublin.

During the period of World War Two, Porter's work at Metropolitan Vickers enabled him to continue to play, and
he captained United through several seasons of wartime football. He also made several guest appearances for the
Latics in wartime season 1944–45 when, according to his son Brian, the Chadderton Road stand was not open to
spectators because there was ammunition stored beneath it!

Porter's untimely death occurred at the Manchester Royal Infirmary on 28 April 1946 – he was only 40 years old.
One of the pallbearers at his Fleetwood funeral was his friend and former teammate, England international
goalkeeper Jack Hacking. Also in attendance were Jimmy Naylor, a former Athletic teammate, and Bert Whalley,
representing Manchester United. Jack Hacking's floral tribute was touchingly inscribed 'Deepest sympathy and
lasting memory for one who was more than a teammate.'

Albert Pynegar

Date of birth: 24 September 1895, Basford, Notts
Died: 26 March 1978, Basford, Notts

Oldham Athletic record:
Appearances: League 131, FA Cup 7
Goals: League 51, FA Cup 4
Debut: Barnsley (h) 29 August 1925, won 2–1

Also played for: Eastwood Rangers, Sutton Town, Leicester City, Coventry City, Port Vale, Chesterfield, Rotherham United, Sutton Town (again)

Albert Pynegar was a miner at Watnall Colliery when he began with Eastwood Rangers, a Nottingham Combination side. After 18 months he left to join Central Alliance team Sutton Town, where his goalscoring abilities brought a move to Leicester City in May 1920. Despite his relatively late start in senior football – he was about three weeks short of his 25th birthday when he made his debut – he made speedy progress. In all competitions he scored 61 goals in his first season at Filbert Street, his total including six goals on his reserve-team debut and two against Bury when he made his League debut. Despite his excellent record as a marksman, he lacked first-team opportunities and left after almost four years, having scored 21 goals in 48 League and Cup matches.

Pynegar's 27 goals in 54 League matches for Coventry City were well up to his usual standards, but it was insufficient to prevent his team from being relegated from Division Two in season 1924–25. He joined Athletic in July 1925 for a fee of £1,200 and was initially fielded at centre-forward but moved to inside-right to accommodate Arthur Ormston after three matches. The positional change was immediately successful as Ormston, who cost a paltry £25 from Wigan Borough, scored a hat-trick on his debut against Fulham and followed with five against Stoke City just two days later.

Pynegar took eight matches before scoring his first goal at Middlesbrough but thereafter was regularly among the scorers, ending his first season at Boundary Park by netting four in an 8–3 win against Nottingham Forest in the final fixture. His 16 goals for the campaign included three in four FA Cup ties, and he remains in the club's record books to this day. The 10–1 third-round victory against Lytham – in which he scored twice – still stands as Athletic's record Cup victory.

In the following two seasons, the lightly-built and balding inside man led the scoring charts with 19 goals in both 1926–27 and 1927–28. A spirited forager, despite his lack of physical advantage, many of his goals were scored from close range. His deft footwork when in sight of the goal resulted in a high proportion of his strikes as the outcome of 'one-on-one' confrontations with opposing goalkeepers.

In what proved to be Pynegar's final season at Boundary Park, the team, little changed from the side that finished 7th in the Second Division, lost their opening fixture at Tottenham Hotspur 1–4. After 10 matches they were at the foot of the table with a record of: Won 1, Lost 9, For 8, Against 23, Points 2. Pynegar lost his place in the struggling side and in January 1929 was part of a player-exchange deal, including a cash adjustment, involving Port Vale's centre-forward Stewart Littlewood.

Neither player had managed to secure a regular place in the first team of the club concerned, but following the exchange both scored freely in the Second Division, leaving both parties in the transaction well satisfied. Pynegar made his debut at inside-left for Port Vale at Millwall on 19 January 1929 in a 1–2 defeat. Despite his contribution of 10 League goals in 18 matches, Vale suffered relegation from Division Two that season. Their stay in Division Three was of the shortest duration, however, as in 1929–30 they won the Championship of the Northern Section, with Pynegar scoring 20 League goals in 29 appearances.

In October 1930 Chesterfield paid £250 for the veteran sharpshooter, and he picked up a second consecutive Northern Section Championship medal, his contribution an impressive 26 goals in 29 games. On the eve of his 37th birthday, he made his final move in League circles when he joined Rotherham United in August 1932. He retired in the close season with career aggregate figures of 174 League goals in 366 matches. Incidentally, his curious surname is correctly pronounced if rhymed with vinegar.

Mike Quinn

Date of birth: 2 May 1962, Liverpool

Oldham Athletic record:
Appearances: League 78(2), FA Cup 2, League Cup 4
Goals: League 34, FA Cup 1, League Cup 2
Debut: Cambridge United (h) 4 February 1984, drawn 0–0

Also played for: Derby County, Wigan Athletic, Stockport County, Portsmouth, Newcastle United, Coventry City, Plymouth Argyle on loan, Watford on loan, Hong Kong football, PAOK (Greece)

After being watched repeatedly by Athletic in the early months of season 1983–84, manager Joe Royle eventually agreed to pay Stockport County £52,000 for the 21-year-old Liverpudlian centre-forward. Although modest enough by today's standards, the fee involved was a huge investment for a club struggling to survive in Division Two, with home attendance figures hovering around the 4,000 mark. Quinn's abilities as a goalscorer were not in doubt, but the fact that he was moving up two Divisions brought into question whether his rich vein of goals would continue at a higher level.

Quinn began with Derby County but did not graduate beyond apprentice level. He was signed by Wigan Athletic in September 1979 and assisted the other Latics to their first-ever promotion in League circles when they finished third in Division Four in 1981–82. He left Springfield Park in July 1982 and made an immediate impact with Stockport County, scoring 24 goals in his first season. At the time of his move to Athletic in January 1984, he had already scored 17.

After an initial run-out with Athletic Reserves, when he scored one and laid on another in a 3–1 win against Barnsley Reserves, Quinn made his first-team debut against fellow strugglers Cambridge United. Only 3,943 spectators turned up for the scoreless encounter that featured heroics from the visitors' goalkeeper Malcolm Webster, who denied Quinn a debut goal three times. One week later, in a display of power and aggression, he brought Athletic their second away win of the season at Huddersfield Town, his first goal for the club ending a miserable sequence of away defeats. Three wins in the season's final four matches steered Athletic away from the threat of relegation.

Five goals in 14 matches constituted a modest start for Quinn, but in the following two seasons, prior to his £150,000 transfer to Portsmouth, the burly Scouser exhibited an in-built radar for goals. Powerful, aggressive and hard working, he was also most adept at turning defenders when in 'back-to-goal' positions, a tactic that created many of his scoring opportunities. Quinn led the scoring charts in 1984–85 with 18 League goals, one in the FA Cup and two in the League Cup. He rounded off the season with a magnificent hat-trick at Carlisle United in a stunning 5–2 victory. His 21 goals made him the third-highest marksman in the Second Division behind John Aldridge of Oxford United and David Geddis of Birmingham City, two players whose clubs won promotion that season.

Athletic transferred talented midfielder Mark Ward to West Ham United for £250,000, three days before the opening fixture of 1985–86. Incoming summer transfers included Ron Futcher from Barnsley for a bargain fee of £15,000, and the big, blond striker soon forged a good understanding with Quinn. In the first three months of the season the side scored plenty of goals, with Palmer, Futcher and Quinn scoring most of them. In October goalkeeper Andy Goram – born at Bury – was called up to Scotland's squad on the recommendation of manager Joe Royle. Not to be outdone, Quinn asked his manager to recommend him to Italy! Normally chatty, Joe Royle was stuck for words, although Quinn's mother was of Italian stock, and his father Irish.

At the time of Quinn's £150,000 transfer to Portsmouth, Athletic were reported to be losing in the region of £3,000 per week. All were sad to see him depart, but his transfer was absolutely necessary in the circumstances. It was denied by Athletic at the time, but one felt that the upcoming outlay of around £385,000 for the new artificial pitch in the summer of 1986 had some bearing on the decision to part with their star forward.

Quinn's subsequent success was reflected in his escalating value on the transfer market. Newcastle United paid £680,000 for him in August 1989, and he scored four goals against Leeds United on his debut – 34 goals in total – a figure that made him the Football League's leading scorer for the season. In terms of League goals alone, he totalled 228 in 481(34) matches. After leaving football he switched to horse racing, initially joining Mick Channon at his Hampshire training complex.

Beau Ratcliffe

Date of birth: 24 April 1909, Bolton-on-Dearne, Yorkshire
Died: 30 March 2003, Overpool, Cheshire

Oldham Athletic record:
Appearances: League 156, FA Cup 6
Goals: League 1
Debut: Mansfield Town (a) 31 August 1935, lost 0–1

Also played for: Bradford Park Avenue amateur, Charlton Athletic trial, New Brighton, Le Havre (France), Reading, Watford, Runcorn (player-manager), Earlestown (player-coach)

Standing at 5ft 11in and weighing 13st, Beau Ratcliffe was a commanding presence at either full-back or centre-half. With a heart to match his physique, he became an inspiring captain as well as a keen student of the game. He began as an amateur with Bradford Park Avenue, but his League career commenced with New Brighton – a Third Division North club at that time. He made his debut against Hartlepools United on 10 October 1931 and in four seasons with the Rakers made 131 League appearances and scored four goals.

After a brief spell with Le Havre in France, Ratcliffe returned to New Brighton where the club were appealing for financial help in order to keep going. It was therefore not surprising that the club were obliged to sell off several of their best players. Three of them joined the Latics; in addition to Ratcliffe, centre-forward Tommy Davis and wing half-back Charlie Butler were added to the Latics pay roll.

At the close of season 1934–35, following relegation from Division Two, Athletic handed free transfers to 11 professionals and placed centre-forward Tommy Reid 'open to offers' on the transfer list. Their trio of signings from New Brighton formed only part of a concerted recruitment drive, the first League match in Division Three North featuring six players making their debut.

During his first season at Boundary Park, Ratcliffe occupied both full-back berths and missed only four first-team matches during the campaign. He also scored his only Latics goal against Southport in a 4–0 victory at Boundary Park in the penultimate League fixture of the season.

Seventh place was deemed disappointing as all had hoped for a quick return to the Second Division. Billy Walsh had enjoyed a prolific season from centre-forward with 32 League goals, two in the FA Cup and three in the Third Division North Cup. Sadly, his prowess had not gone unnoticed, and he was snapped up by Heart of Midlothian in the close season.

In 1936–37 Ratcliffe switched to centre-half, a position he retained until the outbreak of World War Two. Successive finishes of fourth, fourth and fifth in the table had seen the Latics as serious contenders for the title of Champions, but with only one promotion place available their best chance came in 1937–38 when Tranmere Rovers took the title with 56 points – Athletic, in fourth place, had 51.

Ratcliffe's Latics career ended on 4 September 1939 when club secretary-manager Bob Mellor called him into his office, along with vice-captain Billy Hilton, to advise them that all players' contracts had been terminated due to the war situation and the suspension of League football by the Government.

Ratcliffe had an eventful war, in which he served as a Corporal in the RAF. At various times he made guest appearances for New Brighton, Reading, Southport, Manchester United, Tranmere Rovers and Arsenal. He also played in representative football for the Central Mediterranean Forces in Italy before being hospitalised with a shoulder wound and then taken as a prisoner of war. In late March 1945 he returned home following his release from captivity and was immediately selected to play for Tranmere Rovers on the following Saturday!

When League football resumed in season 1946–47, Ratcliffe joined Reading and was 39 years old when Watford signed him in May 1948. Outside of football, he was for many years a butcher in Birkenhead.

Neil Redfearn

Date of birth: 20 June 1965, Dewsbury

Oldham Athletic record:
Appearances: League 56(6), FA Cup 7(1), League Cup 3
Goals: League 16, FA Cup 3, League Cup 1
Debut: Swindon Town (a) 13 January 1990, lost 2–3

Also played for: Nottingham Forest (apprentice), Bolton Wanderers, Lincoln City, Doncaster Rovers, Crystal Palace, Watford, Barnsley, Charlton Athletic, Bradford City, Wigan Athletic, Halifax Town, Boston United, Rochdale, Scarborough, Bradford Park Avenue
Managed: Scarborough

One of soccer's happy wanderers, Neil Redfearn's stay at Boundary Park was relatively brief – January 1990 to September 1991 – but he certainly etched his name in Athletic's folklore. In what manager Joe Royle memorably described as his 'pinch-me' season, his sweetly struck, injury-time penalty-kick against Sheffield Wednesday in May 1991 snatched the Second Division Championship in true 'Roy of the Rovers' fashion. A goal down after just two minutes and two goals behind within five minutes of the resumption of the second half to a slick Wednesday side, the writing appeared to be on the wall. The amazing comeback began with a goal from Ian Marshall, his 18th of the season. On 80 minutes, teenager Paul Bernard celebrated what was only his second League appearance with a fortunate equaliser, his snap shot taking a deflection past goalkeeper Kevin Pressman.

The moment of destiny was at hand. Late into injury time a surging run by Andy Barlow was abruptly halted inside the penalty area by a clumsy tackle from John Sheridan. It seemed that a lifetime had elapsed before the referee finished booking Wednesday's Danny Wilson for dissent and the police had cleared the already celebrating Latics fans from the pitch. As Redfearn's spot-kick arrowed into the bottom corner of the net, Boundary Park erupted. Athletic had pipped West Ham United by one point to take the Second Division title and a wonderful afternoon at Boundary Park was crowned when skipper Earl Barrett was presented with the Barclays League Eagle trophy.

Athletic were lying third in the table in January 1990 when Redfearn was signed from Watford for a fee of £150,000. In joining, he linked up again with his friend and former Vicarage Road colleague Rick Holden. He had played for Watford in an early round of the Littlewoods Cup, a factor that denied him a place in Athletic's run through to the Wembley Final against Nottingham Forest. He did, however, play in both the FA Cup semi-final and the replay against Manchester United. He made his Athletic debut, one day after signing, at Swindon Town. Athletic lost the promotion battle 3–2 in a game that also marked the first (and only) League appearance of defender Wayne Heseltine, who was substituted after 51 minutes. His replacement, Scott McGarvey, reduced the arrears when he scored his first goal for the club with a diving header.

Redfearn scored his first goal in the 3–0 win against Aston Villa in the sixth-round FA Cup tie at Boundary Park on 14 March. His first League goal followed six days later in the 4–0 victory against Bournemouth, and he also netted Athletic's goal in the season's final fixture, a 1–1 draw at Bradford City. The same opponents opened Athletic's 1990–91 season with a friendly match at Boundary Park, and the visitors won 3–2. When the serious business began, however, five straight wins commenced with a stunning 3–2 victory at Wolverhampton Wanderers, where Ian Marshall upstaged England centre-forward Steve Bull with two late strikes to complete his hat-trick. Redfearn scored 17 goals during the season, a wonderful return for a central midfielder. He helped himself to three goals within the space of three matches in December, commencing with Athletic's fifth in the 6–1 hammering of Brighton. A 4–1 victory and a League double against Wolves was followed by a 5–3 attacking extravaganza against Plymouth Argyle. Redfearn opened the scoring after just 80 seconds and followed with his 10th goal of the campaign on the hour. A second double followed in the 3–1 win in the third round of the FA Cup against Brentford. Both of his goals were penalties, and he commendably held his nerve when his second spot-kick was ordered to be retaken. Having beaten the 'keeper to his right, he stepped up again and calmly netted to the goalkeeper's left.

The return of Mike Milligan, after a season at Everton, brought Redfearn's time at Boundary Park to a close. He was transferred to Barnsley for £150,000 in September 1991 and remained at Oakwell for almost seven years, helping them to win promotion to the Premier League. He cost Charlton Athletic £1 million in July 1998, and when his League career finally ended at the age of 38 he had appeared in 852(37) League and Cup matches and scored 180 goals for 13 different clubs.

Steve Redmond

Date of birth: 2 November 1967, Liverpool

Oldham Athletic record:
Appearances: League 195(10), FA Cup 10(2), League Cup 20
Goals: League 4, League Cup 1
Debut: Chelsea (a) 15 August 1992, drawn 1–1

Also played for: Manchester City, Bury, Leigh RMI

Steve Redmond represented Liverpool and Merseyside Schools then joined Manchester City on schoolboy forms in October 1982. He signalled his immense promise by leading City's youth team to an aggregate 3–1 victory against Manchester United youth in April 1986. He had already made his Football League debut in a 2–0 win against Queen's Park Rangers (h) on 8 February 1986. In the following month he appeared at Wembley in the Full Members' Cup Final, won 5–4 by Chelsea. Redmond was ever present in season 1987–88 when he was voted City's Player of the Year and was named as the Blues youngest-ever skipper in 1988. He won England Youth and Under-21 caps and was captain of the Under-21 side in the qualifying stages of the European Championship matches in the autumn of 1988. In terms of League matches alone, he had totalled 231(4) and seven goals by the time of his transfer to the Latics.

Redmond arrived at Boundary Park in July 1992 in a somewhat complex 'exchange plus cash' deal. Manager Joe Royle was obviously intent on strengthening his defence for the club's first season in the newly formed Premier League; he took Redmond and Neil Pointon from Manchester City in exchange for Rick Holden, plus an adjustment in cash. Redmond made his debut on the opening Saturday of the 1992–93 season. 20,699 spectators saw Athletic draw with Chelsea thanks to an equalising goal from Nick Henry on 86 minutes – two minutes after Mick Harford had given Chelsea the lead. The Latics' first Premier League line up was as follows: Hallworth, Redmond, Barlow, Henry, Jobson, Marshall, Halle, Palmer (sub Tolson), Sharp, Milligan, Bernard. Athletic ended the season in 19th place, avoiding relegation with a late flourish of three wins against Aston Villa (a), Liverpool and Southampton (h). In the latter match, Redmond's former Manchester City colleague Neil Pointon opened the scoring in rather unusual fashion, direct from a corner-kick.

The 1993–94 season opened with a tour of Norway and Sweden and a testimonial match against Burnley for long-serving coach Billy Urmston. When the serious business commenced, Ipswich Town won 3–0 at Boundary Park on the opening day, with former Latics favourite Ian Marshall opening the scoring for the Suffolk club. A 1–0 win at Swindon Town followed, and in December the same opponents were beaten 2–1, Redmond scoring his first Athletic goal, which was the decider in a 2–1 win. He missed the Wembley FA Cup semi-final against Manchester United and was a substitute in the Maine Road replay, won 4–1 by United. A season plagued by injuries finally ended in relegation.

Back in Division One, Redmond made his 100th League appearance on 29 April 1995 in a 3–1 win against Bolton Wanderers. Athletic finished in 14th place, Redmond playing in 43 of the season's League matches and winning the Player of the Year award. He lost his central-defensive partner Richard Jobson, who was transferred to Leeds United in late October 1995 – a situation that left him very much the senior partner in a new combination with 19-year-old Richard Graham.

As Athletic kicked-off their 50th season of post-war football with a home Division Two match against Stoke City, I was reminded of my attendance, via the boy's entrance, for the first post-war match – a 0–2 home defeat by Carlisle United. The attendance figures for the two games were not dissimilar, with 7,696 versus Carlisle United and 8,021 versus Stoke City. Although 50 years apart, both sets of supporters went home disappointed as Stoke City took the points on 17 August 1996, despite a rare goal from Redmond in the 1–2 defeat. In a dire season for both him and the club, Division One status was lost and he suffered a serious knee-ligament injury mid-season, missing the remainder of the campaign.

Season 1997–98, back in Division Two, proved to be Redmond's last at Boundary Park. Although the team stood third in the table at the end of December, the promotion push faltered and the side finally finished 13th. In July 1998, after six years of consistent and totally committed service, he joined Bury on a free transfer. In five years at Gigg Lane he completed 145(6) League appearances and scored six goals to take his career aggregate to 571(20) League matches and 17 goals. Sadly, his final senior match for Bury was a 1–3 defeat by Bournemouth in the Division Three Play-off semi-final on 13 May 2003.

Paul Rickers

Date of birth: 9 May 1975, Pontefract

Oldham Athletic record:
Appearances: League 242(19), FA Cup 17(2), League Cup 13
Goals: League 20, League Cup 2
Debut: Stoke City (h) 22 October 1994, drawn 0–0

Also played for: Tadcaster FC, Northampton Town, Leigh RMI on loan, Farsley Celtic

Paul Rickers began with Leeds Schoolboys, where youthful colleagues included England Under-21 cap Noel Whelan (whose subsequent clubs have included Leeds United, Coventry City and Middlesbrough) and Richard Graham, the Athletic central-defender. Graham's career ran parallel with Rickers's at Boundary Park for nine seasons before he was forced to retire at the early age of 26 due to injury.

Rickers attended the Latics School of Excellence from the age of 14 and was signed on associate schoolboy forms in July 1990 despite overtures from several other interested parties, including Leeds United, Sheffield Wednesday and Bradford City. In the season of his senior debut, Rickers was a member of the Athletic party who toured the Isle of Man in July 1994. He scored twice against an Isle of Man XI in a 7–1 victory, and although replaced after 69 minutes by Nick Henry, he won the sponsor's Man of the Match award. In the following month he scored Athletic reserves' first goal of the Central League Division Two season against Sheffield Wednesday reserves.

Tireless and always busy in midfield, Rickers displayed excellent skill and awareness. Despite his relatively tender years he always appeared comfortable in possession and at the age of 19 made his senior debut, replacing Lee Richardson in the number-seven shirt, in the goalless encounter with Stoke City at Boundary Park. A glance at the line up reveals a team in transition, having lost their Premier League status in the previous season. The Athletic team that day was: Paul Gerrard, Gunnar Halle, Neil Pointon, Nick Henry, Richard Jobson, Steve Redmond, Paul Rickers, Nicky Banger, Richard Graham, Sean McCarthy, Rick Holden. They ended the season 14th in Division One; Rickers played in four matches and scored his first League goal against Bolton Wanderers in a 3–1 win at Boundary Park on 29 April 1995.

In 1995–96 Rickers appeared in half of the season's League matches, with his best run coming in late season when Athletic clawed their way out of the drop zone to finish 18th. Three wins and a draw in the final four matches ensured another season in Division One; however, the stay of execution proved short lived. Despite his best efforts – he never missed a match during the season – Athletic failed to avoid the drop into Division Two. His four League goals included a first-minute strike against Ipswich Town, which earned Athletic their first point of the season in a 3–3 draw and a double against the Wolves in the 3–2 win at Boundary Park in March.

For the next four seasons Rickers was consistency personified, averaging 41 League matches per season. He missed just one match – due to being involved in a car accident – in 1998–99. Most valuable among his four goals during that season was his strike in the 2–0 win against Reading on the last day of the campaign, a result that kept Athletic in the Second Division. He passed the milestone of 200 senior appearances in 1999–2000, while operating in a variety of midfield roles and at wing-back. A rare double strike by the industrious midfielder in 2000–01 advanced Athletic into round two of the Worthington Cup with First Division opponents Huddersfield Town being defeated in both legs – 1–0 at Boundary Park and 2–0 at the McAlpine Stadium.

For the first time since embarking on his five-year run of near ever-present senior action, Rickers was restricted to 13(11) League matches in 2001–02. At the close of the campaign, the 27-year-old rejected manager Ian Dowie's offer of a further one-year contract and in early July signed a two-year contract with Second Division rivals Northampton Town. His return to Boundary Park with his new employers on 29 October proved totally unrewarding. At 2–0 down after an hour's play, he was substituted as the Cobblers threw on an extra striker; however, the ploy misfired and Athletic ran out 4–0 winners. Worse was to follow as he suffered a broken leg mid-season. After just one substitute appearance in 2003–04, he was loaned to Conference members Leigh RMI in December, and in February of the same season his contract was cancelled by mutual consent. Sadly, he was unable to resurrect his career despite spending trial periods with Macclesfield Town, Dundalk and Bury. He subsequently stepped down into non-League football with Farsley Celtic of the Northern Premier League.

Andy Ritchie

Date of birth: 28 November 1960, Manchester

Oldham Athletic record:
Appearances: League 201(42), FA Cup 9(4), League Cup 20(2)
Goals: League 84, FA Cup 4, League Cup 19
Manager: May 1998–October 2001
Debut: West Bromwich Albion (a) 15 August 1987, drawn 0–0

Also played for: Manchester United, Brighton & Hove Albion, Leeds United, Scarborough
Also managed: Barnsley

On the eve of the 1987–88 season, Athletic had no fewer than 13 players under treatment for various injuries. Desperately short of numbers, manager Joe Royle was forced to gamble when he signed Andy Ritchie from Leeds United in mid-August. The gamble surrounded the fee to be paid, as Leeds valued the former Manchester United striker at £100,000, while Athletic offered around half of that. The issue was settled – very much in Athletic's favour it has to be said – when an independent tribunal ruled that the fee should be £50,000.

The start of what was to become a very long and successful association commenced at the Hawthorns on 15 August 1987. In weather more suited to cricket than football, a small crowd of 8,873 witnessed a scoreless encounter. Although Athletic's new Scottish international goalkeeper Andy Goram took the main honours, Athletic's 2,000 travelling supporters were instantly appreciative of the assured touch and obvious class of their team's most recent signing. In 36 League and two Cup matches in his first season, Ritchie tied with Roger Palmer as leading scorer, each netting 20 goals. It was the first time since 1970–71 that two marksmen had reached the 20 mark, Jim Fryatt (24) and David Shaw (23) being the last to do so in the Fourth Division promotion season. In 1988–89 Ritchie was top scorer with 16 goals in 34 appearances; Roger Palmer scored 15 and extended his overall total to 113, overtaking Eric Gemmell's 35-year-old all-time record of 109 League goals.

Ritchie's 28 goals in 1989–90 – the best of his career – included 10 in the Littlewoods Cup, a huge contribution towards Athletic's first-ever trip to Wembley. Despite a lengthy lay-off in the 1990–91 Second Division Championship season, he scored 15 goals in 30(2) matches. Probably accustomed to being a pin-up on fan's walls, local artist Walter Kershaw took the concept a stage further when he captured Ritchie for posterity in a 30ft mural, covering almost one wall at the Briar Mill at Shaw. Competition for first-team striking places increased when Athletic's ex-Everton contingent was further boosted by the signing of centre-forward Graeme Sharp, as the team prepared for life in the top flight. Ritchie suffered a calf muscle strain pre-season and missed the six-match tour of Sweden. Although he celebrated his first senior start of the season by scoring four goals in the 7–1 demolition of Torquay United in late September, an injury-hit season saw him restricted to just 7(7) First Division matches.

Increasingly troubled by injuries in subsequent seasons, Ritchie nevertheless celebrated his 100th goal for the club during season 1994–95, his 13 League and Cup goals including a hat-trick against Port Vale (h) in the 3–2 win on 10 December 1994. He joined Scarborough on a free transfer in August 1995, but he was back at Boundary Park as player-coach in February 1997. The move coincided with Graeme Sharp's departure and the appointment of Neil Warnock as manager. His playing days were drawing to a close, his last goal coming in the 3–0 win against Wrexham (h) on 27 January 1998. In May of the same year he succeeded Neil Warnock, whose contract was not renewed.

Athletic avoided relegation by the narrowest of margins in Ritchie's first season in charge. They finished in 20th position, one point above the drop zone. After losing the first five matches of 1999–2000, a better second half of the campaign saw them finish in 14th place in Division Two. A very similar season in 2000–01 started badly – one win in 11 matches – and ended in another mid-table finish. In August 2001 new chairman and owner Chris Moore somewhat rashly 'guaranteed' that Athletic would be back in Division One within three years. Early indications were that his predictions might have some basis in fact, as the side stood proudly atop the table on 29 September with a record of six wins, five draws and one defeat. At the end of the following month, however, only one point had been taken from five matches, and Ritchie was sacked. He was offered, but declined, a position on the board as technical director. Moving into coaching, after a spell at Leeds United he joined Barnsley and in May 2005 was appointed manager. Twelve months on, he has led his team to promotion from Division One by overcoming Swansea City in the Play-off Final at the Millennium Stadium.

Charlie Roberts

Date of birth: 6 April 1883, Darlington
Died: 7 August 1939, Manchester

Oldham Athletic record:
Appearances: League 72, FA Cup 7
Goals: League 2
Manager: June 1921–December 1922
Debut: Bolton Wanderers (a) 6 September 1913, lost 2–6

Also played for: Bishop Auckland, Grimsby Town, Manchester United, England (3 caps)

Just prior to the 1913–14 season, the Latics pulled off a deal that shook the soccer world and came as a bombshell to the supporters of Manchester United. One of the very best centre-halves of his day, Charlie Roberts had been the backbone of the United defence for nine years, and it was generally expected that he would finish his career at Old Trafford. Apparently in disagreement over a second benefit with United's directors, it was nevertheless a shock when it was announced that he had been transferred to the Latics for a fee of £1,750. Mr David Ashworth was the Latics manager responsible for his signing, and Roberts proved to be worth every penny of the club record fee.

Tall, slim and pale faced, Roberts tackled, passed and controlled the ball with exceptional ability and was also virtually unbeatable in the air. All in all, he was a superb pivot; in his first season at Boundary Park he did not miss a League or Cup match and led the side to finish fourth from the top of the First Division.

Season 1914–15 commenced with a 3–1 victory against his old club Manchester United, and the side were defeated only once in their first 14 League engagements. The all-international half-back line of Moffatt, Roberts and David Wilson seemed certain to drive the Latics to their first-ever Football League Championship, but a total lapse in form by the forward line prevented the issue from being made safe long before the closing month of the season.

In the event, the club's supporters were left downcast and thinking of 'what might have been'. With ground advantage they needed to take three points from the last two games against Burnley and Liverpool. Both were lost, and Everton took the title by the slender margin of one point, with the Latics finishing as runners-up. Despite missing out on the top prize, the season was a successful one in a playing sense. Financially, however, due to the season commencing with World War One a month old, season tickets sales were greatly reduced as it was doubtful whether football would be able to continue through the season.

League football was disbanded from 1915–16 until the end of the conflict. When it resumed in 1919–20, Roberts was not sufficiently recovered from a serious knee injury sustained at Stoke in a wartime match, and despite further hospital treatment in June 1919 he was unable to play again.

Installed as Athletic's manager in July 1921, in succession to Mr Herbert Bamlett, Roberts found the transition to management a difficult task. He was, in fact, anxiety personified and could often be seen pacing up and down behind the grandstand during a match, quite unable to watch. Only a late revival secured 19th place in Division One when relegation had looked inevitable. Despite a bright opening to the new season, an almighty slump followed, and in December Roberts resigned, to be replaced by David Ashworth, the manager who had first brought him to Boundary Park in 1913.

A founder member of the Players' Union and its chairman until September 1921, Roberts's early involvement in the movement, which found little initial favour with the game's authorities, was always considered a contributory factor to his comparative lack of international recognition.

After leaving the game, Roberts was in business as a wholesale tobacconist. One of his lines was a cigarette named 'Ducrobel', named after the legendary Manchester United half-back line: Duckworth, Roberts and Bell!

Ian Robins

Date of birth: 22 February 1952, Bury

Oldham Athletic record:
Appearances: League 202(18), FA Cup 12(1), League Cup 4(2)
Goals: League 40, FA Cup 3, League Cup 3
Debut: Port Vale (a) 13 December 1969, lost 0–1

Also played for: Bury, Huddersfield Town

In his first season at Boundary Park, Ian Robins played regularly for the A team and made his debut for the reserves against Chorley reserves on 14 October 1967, at the tender age of 15. In the following month he scored in the first round of the FA Youth Cup against Eccleshill (Bradford) Youth in a 4–1 win at Boundary Park. In his earliest days an orthodox outside-left, he was considered an outstanding prospect with nice balance, plenty of confidence and a sweet left foot. It was a testament to Athletic's youth policy of that time that all 11 players who opposed Eccleshill subsequently reached senior level, with Ronnie Blair the other outstanding prospect.

Robins was selected for England Youth trials and made his first-team debut at Port Vale on 13 December 1969, in the final month of Jack Rowley's second spell as Latics manager. Steve Hoolickin – elder brother of Garry – also made his debut in the same match. A single goal scored by Ian Buxton, perhaps better known as the Derbyshire cricketer, settled the issue in Port Vale's favour. Robins retained his place for the Boxing Day meeting with Workington. Too much Christmas cheer was suspected when goalkeeper Alan Taylor, on loan from Blackpool, was beaten twice within 19 minutes of the kick-off. In the second half Keith Bebbington missed from the penalty spot, his kick clearing the bar by some distance. Although Robins marked his home debut with a goal in the 75th minute, despite sustained late pressure Athletic could not find an equaliser and went down 2–1.

As new manager Jimmy Frizzell successfully set about lifting the side from the doldrums, Robins continued to develop at reserve level and saw little first-team action until 1971–72. The departure of Jim Fryatt to Southport in November 1971 left a vacancy that Robins seized to great effect. He was first tried in the number-nine shirt in a friendly match against Huddersfield Town on 30 November, to mark the opening of the new Ford Stand on the Broadway side of Boundary Park. Robins retained the position for the trip to Blackburn Rovers on 4 December, where Athletic took the points with a 1–0 victory. This was achieved despite the loss of goalkeeper Harry Dowd after 25 minutes, with Maurice Whittle starring as his deputy. He scored eight League goals in 23(1) matches, two of them coming in the season's best victory – 6–0 against Barnsley.

Robins scored 10 League goals in 1972–73 when Athletic reached fourth place in Division Three. Although his scoring touch was less evident in 1973–74, his shrewd promptings from central midfield were a key element in the team's Championship success. Throughout the campaign, goals were scored from almost every position on the field, no fewer than six players ending the season with a double-figure total. As Athletic strove to establish themselves in Division Two, Robins was leading goalscorer in their first season among higher company with nine, the most memorable being scored at Old Trafford in a stirring encounter that ended 3–2 to Manchester United, witnessed by a crowd of 56,618.

Robins made his 200th League start for the Latics against Chelsea at Boundary Park on 19 April 1977. It is interesting to reflect that the side fielded in the goalless encounter contained no fewer than five players with the experience of 200 or more League matches in the Latics colours. Heading the list was Ian Wood (408), followed by Maurice Whittle (305), Ronnie Blair (232) and David Shaw (207).

Robins added little to his total as he was transferred to Bury for £25,000 in July 1977. Thirteen months later he joined Huddersfield Town, and in 1979–80 he scored Town's 100th goal of the campaign in the season's final fixture against Hartlepool, the 2–1 win clinching the Fourth Division Championship ahead of Walsall. He finished as leading scorer in each of his first two seasons at Leeds Road and his 25 in 45 matches in 1979–80 won him a place in the PFA Fourth Division select team for the season. He was a regular goalscorer for four seasons and totalled 67 in 163(23) League and Cup matches. He surprised Town's fans when he announced his retirement in May 1982.

Ten years later, Robins was still playing as a reinstated amateur with Pemberton Central of the Wigan Amateur League and at 40 years of age was awarded the Second Division Player of the Year trophy.

Joe Royle

Date of birth: 8 April 1949, Norris Green, Liverpool

Oldham Athletic record:
Manager: June 1982–November 1994

Also managed: Everton, Manchester City, Ipswich Town
Played for: Everton, Manchester City, Bristol City, Norwich City, England (6 caps)

Joe Royle became the youngest player to represent Everton when he made his debut at the age of 16 at Blackpool in a First Division match on 15 January 1965. He established himself as the Toffees regular centre-forward from season 1967–68, his bustling powerful style and superb headwork netting him 102 League goals and a Football League Championship medal in 1970.

Royle won 10 England Under-23 caps, represented the Football League and was awarded the first of his six full England caps against Malta in 1971, with his last coming against Luxembourg at Wembley in 1977. He joined Manchester City in December 1974 and was a Football League Cup winner against Newcastle United in February 1976. Spells with Bristol City and Norwich City followed, but two major back operations and finally a knee injury enforced his retirement in April 1982. His career aggregate figures totalled 467(7) League matches and 152 goals.

The ever-smiling and affable Royle arrived at Boundary Park on the back of a lorry, after his maroon-coloured Daimler broke down en route to Oldham, and he had to thumb a lift to get to the press conference scheduled to announce his surprise appointment. He was selected from a shortlist of three, whittled down from 30 applicants. Athletic's directors had advertised for a player-manager, but they were unanimous in their selection of Royle, despite the fact that he had no managerial experience and his playing days were over. His request for a one-year contract – which he felt would be long enough for both parties to decide whether he was up to the job – was approved by Athletic's board, whose earlier decision to remove the hugely popular Jimmy Frizzell had left a bitter taste.

Royle's first signing was goalkeeper Martin Hodge on a three-month loan agreement from Everton. For his first competitive match in charge, he selected the following XI to oppose Shrewsbury Town at Boundary Park on 28 August 1982: Hodge, Sinclair, Ryan, Keegan, Clements, Futcher, Heaton (sub Steel), Atkinson, Humphries, Wylde, Palmer. A powerful left-foot shot from John Ryan, deflected off Shrewsbury's Ross MacLaren, proved sufficient to get Athletic's new boss off to a winning start by 1–0. Despite losing Paul Futcher in January – sold to Derby County for £114,000 to relieve cash-flow problems – promotion hopes remained alive for much of the season, but, despite only nine League defeats, too many drawn matches resulted in a seventh-place finish.

A vast change in fortunes occurred in Royle's second season in charge. Injuries took a devastating toll and new signings, with the exception of Mark Ward, failed to impress. A points tally of 47 proved just enough to finish one place above the drop zone. Eighteen League goals from Mick Quinn and the £250,000 transfer of teenage star Wayne Harrison to Liverpool were the main features of 1984–85 when the team finished in 14th position. A season of steady progress and an eighth place finish was rewarded in May 1986 when Royle accepted a new contract to keep him at Boundary Park for a further three years.

A Play-off semi-final defeat by Leeds United in May 1987 was a tragic ending to a season of rich promise, but it proved to be a launch pad to better times. Athletic lost only two of their last 20 games of 1988–89, and in December 1989, Royle was offered a short cut to the First Division by Manchester City, but, to the relief of all, he opted to stay to fulfil his ambition of taking Athletic into the top flight. A season of magnificent Cup exploits saw the side reach the semi-final of the FA Cup and the Wembley Final of the Littlewoods Cup. In May 1991 Royle was named Second Division Manager of the Year, crowning his achievement of finally leading Athletic to the Second Division Championship.

A narrow 2–1 defeat at Liverpool opened Athletic's first season in the top flight, but, on their new grass pitch and new look 'Chaddy End' stand, they thrashed Chelsea 3–0 to record their first win in the top flight for 68 years. The fact that they survived for three seasons among the elite of the football world was greatly to the credit of all at Boundary Park, as was the manager's policy of attacking, entertaining football. At the time of writing, Royle was the last English manager to lift the FA Cup when his Everton side beat Manchester United 1–0 at Wembley in 1995.

John Ryan

Date of birth: 18 February 1962, Failsworth

Oldham Athletic record:
Appearances: League 97(3), FA Cup 4, League Cup 8
Goals: League 8
Debut: Cardiff City (h) 29 August 1981, drawn 2–2

Also played for: Seattle Sounders (US) on loan, Newcastle United, Sheffield Wednesday, Mansfield Town, Chesterfield, Rochdale, Bury, Stalybridge Celtic, Radcliffe Borough

A product of Manchester schools football, John Ryan signed apprentice forms with the Latics in June 1978. In a somewhat unusual career move, he was loaned to Seattle Sounders of the North American Soccer League before signing professional forms at Boundary Park. At the start of his American adventure, he scored against Tulsa Roughnecks on his debut at the Kingdrome in a 3–4 defeat on 30 March 1979. He returned to Seattle for a second season in 1980, scoring six goals in 33 matches and appearing in the Play-offs for the National Conference title.

Ryan made his first-team debut for Athletic in the opening fixture of season 1981–82. Both he and the team made a bright start, with five wins and four draws from the season's first nine Second Division fixtures. Form evaporated mid-season, however, with a run of 18 matches that produced just two wins. The slump was to cost popular manager Jimmy Frizzell his job. In his first season Ryan appeared in 37 League matches and five FA Cup ties.

Under new manager Joe Royle, Ryan's distinct promise was fully realised. From the opening match of the season against Shrewsbury Town (h) on 28 August, his adventurous raiding down the left flank earned Athletic the points. His fierce left-foot shot, following a surging run from the halfway line, deflected off a defender to leave goalkeeper Ogrizovic stranded. His first League goal was a stunning strike. Scored just before the interval against Carlisle United (h) on 23 October, it was rifled home from a full 30 yards after Carlisle had partly cleared a corner-kick. In the following week Ryan was on the mark again, scoring the winner against Burnley in a 2–1 victory at Turf Moor.

Ryan's scoring streak continued in the opener against Wolverhampton Wanderers with a curling left-foot volley, giving Athletic a 1–0 lead at the interval. A Rodger Wylde hat-trick in the second half sealed a famous 4–1 victory. Towards the end of the season, Ryan was voted as the best left-back in the Second Division by his fellow professionals. The All-Stars team also included such famous names as Kevin Keegan, Andy Gray and Mick McCarthy. Ryan finished the season with eight goals in 40 League matches and was considered very unfortunate to have been left out of the England Under-23 squad for the European Championship game against Greece at Portsmouth. He was, however, subsequently capped by England Under-21 against Hungary at St James' Park, Newcastle. Some four months later he became a Newcastle United player.

Ever-present financial considerations led to his departure, the Magpies paying £225,000 to take him to Tyneside. Ryan appeared in 22 matches in Newcastle's 1983–84 promotion-winning side, but new manager Jack Charlton transferred him to Sheffield Wednesday within two months of taking over as Newcastle's manager. Despite a bright start at Hillsborough – he scored on his home debut against Leicester City – he failed to hold down a first-team place, and in August 1985 he was welcomed back to Boundary Park. With Paul Atkinson already back in the fold – he returned from Watford a month earlier – the prospect of restoring their partnership of two seasons ago was eagerly awaited. Their first pairing certainly delighted the enthusiastic band of Latics supporters at Sunderland on 26 August. A typical surging run from Ryan and a cracking left-foot drive beat goalkeeper McDonagh but struck the base of the far post. The ever-alert Mike Quinn was on hand to steer home the rebound. Athletic went on to win 3–0 and record only their second ever victory at Roker Park.

Ryan was sent off at Shrewsbury on 7 December and virtually condemned Athletic to their fifth defeat in six matches. His suspension opened the way for Andy Barlow, who held the left-back position for the remainder of the season. In a pre-season friendly at Tranmere Rovers in August 1986, Ryan sustained a double fracture of his left leg. He had scored Athletic's first goal in a 4–2 win before being stretchered off in the 41st minute. Sadly, he was destined to play just one more game, in which he was substituted at half-time, before he embarked on a round of lower Division football, the highlight of which was a Wembley appearance for Chesterfield in the Division Four Play-off Final in 1990.

Graeme Sharp

Date of birth: 16 October 1960, Glasgow

Oldham Athletic record:
Appearances: League 103(6), FA Cup 11(1), League Cup 12(1)
Goals: League 30, FA Cup 2, League Cup 4
Debut: Liverpool (a) 17 August 1991, lost 1–2

Also played for: Eastercraigs FC, Dumbarton, Everton, Scotland (12 caps)
Managed: Oldham Athletic, Bangor City

Athletic's manager Joe Royle had a busy month in the transfer market in July 1991, in preparation for the club's return to the First Division after an absence of 68 years. First to arrive was Mike Milligan, returning after a 12-month stay at Everton, for a fee of £600,000. One week later 30-year-old Graeme Sharp was the next recruit from Goodison Park, signed for £500,000. As Sharp arrived, Paul Warhurst departed to Sheffield Wednesday for a fee of £750,000.

In the year of his transfer, Sharp became the second highest Everton marksman behind 'Dixie' Dean, his Everton record closing with the following figures: League: 306(16) appearances, 111 goals. Cups: 119(5) appearances, 47 goals. He assisted the Goodison Park club to win the Football League Championship twice, as well as the FA Cup, the European Cup-winners' Cup and four Charity Shields.

In earliest days, Dumbarton's manager Davie Wilson nearly got the sack after paying £750 for Sharp, but he well justified the modest outlay as he was soon a regular in the side and scored 16 goals in 34 League games in his second season. He spent a week with Aberdeen and a brief trial period with Aston Villa before Everton manager Gordon Lee swooped for his signature in April 1980.

Although Athletic had been the second highest scorers in the Football League in 1990–91, manager Royle still felt that the team lacked a target man, and he considered that Sharp was still the best one in the country. His confidence was not misplaced, as the experienced front man had all the necessary qualities for his position. He held the ball up well, was excellent in the air and lacked nothing in courage and determination.

Sharp certainly benefitted from Athletic's attacking style of play and the variety of attacking options available. He opened his account against Torquay United in a League Cup tie at Boundary Park, with a 51st-minute header from a floated free-kick by Paul Kane. Athletic's forwards enjoyed a field day, Andy Ritchie scoring four in the 7–1 romp. In April 1992 Sharp scored all four of Athletic's goals in their 4–1 home win against Luton Town and finished his first season at Boundary Park with 15 in 48 League and Cup matches.

In the 1992–93 season, when Athletic effected an unlikely escape from relegation from the Premier League by winning their final three matches, Sharp scored seven Premier League goals in 20(1) appearances, but his consecutive run of 74 games was broken in January when he was relegated to the substitutes' bench. Sadly, in the same month, it was announced that he was to undergo a back operation to cure a disc problem, and he was sidelined for the remainder of the season.

In 1993–94 Athletic progressed to the semi-final of the FA Cup but lost their Premier League status. Sharp made his first full appearance of the season against Aston Villa on 25 September and made 31(3) League appearances. He was leading scorer with nine goals, plus a further two in the League Cup.

In November of the following season Sharp was appointed player-manager following Joe Royle's departure to Everton. Although he had scored in each of the season's opening two matches, he played little following his managerial appointment, his final appearance coming on 14 January 1994 against Sunderland in a 0–0 draw at Boundary Park.

Sharp's managerial career was terminated – along with that of his assistant Colin Harvey – on 11 February 1997. The team had spent the entire season in and around the relegation places of Division One, and Neil Warnock's arrival came too late to avoid the drop into Division Two. As manager of Bangor City, he led his team to victory in the Welsh Cup in May 1998 and qualification for the European Cup-winners' Cup competition of 1998–99.

David Shaw

Date of birth: 11 October 1948, Huddersfield

Oldham Athletic record:
Appearances: League 210(4), FA Cup 9, League Cup 5
Goals: League 91, FA Cup 2, League Cup 2
Debut: Darlington (h) 27 September 1969, drawn 1–1

Also played for: Huddersfield Town, West Bromwich Albion

David Shaw followed family tradition when he joined the Leeds Road ground staff, initially as an amateur in October 1965, before signing professional in January 1967. His famous grandfather was David Steele, the Huddersfield Town and Scotland international player, who won a hat-trick of Football League Championships between the years 1923 and 1926 and later managed the Leeds Road club.

Shaw made his Town debut against Birmingham City at St Andrews on 28 April 1967 and held his place for the final two matches of the season. In the following term he played in 14(2) Second Division matches and scored two goals. His most telling contribution, however, came in the Football League Cup fifth-round replay against Fulham at Leeds Road on 12 December 1967. Six minutes from the end of extra-time, Shaw netted the winner that took Town into the semi-final of the competition.

When Ian Greaves took over from Tom Johnston as manager in June 1968, Shaw found fewer opportunities, and in September 1969 he joined the Latics in an exchange deal that took Les Chapman in the opposite direction. His record of three goals in 24(3) matches for Huddersfield gave little indication of what was to follow, as in two separate spells at Boundary Park his electrifying pace, stamina and goalscoring flair made him a warm favourite. He was one of the foremost players in the club's rise from Fourth Division obscurity, and his goals also played a major part in winning the Ford Sporting League top prize that financed the new stand on the Broadway side of the ground.

Shaw scored the first of his 95 goals for the Latics in his second appearance, a 2–3 home defeat against Wrexham. In the season that Jimmy Frizzell took over from Jack Rowley as manager, he finished with 12 League goals in 34 matches. He was first paired with Jim Fryatt in February of the same season. His strike partner scored 11 goals in just 16 matches as the duo lifted the Latics away from the foot of the table and to the safety of 19th place.

It was in the 1970–71 promotion season that the partnership of Shaw and Jim Fryatt reached its zenith. Shaw opened his scoring account for the season with a four-goal blast against Brentford at Boundary Park and three weeks later scored a hat-trick against Aldershot. In the most prolific forward partnership in the club's League history, Shaw scored 23 League goals and Jim Fryatt 24. It was the first occasion that two players had scored 20 or more League goals in a season; the nearest approach to the record was back in season 1929–30 when Stewart Littlewood netted 27 and Matt Gray 19.

Shaw's excellent goalscoring record earned him an upward move to West Bromwich Albion in a £80,000 transfer in March 1973. He made his debut, from the bench, at Manchester United in a 2–1 defeat before a crowd of 46,735. A week earlier he had played for the Latics in a 3–0 defeat at Walsall when the attendance numbered only 4,515! Shorn of their leading scorer, Athletic's push for promotion petered out – they finished fourth in the table – meanwhile, Shaw was unable to prevent the Baggies descent into Division Two. He failed to find his best form at the Hawthorns, scoring 19 League and Cup goals in 76(17) appearances, but he was welcomed back with open arms by the Latics in October 1975.

In his second match, against Southampton at Boundary Park on 21 October, Shaw rattled in a 26th-minute, first-half hat-trick in a 3–2 win. The game also marked the debut of John Platt in Athletic's goal. Shaw totalled 13 goals in 29 matches in the season of his return, but, increasingly troubled by a knee injury, he had lengthy spells on the sidelines in 1976–77. He made his final appearance, from the bench, against Charlton Athletic at Boundary Park on 17 September 1977.

An ideal player both on and off the field, Shaw was presented with a silver salver from players and staff following his retirement. He was also awarded a testimonial match, with Blackburn Rovers providing the opposition at Boundary Park on 2 May 1978.

John Sheridan

Date of birth: 1 October 1964, Stretford, Manchester

Oldham Athletic record:
Appearances: League 132(13), FA Cup 14(1), League Cup 2(2)
Goals: League 14, FA Cup 2
Debut: Wycombe Wanderers (h) 24 October 1998, drawn 0–0

Also played for: Manchester City associate schoolboy, Leeds United, Nottingham Forest, Sheffield Wednesday, Birmingham City on loan, Bolton Wanderers, Doncaster Rovers, Republic of Ireland (34 caps)

John Sheridan was one of six brothers, which includes Darren, the combative midfielder, who joined John at Boundary Park in July 2001. Sheridan was 34 when he joined Athletic from Doncaster Rovers – a Conference team at that time – linking again with his former Leeds United colleague Andy Ritchie. He qualified for the Republic of Ireland through his Dublin-born parents and commenced with Manchester City on schoolboy forms. He became a professional with Leeds United in March 1982. Next came Nottingham Forest in August 1989, but his unhappy sojourn at the City Ground lasted just three months before Sheffield Wednesday paid £500,000 for him. The Owls were relegated in Sheridan's first season but came straight back up in 1990–91. In the same season, a goal by Sheridan in the Wembley League Cup Final saw Wednesday lift the trophy at the expense of red-hot favourites Manchester United. A loan spell with Birmingham City preceded his £180,000 move to Bolton Wanderers in November 1996. In successive seasons, he experienced both promotion to the Premier League and relegation back to Division One before being released to join Doncaster Rovers. On the international scene, he appeared in two World Cup squads – Italia '90 and USA '94 – winning 34 full caps in addition to other awards at Youth, Under-21, Under-23 and B levels.

Initially signed by Athletic on non-contract terms Sheridan was quickly offered a permanent engagement in October 1998. The creative midfielder quickly established himself; his range of passing and the excellence of his all-round game lifted his teammates in a season when relegation was only narrowly avoided. His first two goals were both scored against Bristol Rovers, the first in the 2–2 draw at the Memorial Stadium and the second at Boundary Park in a vital 2–1 victory on 13 April 1999. He appeared in 30 of a possible 32 League matches and was voted supporters' Player of the Year. The veteran midfielder's first goal of 1999–2000 was an incredible long-range free-kick against his favourite opponents Bristol Rovers, and, for the second year in succession, he received the supporters' vote as the season's best player. His initial 18-month contract was extended mid-season as the influential playmaker continued to make a massive contribution in Athletic's midfield.

Already beyond the personal milestone of 500 League appearances, Sheridan's progress received a setback when he was injured in the first month of season 2000–01 and was sidelined until mid-December. He scored in successive matches in January – the first gave Athletic the lead against Wigan Athletic – but younger brother Darren secured the family bragging rights, with his team running out 3–1 winners. Sheridan netted four goals in 22(3) League matches in the season when Lee Duxbury, with eight, headed the scoring lists. In July 2001 Athletic signed his 33-year-old brother Darren, and it was the first time in their professional careers that the Sheridan's had united. The brothers began together in a rousing, opening day 3–3 draw at Wrexham, Darren receiving the first yellow card of his Latics career. Both brothers fell foul of the authorities in September; Darren was red-carded for his part in a brawl which marred the Worthington Cup tie at Blackburn Rovers, while John saw red at Colchester United as the Latics lost their unbeaten start to the season after eight League matches.

In late October, the sacking of manager Andy Ritchie left the club in turmoil. New head coach Mick Wadsworth took over and swiftly made 13 players available. In May 2002 another change of direction saw head coach Ian Dowie promoted to manager; Sheridan – still registered as a player – was given coaching duties in the re-shuffle. He drifted from the first-team picture in 2002–03, and in April he announced his retirement. With the club close to extinction as the new season opened, he was pressed back into action and quickly made the headlines. A display of true quality and a 6th-minute penalty crowned an emotional return against his former team Sheffield Wednesday at Hillsborough in the 2–2 draw. Following Ian Dowie's resignation, Sheridan – assisted by David Eyres – took over as manager. He subsequently served as assistant to Brian Talbot, and following a successful spell in charge of the reserve team he was promoted to succeed outgoing manager Ronnie Moore on 1 June 2006.

Les Smith

Date of birth: 2 October 1920, Manchester
Died: 6 December 2001, Hazel Grove

Oldham Athletic record:
Appearances: League 178, FA Cup 14
Goals: League 3, FA Cup 1
Debut: Rotherham United (h) 23 August 1949, drawn 2–2

Also played for: Stockport County amateur, Huddersfield Town

Although born and raised within the immediate vicinity of Manchester City's Maine Road ground, Les Smith began in football as a pre-war amateur with Stockport County. World War Two interrupted his progress when he was called up for military service, and he subsequently saw action as an army sergeant in Egypt. On demobilisation, he joined Huddersfield Town in March 1946.

Smith made his League debut for Huddersfield in Division One at Sunderland on 4 September 1946, and it proved a severe introduction. As right half-back he was directly opposed to Willie Watson, who subsequently won caps for England at both soccer and cricket. Sunderland won 3–0, but in the following week Smith collected his first winning bonus as Derby County were beaten 5–2 at Leeds Road.

The signing of Irish international inside-forward Peter Doherty saved Town from relegation – they finished 20th in Division One – Smith appearing in 16 of the season's League matches and in 21 the following term. Although subsequently in reserve, he nevertheless had accumulated a fair amount of top-flight experience when he joined the Latics as a part-time professional in July 1949 – combining football with his job as a carpet salesman in Manchester.

Billy Wootton was Athletic's manager, and he seemed undecided as to Smith's best position. He began as left-half and was then tried on the right wing, before reverting to the middle line as right-half. A six-match run at inside-right was terminated when, on 17 December, he was injured after 20 minutes of play in the home defeat against Lincoln City. The depleted Latics went down 2–0, and Smith's season came to a premature end, although he was eased back in two late season matches for the A Team in the Lancashire Midweek League.

A change of manager in November of the following season – George Hardwick replacing Billy Wootton – lifted Athletic's fortunes, and Smith benefitted from his first lengthy run of first-team football, missing just one match following Hardwick's appointment. Although better in defence than attack and a very infrequent goalscorer, his 25-yard volley against Manchester United in the FA Cup third round at Old Trafford on 6 January 1951 was one to savour – despite the fact that the Latics lost 1–4.

Season 1951–52 opened with a visit to Southport, and the new signing, player-coach Jack Warner, was preferred to Smith at right-half, despite the fact that he was a month away from his 40th birthday. The Wales international became Athletic's oldest debutante (a record broken later by Bobby Collins), but despite his age and greying locks he proved anything but a spent force, completing 35 matches during the season. He began in the Lancashire Combination side but completed 21 first-team matches from mid-season. He scored one of Athletic's goals in the 11–2 rout of Chester at Boundary Park on 19 January and also scored Athletic's goal in the 1–3 defeat at Grimsby Town on 29 March.

Season 1952–53 opened in heatwave conditions at Tranmere Rovers, two new players in Tommy Lowrie and Ian Crawford making their debuts in the 0–0 draw. Smith began at left-half and enjoyed his best season at Boundary Park, as Athletic were crowned Third Division North Champions thanks to an outstanding defensive performance throughout the campaign. Seventeen clean sheets and just 45 goals conceded in 46 League matches was the bedrock on which the season's success was founded.

Sadly, the hard-won promotion was squandered when the side finished rock bottom of Division Two in 1953–54. During the campaign, Smith was switched from right-half to right full-back. He quickly settled into his new position – being the most conspicuous figure in the team's defence – proving a thoughtful and cool defender with the rare gift of anticipation. Younger players challenged in subsequent seasons, and Smith played his final match at Bradford City in the FA Cup first-round tie on 19 November 1955, one month beyond his 35th birthday.

Billy Spurdle

Date of birth: 28 January 1926, St Peter Port, Guernsey, Channel Islands

Oldham Athletic record:
Appearances: League 200, FA Cup 18
Goals: League 24, FA Cup 4
Debut: Carlisle United (a) 26 March 1948, lost 1–4

Also played for: Manchester City, Port Vale

Billy Spurdle was evacuated from the Channel Islands during World War Two and first appeared for the Latics in the Manchester League team on 4 November 1944. He was at inside-right in the 7–2 win against Manchester City A team, a match in which Walter Cotterill – perhaps better known as the Werneth and Crompton cricketer – scored five goals. It is interesting to note that although seven of the 11 players who turned out that day also played in the first team in the Football League North, only Fred Ogden (goalkeeper), Bill Lawton (left-half) and Billy Spurdle eventually graduated to play in League football for the Latics.

Spurdle signed a professional form following his demobilisation from the forces and in early days combined football with his work for a Royton based timber merchant and case manufacturer. He made his League debut on Good Friday 1948, deputising for Bill Hayes at Carlisle United. Directly opposed to Jimmy Dougal, the ex-Preston North End and Scotland international, he was given a severe examination and returned to reserve-team football for the remainder of the season.

When the new season opened, Spurdle was included in the side for the opening match against Rotherham United at Boundary Park. Four new signings made their debut in the 1–2 defeat and for the midweek visit to Hull City, a further three newcomers made their bow. One of them, Viv Aston, was injured after three minutes, and the Raich Carter inspired Tigers won 6–0. It took some time for manager Wootton to find a settled combination, but when he did the side improved to finish sixth in the table. Spurdle played in 35 League matches and scored his first goals in wins against New Brighton and Stockport County.

Spurdle's cultured displays and eye for a scoring opportunity were deserving of a bigger stage as he began the 1949–50 season in sparkling form. By mid-season he had performed equally well at right-half, inside-right and on the right wing. He scored League goals against Doncaster Rovers, Crewe Alexandra and Tranmere Rovers, and FA Cup goals against Stockton, Crewe Alexandra and Newcastle United. In January 1950 Manchester City paid £10,000 for him. In a stay of almost six years he played in 172 League and Cup matches and scored 33 goals. He became the first Channel Islander to appear in a Wembley Cup Final – against Newcastle United in 1955 – and was dreadfully unfortunate to miss the following year's trip to Wembley. Twenty-four hours before the Final against Birmingham City, he developed a number of painful boils and was replaced by Don Revie.

In late November 1956, Port Vale paid £4,000 for Spurdle, but he was unable to prevent their relegation from Division Two, and in June of the following year he returned to Boundary Park. Installed as captain by manager Ted Goodier, he led out Athletic to face Carlisle United on the opening day of the season. A crowd of 11,339 spectators greeted a team with five brand new signings and two who were making their 'second debut'. In addition to their new captain, outside-right Tommy Walker was making his first appearance since returning from his sojourn with Chesterfield.

The new look team opened with a 1–0 victory, Spurdle scoring the only goal. Sadly, the season was a troubled one. By late September, 10 players had been affected by the Asian Flu epidemic. With almost a quarter of the season gone, only two wins had been recorded and the side never recovered sufficiently to avoid finishing in 15th place in the final season of the Third Division North, thereby becoming founder members of the new Division Four in 1958–59. Spurdle's first-team appearances progressively decreased until his retirement at the age of 37 in May 1963. It was, however, totally fitting that his final four first-team games (which took him to exactly 200 League appearances) were made in April and May 1963 when the side celebrated promotion from Division Four. After a brief spell as trainer-coach to Athletic Reserves, Spurdle returned to the Channel Isles in 1967 'to do some coaching, and grow tomatoes'.

Frank Tomlinson

Date of birth: 23 October 1925, Manchester
Died: 20 April 1999, Oldham

Oldham Athletic record:
Appearances: League 115, FA Cup 9
Goals: League 27, FA Cup 2
Debut: Tranmere Rovers (a) 16 November 1946, lost 2–4 (scored one)

Also played for: Manchester United amateur, Bolton Wanderers amateur, Goslings FC, Rochdale, Chester, Ashton National
Managed: Bradford Park Avenue

When Frank Tomlinson was signed by Athletic on 16 November 1946, he had already scored 23 goals for Goslings, despite the season being less than three months old. Combining football with his work at Metropolitan Vickers in Manchester, he had seen teenage service with both Manchester United and Bolton Wanderers on amateur forms.

The ex-Goslings sharpshooter was introduced at outside-right for his League debut and was partnered by Flying Officer Jack Cutting, who was also making his first-team debut. Tranmere were represented by the youngest side in the club's history, the average age being 20. The youngsters were quickly off the mark and opened the scoring after just two minutes. Tranmere continued to make good use of the ball on a heavy surface and were four goals up before Athletic replied with late goals by Tomlinson and Jack Ormandy.

Tomlinson's scoring streak continued throughout the month when he netted one of Athletic's goals in the 2–0 win against Darlington at Boundary Park. He then scored the only goal of the FA Cup first-round match against Tranmere Rovers and followed with the equaliser in the 1–1 draw against Gateshead on 7 December.

Although the 1946–47 season ended on a depressing note – an 8–0 defeat at Rotherham United – Tomlinson had good reason to be pleased with his season's work, which had brought him nine League and Cup goals in 29 appearances. Under new manager Billy Wootton in 1947–48, he did not win a regular first-team place until mid-season, but he regained his place in 1948–49 when Athletic enjoyed a much better season, finishing at sixth place in the table.

Although the campaign began falteringly, Athletic enjoyed an excellent mid-season spell. The usual forward line up of Tomlinson, Stock, Gemmell, Haddington and Jessop was a potent one. Tomlinson's progressive sorties along the right wing contributed greatly to the team's success. His speed and ball control, combined with an ability to swerve past an opponent, made him a very dangerous raider, his 14 goals in 43 matches earning him third place in the season's scoring lists behind Eric Gemmell (23) and Ray Haddington (22).

In the early stages of season 1950–51, when playing against York City at Boundary Park, Tomlinson fractured his right leg and did not play again for the remainder of the season. With the former Manchester City wingman Jimmy Munro firmly established, Tomlinson began 1951–52 in the reserves. In November he became the first departure from Boundary Park, following his request to be placed on the transfer list. York City and Rochdale discussed terms with him and an agreement was reached with both parties, both in general terms and with regard to his benefit monies, to which he was entitled. He opted for the shorter move to Rochdale. By coincidence – as was the case when he made his debut with the Latics – Tranmere Rovers were the opponents and Tomlinson scored in a 3–2 win. His second League goal for the Dale was scored against his former teammates in the 2–2 Boxing Day draw against Athletic at Spotland.

Tomlinson's sole venture into management was short lived. Many years after his playing career ended, he was surprisingly appointed as manager of Bradford Park Avenue in February 1970. With less than three months of the season remaining, he had little opportunity to improve matters, and when the season ended with Bradford in bottom place they failed to gain re-election. In December of the same year Tomlinson was dismissed for economic reasons.

Don Travis

Date of birth: 21 January 1924, Moston, Manchester
Died: February 2002, Yeovil

Oldham Athletic record:
Appearances: League 114, FA Cup 4
Goals: League 62
Debut: Stockport County (a) 20 October 1951, drawn 0–0

Also played for: Ferranti FC, Blackpool amateur, Goslings FC (wartime guest player with Southend United, Plymouth Argyle, St Mirren, Cowdenbeath), West Ham United, Southend United, Accrington Stanley, Crewe Alexandra, Chester, Yeovil Town

Don Travis represented Manchester Schoolboys as a 13-year-old outside-left in 1937 and was on Blackpool's amateur list at the age of 15. During army service he gained a variety of experience in wartime football, before signing his first professional form with West Ham United in September 1945.

A friend of a West Ham scout first heard two soldiers talking about a grand centre-half in their unit side, but the Hammers immediately saw a centre-forward in the young six-footer. Although he had never before filled the position, manager Paynter put him into the reserve team as leader of the attack, and he scored four goals on his debut.

A move north to Accrington Stanley in 1948 brought Travis his first extended run of first-team football, and it was in the Northern Section of Division Three that he scored his goals – 154 in 319 matches.

Standing at 6ft 3in and weighing close to 13st, Travis was ideally built for the position of attack leader. Although lacking a yard of pace, he was remarkably nimble for such a big man and his height enabled him to give most central-defenders a hard time in the air. Strong shooting (mainly with his left foot) as well as good distribution and line-holding qualities combined to make him an extremely dangerous opponent.

With deep-set eyes and an unsmiling, severe countenance, Travis exuded an air of menace. He was indeed a goalkeepers nightmare in the days when the unfortunate custodian often finished in the back of the net, along with the ball, and all quite legitimately!

Travis had two separate spells with the Latics, and the first time round it was his misfortune to cover for the injured Eric Gemmell, a huge favourite at Boundary Park and an altogether more polished performer. His second spell, three years later in 1954, served to confound his earlier critics in the most emphatic manner. He joined a side who had been newly relegated after just one season in Division Two. Although the new term started in a disappointing fashion – one win in the first eight League matches – the side rallied to finish in 10th place in the table.

Travis netted 32 goals in 40 League matches and came within a whisker of equalling Tommy Davis's club record of 33 – recorded in the 1935–36 season. A personal highlight was a four-goal blast against Bradford Park Avenue in a 5–0 victory during a midweek night match in April 1955.

Although the team's fortunes were in serious decline with a 20th-place finish in 1955–56 – which led to the resignation of player-manager George Hardwick – and an equally disappointing 19th placing in 1956–57 under new manager Ted Goodier, Travis continued to find the net. Without managing to reach the same heights as in 1954–55, he was nevertheless the club's leading scorer in the following two seasons.

An elder brother, Harry Travis, was on Latics' books for a season in 1932–33 but made several moves before winning his spurs with Bradford City, for whom he was leading scorer in 1935–36, with 16 goals in only 24 appearances. Both brothers had started their working lives as butcher's boys, and, as one correspondent noted, they both put plenty of 'beef' into their shots!

David Walders

Date of birth: c.1880, Barrow-in-Furness
Died: April 1929, Burnley

Oldham Athletic record:
Appearances: League 112, FA Cup 17
Goals: League 8, FA Cup 2
Debut: Hyde, FA Cup first qualifying round (h) 6 October 1906, won 5–0 (scored one)

Also played for: Barrow, Burnley, Southport Central (World War One guest player with Burnley)

Athletic's first captain in the Football League, David Walders had joined in May of the previous season from Burnley, along with his brother Jack. While the appearance statistics above refer to League and FA Cup matches, Walders additionally appeared in 37 Lancashire Combination matches in 1906–07 and scored six goals. His first outing was on 1 September 1906 against Colne, and he opened the scoring in a 2–0 win. Although his position was centre-half, his role in those far-off days could best be likened to that of an attacking central-midfielder. Operating almost as a sixth forward, he scored six League goals and two in the FA Cup in 1906–07, backing up an already potent attack that recorded 105 goals in 38 Lancashire Combination matches to lift the Championship trophy.

When Athletic began life as a Football League club, Walders had the honour of captaining the first XI selected to represent the club at Stoke on 9 September 1907. The line up was as follows: Hewitson, Hodson, Hamilton, Fay, Walders, Wilson, Ward, Dodds, Newton, Hancock, Swarbrick. It varied in one position – Newton for Brunton at centre-forward – from the team that had beaten Rochdale 4–1 in a friendly match at Spotland four days earlier.

Billy Dodds, Frank Newton and Jimmy Swarbrick were Athletic's scorers in the inaugural 3–1 victory at Stoke. The same XI marked the first League match at Boundary Park with a 2–1 win against West Bromwich Albion before 15,803 spectators, who paid a fraction less than £400 at the gate. Frank Newton was the season's star performer with 28 League goals, two in the FA Cup and a further four in five Lancashire Senior Cup ties. The side came very close to winning promotion at the first attempt, finishing third behind Bradford City and Leicester Fosse.

Walders registered his first League goals for Athletic in April 1909, scoring against Clapton Orient at Boundary Park and against Hull City at Anlaby Road. A busy end-of-season programme saw nine matches contested within 26 days, and Athletic won only one of them. They used 29 players in League matches, and despite a season of many team changes the famous half-back line of Fay, Walders and Wilson was largely undisturbed. The team finished sixth in Division Two, but they were on the threshold of great achievements.

Season 1909–10 opened with a 2–2 draw at Birmingham, in which Howard Matthews saved a penalty-kick from Blues debutante Charlie Millington. John Mitchell, Athletic's new inside-right from Glentoran, scored on his debut, and their second came courtesy of an own-goal by Birmingham's full-back Frank Stokes. Five matches into the new season, Athletic were without a victory, but the campaign that had started so poorly was turned around to such effect that promotion to the top flight was secured after the team remained undefeated in all but one of their last 21 Second Division fixtures.

Walders lost his place early in the season when Alex Downie was signed from Manchester United. However, an inspired tactical reshuffle by manager Ashworth saw him reinstated at centre-half, with Downie being moved across to right-half and Jimmy Fay moved forward to inside-right. Athletic clinched the runners'-up spot with a run of six consecutive victories, Walders scoring in each of the final three matches, while Jimmy Fay finished the season with 26 League goals in 38 matches.

Walders remained at Boundary Park long enough to earn a benefit match, with a guarantee of £250, against Sheffield Wednesday in March 1912. In October 1912 he left Athletic to take up the post of trainer-coach at Sparta Rotterdam. In May of the following year he joined Southport Central and on 11 October 1913 scored twice in their record FA Cup victory, a 9–0 win against Portsmouth Rangers. His career was ended by a severe leg injury, sustained during World War One. His brother Jack died at the early age of 42 in January 1924 as a direct result of severe privation suffered as a prisoner of war.

Tommy Walker

Date of birth: 14 November 1923, Cramlington, County Durham
Died: 14 June 2005, Middleton

Oldham Athletic record:
Appearances: League 158, FA Cup 6
Goals: League 23
Debut: Doncaster Rovers (h) 6 February 1954, drawn 2–2

Also played for: Newcastle United (World War Two guest player with West Ham United), Chesterfield

The signing of the Magpies outside-right Tommy Walker added 2,000 spectators to the gate for the visit of Doncaster Rovers, providing a welcome boost for an Athletic side firmly rooted to the foot of Division Two. Despite having travelled down from Newcastle on an early-morning train, Walker played a big part in the match. The visitors were held to a draw in an eventful encounter; Bobby McIlvenny and Frank Scrine scored Athletic's goals, but player-manager George Hardwick had a penalty-kick saved by Ken Hardwick, the Doncaster Rovers goalkeeper.

Despite the signing of another wingman of ripe experience – Harry McShane from Manchester United – the side showed only a marginal improvement over the remainder of the season. They won at Stoke City and West Ham United – in each case completing a double over their opponents – but a hugely disappointing season ended in relegation, after just one term in higher company.

Despite suffering from a duodenal ulcer during 1954–55, Walker missed only four of the season's matches and finished with a scoring burst of three goals within the space of four matches in the month of April. His surging runs along the right wing and inviting centres were a key element in the outstanding scoring record achieved by Athletic's centre-forward Don Travis, who netted 32 League goals during the season.

Despite a season of struggle in what was to become player-manager George Hardwick's last at Boundary Park, Walker was Athletic's most consistent performer in 1955–56. He played in every match and his 11 League goals included one in the season's opener, a 1–1 draw against Bradford City, and one in the final match of the season, another 1–1 draw against Wrexham. The most impressive, however, was his hat-trick against Barrow at Boundary Park on 10 March 1956. I was among the crowd of 5,496 that day and celebrations for my 22nd birthday were greatly enhanced by Walker's treble in the 6–1 demolition of Barrow! Latics' other goals came from Don Travis (2) and George Crook.

Walker's performance brought to mind an earlier visit to Boundary Park – in the colours of Newcastle United – for a third-round FA Cup tie on 7 January 1950. A crowd of 31,706 witnessed a wonderful exhibition by the First Division side, who were two goals up within seven minutes and ran out 7–2 victors. Walker scored twice for the Magpies, Jackie Milburn completed a hat-trick, with Frank Houghton and Bobby Mitchell scoring the other two. Billy Spurdle and Ray Haddington replied for the Latics, but, much to the disappointment of the home fans, Haddington shot wide from a penalty.

Newcastle went out in the next round, losing 3–0 at Chelsea before a gate of 64,446, but in the following two seasons they reached Wembley and won on both occasions – by 2–0 against Blackpool in 1951 and 1–0 against Arsenal in 1952. Walker gained winners' medals both times. His record with Newcastle United covered 184 League appearances and 35 goals, plus 20 FA Cup matches and three goals. He had joined the Magpies in October 1941, originally as a centre-half.

Walker requested a transfer from Athletic in December 1956, and, among the many interested clubs, Gateshead were keen to recruit him but were unable to raise the asking fee of £1,500. In February 1957 Chesterfield signed him for a fee of £1,250, but he failed to settle at Saltergate and returned to Boundary Park for a second spell in July 1957. He was manager Goodier's seventh close-season capture, but under new manager Norman Dodgin in 1958–59 he appeared only twice and announced his retirement in April 1959. A Methodist lay preacher for many years, Walker ran a successful newsagents in Middleton for almost 30 years following his retirement.

Bert Watson

Date of birth: 26 August 1900, Thelwell, Cheshire
Died: January 1971, Thelwell, Cheshire

Oldham Athletic record:
Appearances: League 233, FA Cup 9
Goals: League 64, FA Cup 8
Debut: Birmingham (a) 10 December 1921, lost 0–3

Also played for: Monk's Hall, Manchester United trial, Witton Albion, Southampton, Rochdale

Bert Watson assisted a number of junior clubs, and at one time it was questionable whether he would take up rugby in preference to soccer. At 12 years of age he assisted Arpley Street in both codes, and his first medal was earned in the Lancashire Schoolboy's Rugby Cup, which his team won in 1912, with Watson playing at wing-threequarter.

Watson played little sport until, at the age of 16, he was invited for a trial by Warrington Rugby League club. He declined the offer, decided to concentrate on soccer and eventually turned professional with Monk's Hall of the Cheshire County League. He had two trial games with Manchester United but was not offered a contract, and it was from Witton Albion that he attracted the attention of the Latics, with manager Charlie Roberts paying £300 for his signature.

Watson stepped into First Division football within four days of signing, taking over the left-wing position from Jack Tatton. He scored his first goal against Preston North End in the following month and missed only one match that season. This came about when he missed his train connection for the match against Aston Villa at Villa Park on 29 April 1922. Howard Matthews, the goalkeeper, who was living in Birmingham at the time, was the only reserve present, and he filled the vacant berth.

In a 1926 interview, Watson recalled the match at Crystal Palace on 2 May 1925. It was the last match of the season and, depending on the result, either the Latics or Crystal Palace would be relegated to the Third Division. Oldham won the match with a single goal, scored by Jack Keedwell, but, as Watson said at the time, 'It was a nightmare for a week!'

Watson enjoyed three outstanding seasons between 1925 and 1928, missing only eight first-team matches and scoring successive seasonal totals of 19, 15 and 17 goals. His strengths were his whole-hearted approach, an ability to get the ball across from any angle and, as his record shows, he knew the way to the goal. Although very much right footed, he spent the majority of his career on the left wing. What might have been a disadvantage was in fact anything but, as many of his goals came from his ability to cut inside and shoot with his 'wrong' foot.

The statistics reveal Watson's success as a marksman in FA Cup matches. In season 1925–26 when the offside law was amended – requiring only two players between the attacking player and the goal, rather than the previous requirement of three – he was quick to cash in, scoring six goals in two FA Cup matches. He scored two of Athletic's goals in the 10–1 victory against Lytham in round three (which remains the club's record Cup win) and four at Stockton in the following round in a high-scoring encounter that finished 6–4 in Athletic's favour.

In May 1928 Watson was awarded a benefit match with a guarantee of £500. Hull City were the opponents, and he scored twice within the first five minutes of the match to set up a 5–0 victory that also featured a 16-minute hat-trick by Scottish international centre-forward Neil Harris.

A dreadful start to 1928–29, with only four wins at the mid-season point, led manager Andrew Wilson to almost totally revamp his attacking formation. Among the changes, Watson lost out to Bill Hasson for the left-wing spot and other new faces introduced were Freddie Worrall, Matt Gray and Stewart Littlewood, inside-right Jimmy Dyson being the only forward to survive the shake-up.

In the close season, Watson was transferred to Southampton in a deal that brought 'Spud' Murphy to Oldham. After two seasons he returned north, ending his career with Rochdale where he scored eight goals in just 17 League matches, bowing out as the season's leading scorer.

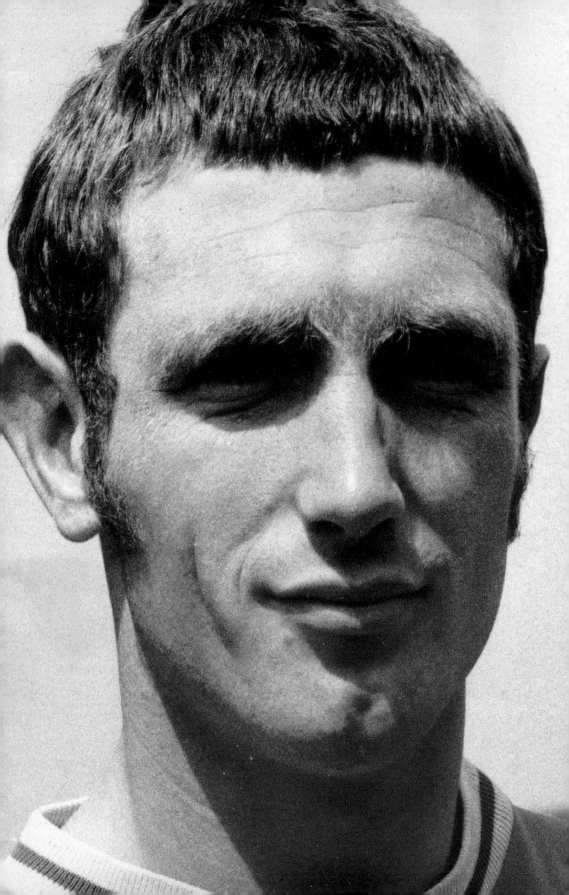

Maurice Whittle

Date of birth: 5 July 1948, Wigan

Oldham Athletic record:
Appearances: League 307(5), FA Cup 17, League Cup 14
Goals: League 39, FA Cup 2
Debut: Southport, League Cup 1 (a) 13 August 1969, lost 1–5

Also played for: Blackburn Rovers, Fort Lauderdale Strikers (US), Wigan Athletic, Bangor City, Stafford Rangers, Barrow, Macclesfield Town, Lytham, Atherton
Managed: Barrow, OBS (Finland)

Maurice Whittle began as a 15-year-old wing half-back with Blackburn Rovers and won a Central League Championship medal in 1967. He made his League debut from the bench at Portsmouth on 21 August 1968 in a 1–0 win. During the season he made five starts and two substitute appearances, playing alongside Jim Fryatt, Dick Mulvaney and Jim Beardall, all of whom where later associated with the Latics.

Whittle joined Athletic on 15 May 1969, and one week later manager Jack Rowley returned to Ewood Park to sign centre-forward Jim Beardall. The two newcomers first donned Athletic's colours at Rochdale on 26 July for the annual Rose Bowl friendly. Athletic fell apart in the second half and were soundly beaten 5–1. Jim Beardall was the Latics scorer, while Whittle was replaced by Eric Magee after 75 minutes. The fortunes of the two ex-Rovers players continued along similar lines for several months. Whittle failed to impress in spasmodic outings, while Beardall scored six League goals in his first seven matches.

By mid-season the team were languishing at the foot of Division Four; Jim Beardall was dropped from the side and was shipped out to Great Harwood in February. Whittle, meanwhile, had been switched to left full-back to take over the role of the injury-plagued World Cup-winning defender Ray Wilson. Given a very hard act to follow, he nevertheless adapted well to his new position and, benefitting from a regular run in the side, his form and confidence improved beyond recognition.

In the promotion season that followed, Whittle scored his first goal at Newport County in a 4–1 win on 12 September 1970, but it was his goal at York City on 19 April that virtually sealed Athletic's promotion. The best attendance at Bootham Crescent for five years (14,426) gathered to witness a stirring encounter between two teams very much in the frame for promotion. The clubs were occupying third and fourth places in the Division, York City being one point behind Athletic but with a game in hand. The only goal of the match was struck sweetly by Whittle, who was fed by Tommy Bryceland for a shot from just outside the penalty area.

Three years on, Whittle was again a key element in a second promotion, this time as Champions of Division Three. In almost a carbon copy of the earlier promotion campaign, Athletic travelled to York City for their 44th League match of the season with both teams well in contention for the Championship. Despite losing Ian Wood to a shoulder injury after just 90 seconds and going a goal down after 55 minutes, Athletic's chance came 10 minutes later when George McVitie was fouled just five yards outside the penalty area. As York City's defenders formed a human wall in expectation of a trademark thunderbolt from Whittle, he stepped up and curled a delicate chip over the wall and into the top corner of the net.

At the conclusion of the successful campaign, Whittle had appeared in four full seasons and had missed only one match in all that time. He was to remain at Boundary Park for a further three seasons as Athletic established themselves in the Second Division. In the opening weeks of season 1975–76, Whittle scored from open play against Hull City – an 89th-minute winner – and one week later he salvaged a point at Blackpool with another late strike when Athletic were down to 10 men after Alan Groves had been sent off.

The arrival of defender John Hurst from Everton in June 1976 stepped up the competition for places, and in what proved to be Whittle's last season he played in only 24 League matches, his final appearance coming in a 3–0 defeat at Nottingham Forest on 27 April 1977. Three weeks later, 19-year-old Garry Hoolickin partnered Ian Wood at full-back for the first time, and Whittle departed, initially into non-League football, although he returned in March 1980 to play in 21 matches for Wigan Athletic.

Archie Whyte

Date of birth: 17 July 1919, Redding, Stirlingshire
Died: 1 October 1973, Middleton, Lancashire

Oldham Athletic record:
Appearances: League 234, FA Cup 14
Goals: 0
Debut: Rotherham United (h) 19 August 1950, lost 4–5

Also played for: Armadale Thistle, Barnsley

One of a number of Scots recruited by Barnsley's manager Angus Seed in the close season of 1938, at 18 years of age Archie Whyte was a promising inside-left, but he did not break into the League side in his first season at Oakwell. The outbreak of World War Two put a halt to his footballing career, which was replaced with a six-year stint of army service. His long delayed League debut came on 9 November 1946 in a 3–1 defeat at Plymouth Argyle. His first appearance was at right-half, but he later took over the centre-half berth, replacing club skipper Joe Wilson. At the time of his transfer to the Latics, he had appeared in 92 League and Cup matches and scored two goals.

Whyte was part of a double signing by Athletic, being accompanied by a Barnsley teammate, full-back Ernie Swallow. Both made their Latics debut, along with veteran goalkeeper George Bradshaw from Bury, in the season's opener against Rotherham United. The 19,192 crowd at Boundary Park witnessed a nine-goal thriller, but unfortunately Rotherham scored five of the goals. Defeats at Chester and Barrow followed – where Whyte scored an own-goal in the 2–1 reverse – and rock bottom was reached in a 5–1 defeat during a (not very) friendly match at Merthyr Tydfil in September. Each side finished with 10 men after Alf Lee and a Merthyr player were sent off for fighting. On 4 November the Latics faithful were dismayed when leading scorer Ray Haddington was sold to Manchester City for £8,000. What was not realised was that the monies raised helped to finance the arrival from Middlesbrough of player-manager George Hardwick, who replaced Billy Wootton.

Whyte was to become a key player in the team's improved side, which ultimately took them to the Championship of the Third Division North in season 1952–53. He was a powerful and commanding presence in the heart of Athletic's defence. Afraid of nothing, his height made him very effective in the air, and he was a quick and forceful tackler who cleared effectively with either foot. He missed only three matches in his first season, when the influence of player-manager Hardwick gradually lifted the side away from the foot of the table. They also enjoyed a run to round three of the FA Cup, which brought a lucrative draw, a visit to Manchester United's Old Trafford enclosure – still with some makeshift facilities – necessitated by the ongoing rebuilding of the ground following wartime bomb damage. In their first senior appearance at Old Trafford for 15 years, the Latics were beaten 4–1, but a share of the gate money from the 37,161 attendance was welcome.

For the opening fixture of 1951–52, a goalless draw at Southport, Athletic fielded three debutantes in Jack Warner (Manchester United), Peter McKennan (Middlesbrough) and Jeffrey Williams, an 18-year-old soldier from Catterick Camp who failed to add to his single senior outing. The undoubted highlight of the League season was the record 11–2 victory against Chester at Boundary Park on 19 January, and a final placing of fourth in the table represented real and heartening progress.

I was handily placed to attend the first match of the 1952–53 season at Tranmere Rovers from nearby RAF West Kirby. In stifling heat, neither team raised much of a gallop throughout the 0–0 draw, and I could have wished for more suitable attire for the heatwave conditions than my RAF uniform. During the season, Whyte completed his 100th League appearance at Carlisle United in late October, with the team riding high at the head of the table. In the season's 46th and final League game, Athletic travelled over the Pennines to Bradford City. A packed Valley Parade witnessed a nervous encounter, and although Athletic never really got going they clinched their first-ever Championship in a scoreless encounter, in which Whyte and goalkeeper George Burnett were the heroes. He went on to record a run of exactly 100 consecutive appearances, only terminated by injury in January 1954. He retired in June 1956 and was appointed assistant-trainer, an appointment that lasted until 1960 when new manager Jack Rowley replaced him with former England international wing-half Henry Cockburn.

Whyte was a popular landlord at a local hostelry – the Hare and Hounds at Chadderton – and he also coached Oldham Ladies football team.

Tommy Williamson

Date of birth: 16 March 1913, Salford
Died: 28 June 1992, South Lowestoft

Oldham Athletic record:
Appearances: League 157, FA Cup 12
Goals: League 4
Debut: Tranmere Rovers (h) 25 December 1935, won 4–1

Also played for: Pendleton Wednesday, Leeds United, Northwich Victoria, Fleetwood

Tommy Williamson first played as an amateur with Pendleton Wednesday. He then spent a season in the reserves with Leeds United from the age of 19, arriving at Boundary Park after two seasons with Northwich Victoria. Fair haired and dashing, he began as a bustling right-half, often dubbed 'Mr Perpetual Motion' by the local press. He later developed into a strong, commanding centre-half and was the first Latics captain when League football recommenced after World War Two.

Williamson's Christmas Day debut in 1935 was a memorable one: a hat-trick from centre-forward Billy Walsh was the feature of a comfortable 4–1 home victory against Tranmere Rovers. Any hopes of a double in the return fixture at Prenton Park on Boxing Day swiftly vanished as the Rovers ran riot, winning by a record score of 13–4. Tranmere's centre-forward 'Bunny' Bell scored nine goals, which could have been double figures had he not managed to miss from the penalty spot. Williamson's own memories of the game mainly surrounded the state of the pitch. 'As we took to the field, we were immediately ankle deep in mud.' He also remembered that the overworked Latics goalkeeper Lewis Caunce – playing in only his fourth match for them – had played a blinder. One hates to think what the score might have been if he hadn't!

A few weeks later, Williamson sustained a knee injury that required surgery, and he was to undergo a second operation before the problem was finally cleared up. Despite the early setback, he went on to enjoy a long and successful career at Boundary Park. Employed in aircraft engineering during the war years at the local A.V. Roe works, he was able to continue to play football throughout the period of hostilities, bringing his total appearances for the club in all competitions to 412.

To mark his long service with the club, Williamson was awarded a benefit. On 15 April 1947 his sparkling career was recognised by the club's supporters and personalities of the game when his benefit match drew a crowd of approximately 22,000 spectators to Boundary Park. Included in the 'International XI' were Stanley Matthews and Stanley Mortensen (Blackpool), Frank Swift and Eric Westwood (Manchester City) and George Hardwick (Middlesbrough). Guests appearing in the 'Oldham Athletic XI' included the Arsenal goalkeeper George Swindin and Bert Whalley, the Manchester United wing-half who was to lose his life in the Munich air disaster in February 1958. The gate receipts from the match amounted to £1,149, of which Williamson was paid £750, the maximum payment allowed for a player's benefit at that time.

In June of the same year Williamson requested his release in order to set up a business in Fleetwood. Athletic's secretary Bob Mellor said at the time 'We are parting on the very best of terms. The club has no desire to part with Williamson. We were prepared to sign him on as good terms as anybody else, but at his own request he has been allowed to leave to take up a business where there is a Lancashire Combination club.' He became player-coach to Fleetwood FC and was first welcomed back to Boundary Park in September 1947 when the Latics Reserves, fielding nine men with first-team experience, won 4–0. Later in the same month, however, he gained revenge when his team won the return fixture by the same 4–0 scoreline.

Williamson was back in the soccer headlines in 1960. At the time he was living in Lowestoft and managing a works team – Richards Ironworkers FC – a shipbuilding firm where he was employed. Getting together a scratch side at the start of season 1959–60, his coaching and influence moulded together a team that won the Suffolk Primary Cup at the first attempt. Over 250 clubs from the whole of Suffolk entered the competition, and no fewer than six of the team's Cup ties were played away from home.

In 1990 Williamson was invited by Granada TV to take part in a programme to celebrate Oldham's appearance at Wembley. Much to his regret, severe arthritis prevented his acceptance. He modestly said at the time: 'One still feels to be a little part of the club.' He was certainly more than that.

David Wilson

Date of birth: 14 January 1884, Irvine, Ayrshire
Died: Unknown

Oldham Athletic record:
Appearances: League 368, FA Cup 37
Goals: League 16, FA Cup 4
Debut: Hyde FC, FA Cup first qualifier (h) 6 October 1906, won 5–0

Also played for: St Mirren, Hamilton Academical, Bradford City, Nelson, Scotland (1 cap)
Managed: Nelson, Exeter City

One of the finest wing half-backs in the club's long history, David Wilson was from a family of footballers, the head of which was Andrew, a Scottish international centre-forward with Sheffield Wednesday who scored 216 League and Cup goals in a 20-year stay at Hillsborough. He also managed Athletic for five years from July 1927, narrowly missing out on promotion with a third-place finish in Division Two during season 1929–30.

   Wilson arrived at Boundary Park after experience with St Mirren, Hamilton Academical and Bradford City, and while he was with the Yorkshire club he came under the shrewd eye of Athletic's manager David Ashworth, who paid just £90 for his signature. Wilson had made his Football League debut for Bradford City at Blackpool on 17 December 1904. He played in five matches – scoring one goal in his first season at Valley Parade – and in only seven matches in 1905–06. Although he dropped into non-League football to join the Latics, he helped them win the Championship of the Lancashire Combination in his first season, playing in every match, including Lancashire and Manchester Cup ties.

   Wilson proved to be a player with remarkable stamina and without equal as a defender; his tireless energy and enthusiasm were a great incentive to his colleagues. He was also remarkably free from injury, and in one spell of four and a half seasons he clocked up 180 consecutive League and Cup appearances. Very early records credited him – mistakenly – with a record of 264 consecutive League appearances. He did in fact appear in 263 consecutive matches for the club, but these included minor Cup and friendly matches.

   In April 1913 Wilson achieved the great ambition of all Scots: his cap against England. The honour gave immense satisfaction to his many friends in Oldham, where he was deservedly a great favourite. At the close of the 1914–15 season, he announced his intention to retire and moved back to Scotland. He changed his mind, however, and in October 1915 he was back in Oldham keeping a tobacconist's shop in Oldham market place during the period of World War One. It was not his first business venture, as in 1908 he was granted sole rights to sell cigarettes at Boundary Park while the proprietor of a tobacconist's shop in St Domingo Street in Oldham.

   Athletic's directors fought hard to retain Wilson's services in the summer of 1919, when he again announced his intention to retire and went to live on a farm in Scotland. Thankfully, he was induced to return and was installed as player-coach. He finally did leave Boundary Park in May 1921 when he accepted the post of player-manager to Nelson FC, who at that time were newly elected members of the Football League, about to embark on their first season in the new Third Division, Northern Section.

   In his second season at Seedhill, Wilson led his team to the Championship. Sadly, they struggled in Division Two and were relegated after just one season. Having reached the age of 40, he retired from playing but continued as manager for a further season, coming close to a second promotion in 1924–25 before the team ultimately finished as runners-up to Darlington, when the rules allowed for only the Champions to be promoted.

   A three-year spell out of the game followed when Wilson ran a stocks and shares business in Blackpool. He returned to the game as manager of Exeter City in March 1928 but was sacked after less than a year in charge. His movements thereafter have remained a mystery, although in September 1925 it was rumoured that he was about to take a coaching job on the continent. Perhaps he followed his brother James, who coached in Holland and Belgium in the period following World War One. To add to the mystery, his son – David Arthur – who was born in Oldham but left when he was barely a year old, was in Oldham in June 1957 trying to trace a sister, May, who he had never seen. He also failed to find any trace of the Wilson family despite several days spent in the town.

Ian Wood

Date of birth: 15 January 1948, Radcliffe, Lancashire

Oldham Athletic record:
Appearances: League 517(7), FA Cup 27(1), League Cup 18
Goals: League 22, FA Cup 3, League Cup 1
Debut: Queen's Park Rangers (h) 25 May 1966, lost 0–2

Also played for: Park Lane Olympic, Denver Dynamo (US), San Jose Earthquakes (US), Burnley, Whichita Wings (US), Radcliffe Borough

Ian Wood was first noted when playing in Sunday League football in his native Radcliffe and was signed on amateur forms in November 1965. The manager who signed him, Gordon Hurst, had a short and relatively unhappy spell in charge at Boundary Park, being replaced by Jimmy McIlroy after less than a season at the helm. He did, however, have the satisfaction of seeing his youthful protégé embark on a record-breaking career.

Blond-haired and energetic, Wood began as a budding centre-forward, making his League debut at 18 years of age. In the season that Jimmy McIlroy took over from Gordon Hurst as manager and chairman Ken Bates splashed out in the transfer market, Wood was the eighth player to be tried as attack leader when he made his debut in the final fixture of the season.

After half a season of reserve-team football in 1966–67, an opportunity presented itself when Frank Large was transferred to Northampton Town after just 12 months at Boundary Park. In his second appearance of the season, Wood scored his first senior goal in the 3–0 home win against Workington on 27 December. He played in 14 of the season's League matches, notching further goals against Gillingham – the winner in a 2–1 victory in March – and two against Darlington in a 3–2 win in April.

The 1967–68 season opened in a bizarre fashion. One win in the first 12 Division Three matches was immediately followed by seven straight victories. As manager McIlroy rang the changes (only goalkeeper David Best retained his place throughout the season), Wood's 25(3) League appearances encompassed all three inside-forward positions and both berths as full-back and wing half-back. It was not until Jimmy Frizzell took over as manager that he was allowed to finally settle at right full-back, and an incredible run of consecutive appearances ensued.

It was on 27 April 1974, towards the close of the Division Three Championship season, that Wood dislocated a shoulder when he fell in the penalty area at York City and was carried off the field. He missed the final two matches of the season, bringing to an end a brilliant, unbroken run of 161 League and Cup matches. The last match he missed was at Lincoln City on 13 March 1970. Happily, he was sufficiently recovered to join teammates Andy Lochhead and Ian Robins for their flight to America to play for Denver Dynamo in the North American Soccer League.

In season 1975–76, Wood became the holder of the club's all-time League appearance record, when he overtook David Wilson's total of 368. He was to greatly extend the margin before he bowed out with a final appearance – as a substitute – against West Ham United at Boundary Park on 29 April 1980. Consistent to the end, he had played in all but five of the season's fixtures.

Wood, along with full-back partner David Holt, joined newly-relegated Burnley in the summer of 1980. While Holt remained at Turf Moor long enough to collect a Division Three Championship medal in 1982, Wood left Burnley in November 1981 having failed to hold down a first-team place. He subsequently worked in America and continued to play football on a part-time basis. He later returned home and joined his home-town club Radcliffe Borough as a player and then as chairman. His son, Clark Wood, signed trainee forms with Athletic in July 1987 but did not reach senior level.

George Woodger

Date of birth: 3 September 1884, Croydon
Died: 6 March 1961, Croydon

Oldham Athletic record:
Appearances: League 115, FA Cup 15
Goals: League 22, FA Cup 4
Debut: Woolwich Arsenal (a) 1 October 1910, drawn 0–0

Also played for: Thornton Heath Wednesday, Croydon Wanderers, Crystal Palace, Tottenham Hotspur, England (1 cap)

George Woodger would comfortably qualify as a Latics Legend on the strength of his being the first player to be selected for England while on the club's books. He became the first Latics player to win full international recognition when he represented his country in the 2–1 victory against Ireland at Derby on 11 February 1911. He was swiftly followed by centre-forward Evan Jones, who won the first of his Wales caps on 6 March 1911, against Scotland at Cardiff.

The 1910–11 season was Athletic's fourth as a Football League club and their first in the top flight following promotion from Division Two in 1909–10. Athletic began the season with Jock McTavish, the former Falkirk and Scotland star, at inside-right. Sadly, in his home League debut against Newcastle United, McTavish was injured in the first few minutes, and after two spells off the field in the first half he returned in the second half as a passenger on the right wing. Athletic moved swiftly to replace the unfortunate Scot, who departed Boundary Park mid-season, after playing in only 10 League matches. They replaced one ball juggler with another when Woodger was signed in late September. An interesting insight into his transfer appeared in a Bradford City programme on 15 October 1915: 'Under the old financial rules, Woodger would never have left Crystal Palace for Oldham. With Oldham offering £750 for him, the player was able to claim a £250 share of the deal, an advantage that altered his view considerably.'

In five years with Palace, Woodger had recorded 150 Southern League appearances and 36 goals, with an additional 16 FA Cup matches and three goals. He rejoiced in the nickname 'Lady' and was an unlikely looking footballer, prematurely balding and with an almost frail physique. He was, nevertheless, a player with splendid footwork, polished style and with great tactical awareness. His left-wing partnership with Joe Donnachie, ably backed up by the sturdy David Wilson at left-half, provided a potent springboard for incisive attacks.

Woodger made his Athletic debut in the goalless draw with Woolwich Arsenal at Plumstead on 1 October 1910. He took some time to score his first goal for Athletic, but then scored in three consecutive matches within the space of three days over the Christmas holiday period and ended his first season with six goals in 30 League and Cup matches.

The 1911–12 season opened with a visit from Sheffield United. Athletic fielded two new players: left-back Stephen Buxton and inside-right Tom Marrison. They were disappointingly beaten 3–2, with Hugh Moffat failing from the penalty spot in the second half. League form was inconsistent throughout the season, and the team avoided relegation by a whisker, one point better off than Preston North End in 19th place, who accompanied Bury through the relegation trapdoor.

Woodger enjoyed his best season at Boundary Park in 1912–13, scoring eight League goals and one in the FA Cup. Athletic finished ninth in Division One and reached the semi-final of the FA Cup for the first time, but lost 1–0 to Aston Villa at Ewood Park, Blackburn. He came close to equalising late in the game but was thwarted by a fine save at the foot of his post by Sam Hardy, Villa's international goalkeeper.

The 1913–14 season opened with a thumping defeat at Bolton Wanderers by 6–2, after Woodger had equalised Bolton's first goal. Two weeks later he scored within a minute of the kick-off in the 3–0 home win against Tottenham Hotspur. His display had obviously impressed the Spurs directors, who signed him in the close season for a fee of £325. He retired from playing during World War One and was then employed as a fitter by Croydon Common Works Department.

Freddie Worrall

Date of birth: 8 September 1910, Warrington
Died: 13 April 1979, Warrington

Oldham Athletic record:
Appearances: League 105, FA Cup 2
Goals: League 21
Debut: Millwall (h) 26 December 1928, won 4–1 (scored one)

Also played for: Witton Albion, Nantwich Town, Bolton Wanderers (but registration cancelled by the Football League), Portsmouth (World War Two guest player for Oldham Athletic, Droylsden, Blackpool, Manchester United), Crewe Alexandra, Stockport County, England (2 caps)

Freddie Worrall was recommended to the Latics by their wingman Bert Watson, and he duly turned out in a Northern Midweek League match at Blackpool. After a sparkling display, he was signed on amateur forms on the return coach journey from the match. At this point complications arose, as it was then discovered that he was already registered with Nantwich Town. In breach of Football League regulations, the Latics offered Nantwich £50 for his services. As something of a nursery club for Bolton Wanderers, Nantwich tipped off Bolton about the offer, and they acted swiftly, signing Worrall on a professional form, with a fee of £250 being paid to Nantwich. The Football League, however, refused to accept his registration and held an inquiry into the matter. Bolton Wanderers were found guilty of breaking League rules and were fined £50, while Nantwich were ordered to repay the £250 transfer fee. The Latics were fined £10, but on Christmas Day 1928 the League contacted the club and agreed to accept their registration of the player.

Worrall made his debut at outside-right on the following day and capped a scintillating display by scoring in a 4–1 win against Millwall. The former cotton mill worker went on to give almost three years of outstanding service before commanding a fee of £3,000 when sold to Portsmouth – an outstanding return, considering the fact that the only cost to the Latics had been the original £10 fine.

The 1928–29 season had opened in disastrous fashion for the Latics, with only three wins from the first 20 League matches. The Boxing Day introduction of Worrall, however, had an immediate impact, with six wins in his first seven matches. With the threat of relegation lifted, confidence soared and for much of the following 1929–30 season promotion from Division Two seemed assured. Sadly, injuries to key players and a loss of form from Easter onwards left the side in third place, two points away from promotion.

An injury to centre-forward Stewart Littlewood in November 1930 resulted in Worrall taking over as attack leader for five matches. At only 5ft 6in he was not ideally built for the position, but, nevertheless, he obliged with winning goals against Bury and Swansea Town. He also netted twice against the Champions-elect Everton at Goodison Park, but the Latics could find no answer to Dixie Dean, who scored four in a rousing 6–4 victory for the home side.

Worrall signed off by scoring in each of his final two League matches: a 2–0 home win against Swansea Town and a 3–1 win against Burnley at Turf Moor. At the end of October he became a Portsmouth player. He remained at Fratton Park until the outbreak of war, clocking up 337 League and FA Cup appearances and scoring 71 goals. After taking part in the FA Cup Final of 1934, he was capped by England in the match against Holland in Amsterdam, and in the following season he played against Ireland. In 1939 he starred in Portsmouth's shock 4–1 victory in the FA Cup Final against the hot favourites Wolverhampton Wanderers, playing with a lucky sixpence in his boot and a miniature horseshoe in the pocket of his shorts.

Worrall returned to Boundary Park in October 1939 to assist the Latics in wartime football. He scored six goals in his first seven outings in 1939–40, but when normal League football resumed seven years later he was a Crewe Alexandra player. Approaching 36 years of age, he made only a handful of appearances for the Railwaymen, but these included a nostalgic final appearance at Boundary Park on 21 December 1946, almost 18 years on from his introduction to League football with the Latics.

By the Same Author

Oldham Athletic – A Complete Record, 1899–1988 (Breedon Books, 1988)
Exeter City – A Complete Record, 1904–1990 with Alex Wilson and Maurice Golesworthy (Breedon Books, 1990)
New Brighton – A Complete Record, 1922–1951 (Breedon Books, 1990)
Accrington Stanley – A Complete Record, 1894–1962, with Mike Jackman (Breedon Books, 1991)
The United Alphabet – A Complete Who's Who of Manchester United FC (Polar Publishing, 1994)
All the Lads – A Complete Who's Who of Sunderland AFC, with Doug Lamming (Polar Publishing, 1999)
Latics Lads – The Official Who's Who of Oldham Athletic AFC 1907–2002 (Yore Publications, 2002)
Meadow Lane Men – The Complete Who's Who of Notts County FC 1888–2005 (Yore Publications, 2005)